THE
DEVIL'S VIRTUOSOS:
GERMAN GENERALS AT WAR 1940·5

THE
DEVIL'S VIRTUOSOS:
GERMAN GENERALS AT WAR 1940·5

DAVID DOWNING

BOOK CLUB ASSOCIATES

Contents

Maps

Illustrations

Author's Preface

In this book I have examined the decisive European campaigns of the Second World War from the viewpoint of those German generals who exercised the greatest influence over their planning, direction and outcome. The adoption of such a perspective creates its own emphases, and as these go to make up an overall picture that might seem unbalanced to those weaned on the Anglo-American view that 'we' won the war with a little help from the once-friendly Russians, it seems advisable to explain briefly the virtual omission of several well-known campaigns.

Poland, for the German Army, was an *hors-d'oeuvre* for the final reckoning with France with which this book begins. The campaigns in Scandinavia and the Balkans were of a secondary nature, necessary in terms of German strategy but of little intrinsic interest. The Battles of Britain and the Atlantic were not the concern of the German Army or its generals. The war in North Africa, though containing great strategic possibilities for the Axis powers (which are discussed in depth), was treated by the German High Command as little more than a wasteful side-show, an apt return for a poor choice in allies. The exploits of the Afrika Korps and the Eighth Army have in any case received more than their fair share of attention elsewhere.

The crucial land campaigns of the European War – those with which this book is concerned – were fought out between the Rhine and the English Channel in the West, and between the Vistula and the Volga in the East. Here it was that the German panzer forces, led with dash and distinction by generals like Rommel and Guderian, pursued through the three summers of 1940–2 the mirage of ultimate victory. And here it was, in the eighteen months that followed the Stalingrad debacle, that first Manstein in the East and second Rommel in the West struggled vainly to avoid the reality of ultimate defeat. Until Germany's choices were narrowed to one – in which of these two areas would they yield ground faster? To whom, in effect, would they yield Germany – East or West?

As the book focuses on the German direction of the war, the 'enemies of the Reich' will often appear shadowy and indistinct. The German forces are observed throughout in greater depth; their forces are named and numbered, their equipment and performance evaluated. The forces of their adversaries are normally just forces, their leadership and equipment as anonymous or otherwise as they must have seemed to the German generals. For purposes of clarity the term 'Allied' refers throughout to Anglo-American-French forces, and excludes the Red Army.

My thanks are due to the following authors and publishers for permission to quote from the books named: E. Belfield and H. Essame, *The Battle for Normandy*, Pan; W. Goerlitz, *Paulus and Stalingrad*, Methuen; H. Guderian, *Panzer Leader*, Futura; G. Jukes, *Kursk*, Pan/Ballantine; C. Malaparte, *The Volga Rises in Europe*, Panther; E. Manstein, *Lost Victories*, Methuen; F. W. Mellenthin, *Panzer Battles*, Cassell; E. Rommel, *The Rommel Papers*, Collins; C. Wilmot, *The Struggle for Europe*, Collins.

I would also like to thank the staffs of the British Museum and Imperial War Museum for their assistance, and Peter Calvocoressi for reading the manuscript and offering the benefit of his wisdom. Finally I would like to express my indebtedness to Wendy and Michèle, who made living, and thus writing, a more satisfying endeavour.

David Downing (November 1976)

PART 1

Quest for Victory

No time ago along the thoroughfare shot a hellish messenger
amid the chant-chanting of henchmen, a mystic gulf lit
and hung with crosses caught and swallowed him,
the shop windows are closed, poor
and harmless though they too are armed
with cannons and toys of war
the butcher has closed his shutters – he would take berries
and decorate the heads of slaughtered kids,
the rite of mild executioners who do not yet know blood
has turned to a foul reeling of shattered wings,
of wraiths at the river's edge, and the water goes on gnawing
the banks and no one now is guiltless.

(from *Hitler Spring* by E. Montale)

Chapter 1

SICHELSCHNITT – THE FLAWED MASTERPIECE

When the thunderclap comes there is no time to cover the ears.

(Sun Tzu)

In the early morning of 10 May 1940 a long black Mercedes, led and followed by armed motorcyclists, climbed slowly up the steep and winding roads of western Germany's Eifel Mountains. It was a clear night, the stars bright in the heavens above. The man in the back of the car had been travelling since the previous afternoon, mostly in his personal train, from Berlin. He was not sleeping though, glancing nervously out of the windows, making gestures of tension with his hands.

For the last two decades this man had been informing all and sundry of the mission he was destined to fulfil in Europe. In beer halls, on street corners, in a courtroom dock. Locked in Landsberg Prison he had written a book about it, called *My Struggle*. Raised to supreme power in Germany he had made his struggle the state policy. The German race would be unified, exalted, raised to its rightful place as the continent's hegemonic power. Its implacable enemy, the Jewish race, which like a virus had infested the corporate bodies of decadent capitalism and Bolshevism alike, would be destroyed. That this would involve war was beyond doubt. Though Germany's destiny lay in the East, the West would not stand aside. The West would have to be bullied, browbeaten, trampled upon, before the thousand-year Reich could move to claim its living-space in the eastern plains between the Vistula and the Volga.

Much had already been achieved. The Germans of Austria and the Sudetenland had been returned to the *volk* fold. The rump of Czechoslovakia had fallen like a ripe fruit. The colossus in the East had been bought off – for a while – and Poland swallowed by the two of them. The Western powers had declared war. And done what? 'Our enemies are little worms; I saw them at Munich.' Now was the reckoning; now they would feel the slice of the sickle, *das sichelschnitt*.

At this moment, as the Mercedes ascended the mountain, Cologne's two airfields were alive with activity. Junkers 52 transport planes were rumbling down the runway, towing gliders into the air, their cargo the élite formations of Student's airborne battalions. In little more than half an hour the gliders would uncouple, and drop into Belgium and Holland, there to accomplish their tasks of securing bridges, muzzling forts, spreading uncertainty behind the lines. Then they would wait for the onrushing German armour. A matter of hours.

On the frontier the 136 divisions of Army Groups A, B and C were poised for the order to march. Ten of these divisions were mobile armoured divisions – panzer divisions – and seven of these were concentrated behind the thickly forested uplands of the Ardennes. Their columns of tanks, troop transports and supply vehicles stretched back in tails beyond the distant Rhine. Soon the engines would be bursting into life, the leading motorcyclists and armoured reconnaissance vehicles driving through the frontier posts en route for France and the English Channel.

The Mercedes reached its destination, a remote mountain dwelling called *Munstereifel*, the Crag's Nest. The ex-house painter from Vienna climbed out of his car, returned the salute of the mute SS bodyguard and walked inside. There, for the next few. weeks, he would brood over the vast maps, watch the flags moving west in his name. The stars were still shining, but for him the skies were made for planes. These were now crossing the frontier.

And as the Führer of the Third Reich settled into his new headquarters, three other men of destiny were no less concerned with the imminence of the moment. Two of them, at points fifty miles apart on the frontier, were going through last-minute preparations with their subordinates, perhaps exchanging words with their men sitting on the lines of vehicles, feeling the tension, waiting for the word to go. The third man was asleep, some 420 miles to the east in his Liegnitz home. He was to get the news from the radio over breakfast.

These three did not share their leader's mission, but he was nonetheless their leader. They were soldiers, given to obeying orders, given to ignoring politics. A notion of 'Germany' and a dedicated professionalism were their twin guiding lights. Victory was their objective. Victory for what? was a question they had not begun to ask. They were virtuosos, yet to discover they served a devil.

II

Their code was personal. They were concerned with their own conduct and with the conduct of those for whom they were responsible, their family and their soldiers. They were not concerned with the behaviour of others. They possessed no spark of the nonconformist urge to seek out evil and destroy it, for they were perfectly conformist. They possessed Luther's capacity for separating public and private morality. They disliked and despised the parvenu Nazis, but their only reaction was to confine themselves yet more strictly to their military duties. Like the Pharisees, they passed upon the other side of the road. (1)

So the British lawyer R. T. Paget characterised the Prussian 'soldier-monk'. One representative of this caste, whom Paget would defend after the war, was born on 24 November 1887 in Berlin: Erich von Lewinski. He was a tenth child, and as was sometimes the case in such primitive times, was adopted without fuss by a childless aunt. His adoptive father, a divisional commander in the Imperial German Army, bore the name of Manstein. Young Erich adopted this in his turn.

His eventual choice of career was unlikely to be difficult. In his two families the closest sixteen male relatives had served in the armed forces of either Kaiser or Czar. The family tradition stretched back to the Teutonic Knights, ancient casting-mould of the Prussian military ethic. Erich was destined for soldiering, and brought up with it in mind.

In 1907 he was commissioned as an officer in the Third Guards, the regiment of his uncle, the future President Hindenburg. Through the First World War he served as a junior officer, both in the front line and in various staff capacities. Germany's collapse found him performing frontier guard duties in Silesia. When the Army, at the victorious allies' insistence, was reconstituted in miniature as the Reichswehr, he was one of the 4000 officers selected to carry forward the traditions of the Prussian/German Army.

Implanted within those traditions lay the seeds of the successes and ultimate failure of the German generals with whom this book is concerned. To begin to understand them it is necessary briefly to turn back the clock to 1806. In that year the Prussian Army suffered a catastrophic defeat at Jena, a defeat without parallel in the Napoleonic Wars. Austria had often been defeated; the Empire could stand such shocks to its aging and obese body. England and Russia both defied the Corsican. But Prussia, young and virile, the nation of Frederick the Great, was humbled, occupied, traumatised. In isolation this might have produced nothing more productive than despair, but it occurred at a time when the nature of war was radically changing. The industrial revolution was improving weaponry and shrinking distance; war was widening in scope, deepening in complexity. Amidst the shock of defeat several Prussians – notably Scharnhorst and Gneisenau – recognised that Prussia's recovery depended on a wholehearted embracing of the new methodology of war. Scientific reasoning and the traditions of Prussian military discipline would be welded together into a professional army, one attuned to the spirit of the age, one that would save Prussia from future humiliation.

The central feature of this new army was a streamlined version of the Prussian General Staff. This body, in most armies according to Howard 'no more than a collection of adjutants and clerks for the commander in the field' (2) would provide in peace a continuous study of military science past and present, in war a ceaseless flow of expertise-based recommendations to the relevant commands. The continuous study was more than an endless obsession with old campaigns. As the century progressed it came to involve overall strategic planning, the problems of mobilisation, fortifications, armaments, transport systems, training and manouevres, intelligence, and mapping. The scope was vast, the General Staff determined to encompass it with the utmost thoroughness. The expertise accumulated was spread through the army by the system of dual command, by which each commander would have his own Staff Officer, his own trained expert. When problems of supply or communications or strategy arose the specialist would be at his right hand to tell him what was possible in any given situation. Although the commander was responsible to the Commander-in-Chief and his Chief of Staff to the Chief of the General Staff, the two were ideally expected to form a unit within which their respective attributes could prove mutually supporting. This in turn, via the unifying influence of

General Staff doctrine, spread both unanimity and flexibility throughout the Army.

The efficacy of such a system obviously rested on the quality of the officers involved. The selection of candidates for the General Staff was consequently based on the attainment of Moltke's 'mercilessly high standards'. They had to pass the most demanding physical and intellectual testing before admission to this *corps d'élite*. Low birth might tell against a candidate; high birth would not in itself tell for him. It was a small club, possessed of an open-minded approach to military affairs that was only matched by its narrow-minded approach to everything else.

The price of military flexibility was political rigidity. The General Staff could only function as a partner. In 1914, devoid of political direction, it chose war at the time it made military sense, as it had been trained to do. This apparent political irresponsibility, coupled doubtless with the fear its military expertise had created, led to its abolition by the victorious powers after the war. It survived in disguise as the *Truppenamt*, only to face another political problem. In 1914 it had reluctantly been forced to play the role of master; from 1933 onwards it fought against the equally distasteful role of the servant.

Hitler was at first extremely wary of the Army. In the first year of his Chancellorship a tacit truce was maintained, finally made explicit by the deal negotiated aboard the *Deutschland* in spring 1934. The Army would agree to Hitler's succeeding Hindenburg if the former quieted his rowdy private army, the SA. As Hitler proved slow in fulfilling his side of the bargain the Army, in the person of War Minister Blomberg, arrogantly threatened him with removal should he not speedily bring about an improvement of the situation. This was the last threat the Army would make. They had under-estimated the 'corporal'. Stung by the impudence of such intimidation Hitler acted so fast it took their breath away. Even the Army's own men, like Streicher and Bredow, fell beneath the knives of that long June night. And before they had recovered their breath Hitler, in Alan Clark's apt phrase, 'opened the toy cupboard'. (3) Rearmament, conscription. Promotions came fast and furious as the tiny Reichswehr swelled in size. The military men had so much military work to do that their natural propensity for evading the sordid issues of politics was undisturbed by even the particularly sordid politics taking place in front of their eyes.

When these issues intruded into the Army's domain it was, for the moment, a different matter. In 1934 Manstein, now high in the General Staff hierarchy, received an order on his desk to dismiss certain officers because of their Jewish blood. Now Manstein, as a Prussian gentleman, was not over-fond of republics, Nazis, the Jewish race, or anything for that matter that seemed tainted by vulgarity, populist hysteria or big business. This was not a matter of principle, merely a personal leaning. That officers should be dismissed on account of such leanings was an entirely different affair. They should be judged as soldiers. He refused to pass the order and sent a stinging note of protest hurtling up the hierarchy. Blomberg, by now a more humble Minister of War, demanded his dismissal; Fritsch, the Commander-in-Chief of the Army, stood by Manstein. The Army still had some reserves of power.

These gradual encroachments on their traditional preserves were not, unfortunately, the General Staff's chief preoccupation. This was the planning of German operational strategy in the increasingly likely event of a new European War. Manstein, promoted Deputy Chief of Staff to Beck, was centrally involved in this task, not to say personally and professionally absorbed in the intricacies of the problem. His official interest ended with his demotion to command of an infantry division that followed the fall of Fritsch on trumped-up charges in early 1938. The absorption continued. The following year the Fuhrer's Army, mindful of Manstein's reputation as the Army's leading operational brain, brought him back to the centre of military activity, appointing him Chief of Staff to Rundstedt's Army Group South for the attack on Poland. There Manstein could watch the new Army in action. Victory secured, Rundstedt and he were transferred West to take over Army Group A. There Manstein could ponder in earnest the problem of France.

The obvious prime requirement of German strategy, given its central position between France and Russia, was the *speedy* elimination of one or the other. The dreaded two-front war had to be avoided. Hitler had failed to convince the West to allow him a free hand in the East, but he had now won a reprieve in the East (the defeat of Poland and the Nazi-Soviet Pact) and thus a free hand in the West. But the blow had to be swift and conclusive. If the Army became stuck again in the mud of Flanders the temptation might prove too great for the Soviet Union. France had to be annihilated as a military power in weeks or months, not years.

A similar problem had confronted the General in 1914. They, in the person of Count Alfred von Schlieffen, had devised a *Blitzkrieg* strategy for the West, relying on superior logistics to strike France from the war in six weeks, before the Russian goliath was fully in motion. It had failed. The world was not technically heady for *Blitzkrieg*, and Moltke's execution of Schlieffen's plan had been too timid to compensate for these limitations.

In 1939 the General Staff was considering a repeat performance. Almost. For although the instruments of war were now fast enough for Schlieffen's plan – transforming his foot-slogging *Blitzkrieg* into an armoured scythe – the General Staff lacked Schlieffen's killer instinct. They had no plans for swinging around Paris and ending the war. A right hook through Belgium, and this time Holland, yes. But they looked no further than the plains of northern France and the Channel coast. This time timidity was built into the plan.

The other, more obvious flaw, was the plan's predictability. The British Expeditionary Force and the flower of the French Army would stand in the panzers' path; even should they be beaten they would more likely be pushed back than destroyed. The outcome would be the stalemate that had cost the Germans the First World War.

Could a better plan be devised? The number of annihilative strategic victories, on the scale required, can be counted on the fingers of one hand. The mobility factor has rarely been high enough; the communication and supply system rarely so precious that their severing would prove strategically decisive. One such example, however, occurred in the thirteenth century. It was planned and executed by Genghis Khan and his general Subodei Bahadur; the unfortunate target was the Khoresm Empire, then the most formidable military power in the Islamic world. The similarities between this campaign and the coming German assault on France are striking.

In 1219 the Mongols were confronted by a numerically superior enemy who, after an initial rebuff, decided to rely on the lateral defence line of the Jaxartes river. Behind this Maginot Line the state of the Khoresm Empire evinced certain characteristics reminiscent of France in 1940. The society was plagued by open class conflict and reluctant to unite against a common foe. The leadership was not so much incompetent as unable to grasp the novelty of the storm about to wash across its shores. The confidence with which they awaited it owed everything to ignorance, and was consequently prone to collapse in a rush of awareness. Their enemy, like the Wehrmacht, possessed superior mobility and a superior understanding of how to utilise it. They also had a keener awareness of the value of reconnaissance, both before the battle and during its course. The Mongols had no Stukas or airborne troops, but they had a Fifth Column and they used raiding parties as reconnaissance units. They knew the ground and the enemy. The Shah of Khoresm, like Gamelin in his radio-less headquarters at Vincennes, directed his forces without such knowledge, strategically blind. When the Mongols waved the matador's cape, first in the south, then along the Jaxartes, he sent his armies scurrying hither and thither, plunging them into thin air. Meanwhile the matador's sword – Genghis and Subodei with 50,000 men – had disappeared into the Kizyl Kum Desert, to emerge undetected far in the Shah's rear, at the gates of Bukhara. Suddenly facing forces on all sides the Shah's nerve broke. He turned and fled. Khoresm was lost.

It is highly probable that Manstein had studied the Mongols' masterpiece. But how to create a similar masterpiece in France? Where to wave the cape? And where to plunge the sword? The Schlieffen Plan would not do. The French would expect a waving of capes along the Rhine; they would watch for the sword thrusting out of Belgium. Ah, but what better place to wave a cape than where the sword was expected? And if the diversionary attack would be made through Belgium, then where would the real attack come from? Not across the Rhine. The Maginot Line was not to be disregarded in terms of a frontal assault. Only one possibility remained. Manstein began to investigate the Ardennes.

It was rough country. Not mountainous exactly, but neither a gentle range of hills. Narrow twisting roads leading from one potential bottleneck to another. Thick forests. This, though, could work both ways. Such terrain offered concealment as well as difficulties. Would the latter prove too great for the surprise offered by the former? How quickly could the German armour get through the Ardennes? There was one obvious man to ask.

III

Heinz Guderian had been born in Kulm on the Vistula on 17 June 1888. Like Manstein he would grow into a Prussian gentleman, if without a 'von' or a long family tradition of military service. His father was an army officer, but most of his close relations were professional men or landed gentry. Unlike Manstein his outstanding intelligence did not express itself in the conventional field of operational strategy; Guderian was always a rebel in his profession, his mind always attuned to the possibilities of innovation. Fortunately for Germany he also possessed a single-minded determination that would not suffer his thoughts to remain just thoughts.

The last two years of the First World War had offered a number of clues to solving the principal problem which had beset both sides: the immobilisation of armed forces by the overwhelming power of fixed defensive lines. The most obvious of these clues was the future potential of mechanisation, of mobilising both firepower (the tank) and troop movements (motorised infantry). The Germans had achieved little in this respect during the war, but the British successes were not forgotten in its aftermath. The breakthrough at Cambrai in 1917 had given ample demonstration of the tank's potential. The action around Amiens in 1918 had enlarged upon this, demonstrating the role aircraft might play in essentially land warfare, interdicting the movement of reserves, destroying communications and directly bombarding the defensive lines. If the Germans had lagged behind in these areas, in another they had pushed ahead. The 1918 'Ludendorff Offensive' had abandoned blanket artillery bombardments and mass assaults across no-man's-land in favour of concentrated fire against specific targets both on and behind enemy lines, so paving the way for fast-raiding infiltration groups of infantry to break through at selective points and create chaos in the rear.

Both the British and German innovations succeeded in the breakthrough phase but failed in the exploitation phase. The British lacked infantry support; the Germans sufficient mobility. These connections were not made by many at the time but Guderian was one who did, gradually, over the succeeding years. He made others too. During the First World War he spent time in command of a wireless station. Radio was still in its infancy, but someone of Guderian's perspicacity could grasp the possibilities inherent in radio – and only in such a rapid medium – for the control of fast-moving formations. Such communications equipment would allow for leadership from the front, supercession of the old cumbersome structures of command, and hence a further increase in mobility.

In all these apparently isolated factors – tanks, ground-attack aircraft, radio, infiltration tactics – lay the genesis of the panzer division. They were only apparently isolated; all sprang from the contemporary advances in technology. Guderian was a man of his times, rare in the military profession where most lag behind it.

At the end of the war these were still random pieces of knowledge slowly coalescing into an idea. Guderian, to his surprise, secured a place in the Reichswehr, and because of his interests was given a post in the Inspectorate of Transport Troops. In this traditional backwater he began to study the problems of motorisation, discovering *en passant* the writings of Fuller and Liddell Hart, then the *enfants terribles* of the British Army. Realising with a thrill that he was not alone Guderian pressed on, expanding his ideas and communicating them through his role as a military instructor. It was not merely a tactical improvement he was aiming at, he began to realise, but a revolutionary development of awesome implications.

Practical experience was essential. Since Versailles had forbidden the Germans real tanks, Guderian constructed dummy ones, originally made of canvas and pushed around by men on foot, later cars draped in sheet metal. It was not just the weapons which fascinated him; there was also the question of their insertion into the existing structure of the Army.

I became convinced (in 1929) that tanks working on their own or in conjunction with infantry support could never achieve decisive importance. My historical studies, the exercises carried out in England and our own experiences with mock-ups had persuaded me that tanks would never be able to produce their full effects until the other weapons on whose support they must inevitably rely were brought up to their standard of speed and cross-country performance. In such a formation of all arms, the tanks must play the primary role, the other weapons being subordinated to the requirements of the armour. It would be wrong to include tanks in infantry divisions: what was needed were armoured divisions which

would include all the supporting arms needed to allow the
tanks to fight with full effect. (4)

This was easier said than done in view of the entrenched interests of all those likely to be down-graded in the process.

Fortunately for Guderian he had a sympathetic superior at
the Transport Department, Colonel Lutz. Between them, in
February 1930, they created a Motor Transport Battalion.
This formation was designed to fight, not to 'carry flour'. The
four companies, true to Guderian's all-arms theory, were com-
posed of tanks, anti-tank weapons, motorcycles, and armoured
reconnaissance vehicles. Lutz's superior, General Otto von
Stulpnagel, fortunately retired after telling Guderian that neither
of them would 'ever see German tanks in operation in our
lifetime'. (5) The two pioneers had a free run. Their greatest
boon in this respect was a visit from the new Chancellor, one
Adolf Hitler, in 1933. Watching Guderian's units going through
their paces, Hitler could see *Lebensraum* opening up before
his eyes. 'That's what I want! That's what I need!' he said
excitedly. (6) Guderian, as yet not privy to the Führer's dreams,
could only be grateful for such vindication. Hitler had won
him over. At least for the time being.

Accordingly Hitler's expansion of the truncated Reichswehr
contained provision for three panzer divisions. All that remained
for Guderian to do was to convince the Army High Command,
with, if need be, Hitler's assistance, that they be used in a
certain way. Through the first six years of the thousand-year
Reich he published numerous articles to this effect, and a book,
'Achtung! Panzer!' (Attention! Tanks!).

How should the panzer divisions be used? To Guderian the
answer was clear. Their essential asset was their mobility; it
must not be wasted in frontal assaults on prepared defensive
positions. Such work, the pinning down of the enemy front, was
for the less mobile infantry. The panzers, as Sun Tzu wrote in
the fifth century BC, should 'go into emptiness, strike voids,
bypass what the enemy defends'. (7) They must go for the
flanks, for the vulnerable spots. In the nineteenth century the
flanks of a nation at war were no longer the flanks of its
fighting armies; they were the supply lines and command
channels which maintained those armies in existence as a collective force. Imagine a country as a wheel, imagine the rim as
the forces defending it. At the hub is the source of the army's
matérial and direction. Between hub and rim are the spokes –

the roads and railways which carry the goods, the telegraph and telephone wires which carry the orders. It is the spokes that hold the wheel together, psychologically as much as physically.

In the panzer division Guderian saw the wheel's nemesis. It carried a concentration of force capable of cutting the rim; it possessed the mobility and power to sweep through the spokes like a scythe. No matter how much of the wheel's rim remained in being, so long as the breaches were held open for the panzers' own supply lines the slaughter of the spokes would destroy the wheel. To change the metaphor: the panzers would be aimed at the nervous system rather than at the bones and muscles. Death would be by paralysis, not by a physical blow.

The divisions were designed with this in mind. The tanks were the backbone, the motorised artillery. They were not tank-killers themselves; their guns were more for self-protection, for forcing their passage. It was the passage in itself that was decisive. If they needed more firepower to this end the division also carried its own artillery, anti-tank and anti-aircraft guns, and had the constant support of dive-bomber formations. For reconnaissance it had armoured reconnaissance vehicles, a motorcycle battalion, and a wing of reconnaissance planes on call. For covering the ground behind the leading elements – the vital gap between the spearhead and the infantry divisions plodding along in the rear – it had its own motorised infantry regiments, carried in lorries or specifically-designed armoured half-track troop carriers. These troops could be used in situations unsuitable for the tanks, for fighting in built-up areas, for holding the ground won by the advance. And in an advance the one crime was to stop, to give the enemy a chance to locate and concentrate against you. As long as the panzers kept moving the enemy could never regain his balance, would fight in the dark, disconnected from his neighbours, his command, without a route of retreat. His supplies would fail to arrive as the transport system broke down, as the roads became clogged by the civil population in flight from the relentless march of the panzers. In such a way, Guderian reckoned, the ability and the will to continue the fight would be destroyed before the main forces came into action.

Panzer doctrine was a neutral, not an offensive doctrine. But it was used offensively with such success by the Reich in 1940–2 that its defensive capabilities tended to be overlooked. Yet the same principles worked equally well in reverse. The panzer

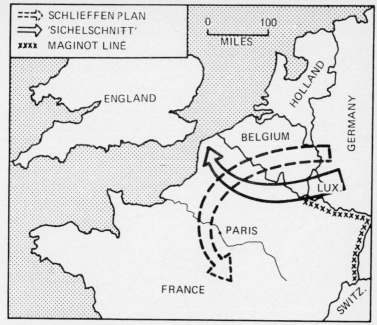

1 FRANCE: ALTERNATIVE PLANS

force cutting through the rim and the spokes could have its own spokes cut by an enemy panzer force. A nation undergoing attack could place its infantry on the frontier with orders to hold any breach as narrow as possible. The panzer forces would be held in the rear to cut off the intruder's lines at this narrow neck of the advance. Again it would be mobility that would prove the decisive factor; the ability to switch forces rapidly behind the front lines to the source of the breakthrough, to counter-concentrate. Then the intruder would himself be immobilised through lack of fuel; once immobilised would be easily locatable; once locatable would be easy prey for a force concentrated against it.

For the offensive though, which was what Hitler had in mind, Guderian asked only for reasonable terrain, good staff work, and an operational plan that would give him the opportunity to let the panzers loose. In Poland, despite the odd cautionary nudges from both superiors and subordinates, he had that chance. The panzers swept through the gallant but archaic Polish Army, spreading the havoc that Guderian had promised. It was all over in three weeks.

France would not be so easy. The French Army, though apparently unaware of the implications posed by mobile armour, was a far more formidable proposition than the Polish. Neither did a re-run of the Schlieffen Plan particularly excite Guderian. The Flanders Plain was unlikely to prove a vulnerable spot. With this in mind it is easy to imagine Guderian's excitement on meeting Manstein in November 1939 and hearing of the latter's plan. He might have echoed Hitler's 'that's what I want! that's what I need!' *Sichelschnitt* it would be called, and 'the cut of the sickle' was what it was. Through the vulnerable spot, a straight drive for the Channel across the plains of northern France, cutting through the spokes that held the French Army together. Yes, he told Manstein, the Ardennes were traversible by armour. The plan would work.

IV

Convincing the Army High Command (O.K.H.) would not prove so easy. For the next six months Manstein would have to fight for his plan and Guderian for the manner of its execution. Before the two met Manstein had already sent off, with Rundstedt's blessing, two memoranda to O.K.H. Neither had produced any response. Only Guderian's Panzer Corps had been transferred to Army Group A – which Manstein envisaged as the concealed sword – apparently on the Führer's specific orders. What was going on?

Through November and December Manstein continued to bombard O.K.H. with the plan, sending another four memoranda before Christmas. Telephoning Halder, the Chief of the General Staff, he was informed that O.K.H. was in substantial agreement with him, but that the Führer insisted on the original modified Schlieffen Plan, *Fall Gelb* (Case Yellow). This was rather strange. Why, in that case, had Hitler transferred Guderian's Corps? Because, Halder informed him, the Führer wanted the option of switching the main point of the attack (the *Schwerpunkt*) south if the situation warranted it.

This was not good enough. Manstein wanted his armoured spearhead from the beginning of the operation. Moving it south in mid-campaign would cost precious time, in which the French could also move their forces south. It had to be all or nothing. He sent off another memorandum, this time with a covering note from Rundstedt asking that, since the Führer seemed to be in charge, he be shown Manstein's plan in person. This suggestion was haughtily refused. O.K.H. might have lost their power, but not their pride.

O.K.H.'s role in the unfolding of *Fall Gelb* was, to say the least, ambivalent. They did not inform Rundstedt and Manstein that as early as October Hitler had been speculating out loud as to whether a thrust south of Liège-Namur might cut off the enemy. A subsidiary *Schwerpunkt* through the Ardennes, he confided to Jodl, might prove decisive. So Guderian's Corps was sent south. Then he began pondering shifting the weight south during the attack. Hitler was obviously fertile soil for Manstein's seed to fall upon. Why did he not see the plan?

On 10 January 1940 a German major crash-landed with the *Fall Gelb* operation plans in Belgian territory. O.K.H. had to assume that these had fallen into Anglo-French hands. But *still* the plan was not changed; a meeting on the 25th made only minor re-adjustments. Manstein, having sent off the seventh and last of his memoranda, found himself removed from his position and kicked upstairs to command an infantry corps assembling in far-off East Prussia. O.K.H. had tired of its monotonous mailbag.

The day before his departure Manstein ran a war game exercise in Koblenz. Halder was one of the observers. The game proved decisively that the proposed use of Guderian's Corps in isolation would achieve little. Halder, according to Manstein, 'was at last beginning to realise the validity of our standpoint'. (8) Guderian, who was also present, was less optimistic.

> I proposed that on the fifth day of the campaign an attack be made with strong armoured and motorised forces to force a crossing of the Meuse near Sedan with the objective of achieving a breakthrough which would then be expanded towards Amiens . . . Halder pronounced these ideas 'sense-less' . . . (9)

This struggle would continue.

The following week Manstein reported to Hitler on assuming his new command. The Führer, probably through the intervention of his adjutant Schmundt, had finally got to hear of the plan. After dinner he dragged Manstein into his study and asked him for a full exposition. The author of *Sichelschnitt* gratefully went through it all one more time. The next day Hitler summoned Brauchitsch (the Army Commander-in-Chief) and

Halder. By 24 February *Sichelschnitt* was the official plan of attack. Manstein was in East Prussia, watching impotently from the wings.

In his absence another war game had been held, with a similar difference of opinion between Halder and Guderian. The Chief of Staff did not think the Meuse could be crossed by the panzer divisions on their own; they would have to wait for infantry support. This was completely at odds with the spirit of Manstein's plan, depriving it of the speed and surprise on which its fulfilment rested. Just how revolutionary a plan it was, and just how few really did understand what it demanded, was evidenced by Rundstedt, its enthusiastic supporter, siding with Halder. Only the panzer commanders – Guderian and Wietersheim – knew what was required. After a heated argument they declared 'that in these circumstances we could have no confidence in the leadership of the operation'. (10) Nothing was resolved. The plan itself would fortunately prove stronger than its opponents.

In mid-March all the Army Group A commanders were summoned by Hitler to outline their tasks. Guderian spoke last, saying that he intended to be across the Meuse by Day Five.

> Hitler asked: 'And then what are you going to do?' He was the first person who had thought to ask me this vital question. I replied: 'Unless I receive orders to the contrary, I intend on the next day to continue my advance westwards. The supreme leadership must decide whether my objective is to be Amiens or Paris. In my opinion the correct course is to drive past Amiens to the English Channel.' Hitler nodded and said nothing more. (11)

According to Guderian he received no more instructions than this as to his course once across the Meuse. O.K.H. was reluctant to commit itself to this daring plan. It would wait and see if it really worked. The consequence of this attitude was the placing of an extraordinary responsibility on the panzer commanders themselves. They would have to take their own decisions. Guderian and Manstein had faith in Guderian, but what of the others? How many had the personal courage to lead from the front, the tactical expertise in wielding armoured formations? How many had the boldness of mind to size up situations correctly at such speed, the will to take those risks that would surely need to be taken? Guderian and Manstein need not have worried. There was no shortage of such officers. One of them, at this time relatively unknown, would become the best known German soldier of the war.

V

Erwin Rommel was born in Heidelheim, near Ulm on the Danube, on 15 November 1891. His father was a schoolteacher, his background neither aristocratic nor Prussian. Young Erwin would never satisfy the requirements of a General Staff officer by birth; he would not do so by inclination either. He was not fired by the rarified air of strategic theory like Manstein; he did not crave the challenges of innovation like Guderian. Rommel would lay his claim to posterity on the battlefield, as a fighting soldier and a human being. To him conceptualisation was something dealt with in the heat of the moment, preferably from an armoured turret. It was his good fortune that the qualities he possessed were those the technology of this war demanded.

He joined the Army in 1910 without, one suspects, any of the predestination experienced by Guderian and Manstein. The four years of war that soon followed found Rommel in continuous active service in France, Rumania, and on the Austro-Italian front. His service record was quite extraordinary, seemingly accumulating medals for bravery every other page. In difficult situations his instinct was invariably to attack, to compensate for any enemy superiority in numbers with the power of surprise and speed. The actions in which he took part and often led, read like a *Boy's Own* extravaganza; scaling mountains, swimming icy rivers, bluffing garrisons into surrender by simulating gunfire from many positions in the darkness. Rommel was a born warrior. As Douglas-Home put it: to Rommel war was a kind of 'wild dance'.

The first 'dance' over Rommel became, on the strength of his fighting record, one of the chosen 4,000. For nine years he remained a company commander stationed in south Germany, enjoying his marriage and his job. The picture of him that emerges from these years of peace-time soldiering is that of an ordinary family man, with rather more physical and mental energy that he could peacefully spend. He drank little, did not smoke, busied himself around the house like a regular handyman. His first thought on acquiring a motorbike was to take it to pieces and put it back together again, without mishap. He and his wife Lucie were canoers, skiers, mountaineers, enthusiastic swimmers and riders. Hardly General Staff material. This picture of the archetypal bourgeois couple, self-absorbed but popular, is completed by an early Rommel judgement on the Nazis. 'They seem to be a set of scallywags' he commented to a friend. (12)

This was not an unorthodox opinion. The German middle class looked down on Hitler's ruffians, shook their heads in anxious wonder at the vulgarity of their discretions, but remained basically grateful that someone should have arrived, even with such a motley-looking crew, to steer the ship back on course. Hitler was seen as an idealist, as the one man who could pull Germany together and save her from communism, as the procurer of the economic 'miracle' and Germany's resurgent pride. To a member of the Army like Rommel he was also, after his ruffian-clearance of June 1934, a patron.

Rommel spent most of the thirties lecturing, first at the Dresden Infantry School, secondly at the War Academy at Potsdam. His experience in the First World War was distilled by these lectures into his celebrated *Infanterie Greift An*, a handbook of infantry tactics. For a while he was also attached to the Hitler Youth, but disagreements over the relative priority given to physical fitness and strength of character led to his amicable removal.

This episode seems to have done him no harm vis-à-vis Hitler, for having consumed Rommel's book the Führer asked for him to command his personal bodyguard. They entered the Sudetenland and Prague together, followed the victorious Army across Poland. This last was too much for Rommel, chafing for active service after twenty years on the wagon. When asked by Hitler what he wanted, Rommel replied 'command of a panzer division'. The wish was granted. In February 1940 he took over 7th Panzer from General Stumme. For ten weeks, in and around its Godesberg headquarters, the division went through intensive training exercises: march procedure, fire tactics, the forcing of river crossings. In the process Rommel got to know his officers, men and equipment. He learned what they were capable of; they learned what he expected of them. Seventh Panzer was not about to lag behind its fellow panzer divisions. Rommel would rather his men erred on the side of recklessness than that of caution.

On that night of 9–10 May the division lay like a snake, its head poised on the frontier, its tail stretching back down the road to the Rhine. Up front the motorcyclists, armoured reconnaissance cars, anti-tank guns and engineer battalions; behind them the infantry carriers and the mass of Rommel's 240 tanks stood in line along the deep valleys of the Eifel. The division's nine Storch reconnaissance planes waited for daylight to spy out the line of march ahead. The Luftwaffe awaited the call for dive-bomber support. Rommel wrote a short letter to Lucie: 'We're packing up at last. Let's hope not in vain. You'll get all the news for the next few days in the papers. Don't worry yourself. Everything will be all right . . . ' (13)

VI

It took three irredeemable days for the French Command to realise the magnitude of the threat burrowing through the Ardennes. Like the Shah of Khoresm their eyes were riveted to the visible threat: the advance of Kuchler and Reichenau's armies through Holland and northern Belgium, the airborne swoops on the Albert Canal bridges and Fort Eban Emael, the swift advances of the three panzer divisions under Schmidt and Hoeppner. The French and British rushed north to meet them, fearful only that the Belgians might crack before they arrived. Meanwhile the long columns of Kleist and Hoth's seven panzer divisions were winding their way along the roads of the *inpenetrable* Ardennes, hidden by the forest and the umbrella of planes that stood guard above them, towards the Meuse.

The weeks of practice manoeuvres in the Eifel Mountains on the German side of the border had not been wasted. The meticulous staff planning which had marked the rail transportation schedules in 1914 now characterised the channelling of armoured columns through the road network of the Ardennes. Every column had its line of march and its schedule. Stoppages were expected to be minor, and they were. Some of the roads had been blocked with felled trees, in places holes had been dynamited in the surface. The engineers leapt from their carriers, cleared or covered the obstacles, and the advance continued. Resistance was limited to small forces of French or Belgian cavalry; those not simply brushed aside were met with tactics soon to be second nature to the panzer élite.

I have found again and again that in encounter actions, the

day goes to the side that is first to plaster its opponent with fire . . . This applies even when the exact position of the enemy is unknown, in which case the fire must simply be sprayed over enemy-held territory. Observation of this rule, in my experience, substantially reduces casualties . . . (14)

And hastens the advance. The young lieutenant who reacted to the sudden appearance of twenty French soldiers in 1914 with a wild charge that sent them scurrying for safety, is now hustling 7th Panzer on towards the Meuse, using identical tactics.

Guderian, fifty miles further south, was doing the same. But he, as early as the first night, was experiencing the drag of the tide as well as the flood. His immediate superior, Panzer Group leader General von Kleist, was nervously expecting a cavalry attack on Guderian's columns, and ordered 10th Panzer off its course to counter the threat. Guderian was not pleased.

I asked for a cancellation of these orders; the detachment of one third of my force to meet the hypothetical threat of enemy cavalry would endanger the success of the Meuse crossing and therefore of the whole operation. In order to anticipate any difficulties . . . I ordered 10th Panzer Division to move along a parallel road north of its previous line . . . The advance went on. The immediate danger of a halt and a change of direction was passed. The Panzer Group finally agreed to this. The French cavalry did not in fact appear. (15)

The moment passed, but not the inclination of the more traditionally-minded Army commanders to exercise over-caution in their use of armour, nor the inclination of such as Guderian to retaliate with insubordination.

By the late afternoon of 12 May Rommel, 'way ahead of my neighbours' as he boyishly wrote to Lucie (16), had arrived on the east bank of the Meuse. The bridges at Dinant and Houx had been blown by the retreating French, but the Motorcycle Battalion discovered an ancient weir near Houx that had not been demolished, for fear that such action would drop the water level and make the river fordable. The motorcyclists scrambled across the weir and found themselves in a mid-river island. On the other side were lock-gates, also intact. Under cover of darkness several companies established themselves on the far bank.

Upstream, at the crossing points selected for the two rifle regiments (the motorised infantry), things were not going so well. The French were well dug in on the far bank, and attempts to force a crossing in rubber dinghies were brought to a standstill with heavy losses. Here Rommel intervened personally, seemingly everywhere at once, supervising and encouraging by his example of unflagging enthusiasm. Houses down-wind were set aflame to provide a smokescreen; the Panzer IVs from the tank regiment were sent up and down the east bank road, their turrets traversed at right angles, their guns at zero elevation pounding the French positions a hundred yards away across the dark water. Under cover of this bombardment the crossing was made, bridgeheads secured. News of French armour in the vicinity did not deter Rommel; he ordered his own armour across that night.

In Guderian's sector things were also proceeding well. 1st and 10th Panzer had reached the Meuse on the evening of the 12th, occupying in the process what the Luftwaffe had left of Sedan on the east bank. Guderian was not very happy with Kleist's decision to substitute the previously-agreed air-strikes against French batteries on the far bank with a mass, and thus less discriminate, bombing attack, but on reaching the river's edge the following afternoon he was pleased and surprised to find that Kleist's orders had failed to reach the Luftwaffe in time. He next drove to the area north of Sedan selected for 1st Panzer's crossing. Here he found 1st Rifle Regiment and elements of *Grossdeutschland* Regiment already across the river, in occupation of the peninsula used as a prison cage for French troops in 1870. The Rifle Regiment's commander, Balck, later to lead panzer divisions and armies with such distinction in Russia, greeted Guderian with a joyfully sarcastic 'joyriding in canoes on the Meuse is forbidden', a reference to one of Guderian's favourite comments in training exercises. (17)

The Meuse had been crossed. At 2 am the following morning a pale General Georges would announce in stricken tones: 'Our Sedan front is broken. There's been a collapse.' (18) Indeed there had. The sword had evaded the frontal armour, pierced the flimsy side-armour. Now it would be driven to the heart.

VII

While General Georges was lamenting, 1st Panzer was widening its bridgehead on the west bank, the engineers busy laying bridges for the tanks to cross at first light. That morning intelligence of a French armoured force moving north-east towards Sedan forced Guderian to send all his available tanks to meet it. 2nd Panzer had also established a bridgehead and was fighting its way up the riverbank.

Guderian visited both units before returning to meet von Rundstedt in the middle of the Meuse pontoon bridge, whilst the do-or-die Allied air attack on the crossing was in progress. It was mostly 'die', the German gunners claiming some 150 Allied aircraft on this day. 'Is it always like this here?' Rundstedt asked. (19) As the generals were chatting and watching the futile heroics of the RAF, 1st Panzer was repulsing the French armour seven miles to the south-west. This threat accounted for, Guderian turned the division west. Together with the quickly-crossing 2nd Panzer it was to advance across the Ardennes Canal and break through the remaining French defences. 10th Panzer and *Grossdeutschland* Regiment would wheel south towards Stonne, to form the hard shoulder of the armoured breakthrough.

North of Sedan, Reinhardt's Panzer Corps had also straddled the Meuse at Monthermé; further north still Rommel was deepening his bridgehead and deep in his element.

Shells landed all around us and my tank received two hits one after the other, the first on the upper turret and the second in the periscope. The driver promptly opened the throttle wide and drove into the nearest bushes. It had only gone a few yards, however, when the tank slid down a steep slope on the western edge of the wood and finally stopped, canted over on its side, in such a position that the enemy, whose guns were in position about 500 yards away on the edge of the next wood, could not fail to see it . . . I therefore decided to abandon the tank as fast as I could, taking the crew with me. At that moment the subaltern in command of the tanks escorting the infantry reported himself seriously wounded with the words: 'Herr General, my left arm has been shot off.' (20)

The enemy resolve did not outlast the arrival of the main tank

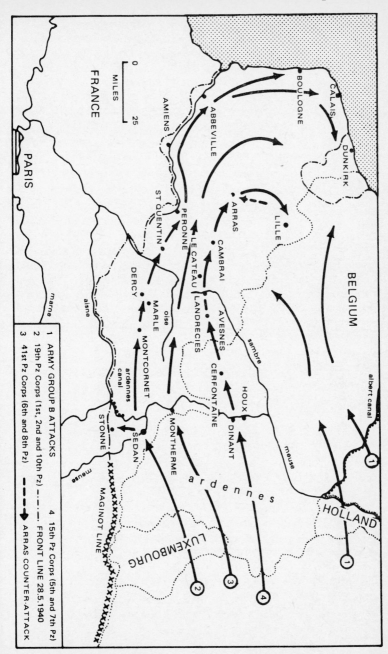

2 FRANCE: PHASE 1

force, and by the evening of 14 May the division had formed a bridgehead extending more than five miles west of the river. The next morning it was ready to thrust outward.

> My intention for the 15 May was to thrust straight through in one stride towards our objective, with the 25th Panzer Regiment in the lead, and with artillery, and, if possible, dive-bomber support. The infantry was to follow up the tank attack, partly on foot and partly lorry-borne. The essential thing, to my mind, was that the artillery should curtain off both flanks of the attack, as our neighbouring divisions were still some way behind us. (21)

For an infantryman Rommel had a keen understanding of the classic *Blitzkrieg* stencil. He went further, introducing an innovatory system of artillery control. As it stood a request for artillery fire on a particular sector required coding, sending by wireless, and decoding. Rommel, with typical handyman logic, simply gathered his artillery officers together, drew a line on the map corresponding to the expected line of advance, divided it into kilometre sections, and numbered them from the starting point. If the artillery received a number '8' they simply trained their sights on the 8 kilometre mark.

15 May was spent in frenzied activity. Rommel accompanied his spearhead straight through the unready French defences to Cerfontaine, some twenty miles beyond the Meuse. He then took some of his force back along the more southerly axis to cut off any French units retreating in that direction. He then reversed again. During this back and fro journey numerous small engagements were fought, as isolated pockets of French resistance came up against the marauding panzers.

> Near Senzeilles we met a body of full-armed French motorcyclists coming in the opposite direction, and picked them up as they passed. Most of them were so shaken at suddenly finding themselves in a German column that they drove their machines into a ditch ... (22)

That evening the forward elements assembled in the hills east of Cerfontaine. Looking back from these heights Rommel could see a dust cloud trailing back to the distant Meuse.

At this point 7th Panzer was still in Belgium, the French frontier looming ahead. Behind the frontier was the so-called (by the Germans) 'extension of the Maginot Line', a less impressive obstacle than its name suggested. Rommel spent the morning of the 16th awaiting a green light from higher authority, and received a visit from von Kluge, who approved his plan of action. This was to reconnoitre with the motorcyclists (already being done), and then move up the artillery to cover the advance of the tanks. These in turn would cover the advance of the rifle regiments, who would storm the fortifications and remove any barricades blocking the road.

By darkness this had been accomplished and the tanks sent through, firing broadsides to right and left, as much for psychological reasons as any other.

The tanks now rolled in a long column through the lines of fortifications and on towards the first houses, which had been set alight by our fire. In the moonlight we could see the men of the Motorcycle Battalion moving forward on foot beside us. Occasionally an enemy machine-gun or anti-tank gun fired, but none of their shots came anywhere near us. Our artillery was dropping heavy harassing fire on villages and the road far ahead of the regiment. Gradually the speed increased. Before long we were 500–1000–2000–3000 yards into the fortified zone. Engines roared, tank tracks clanked and clattered . . . we crossed the railway line . . . swung north to the main road . . . then off along the road and past the first houses. The people in the houses were rudely awoken by the din of our tanks . . . Troops lay bivouaced beside the road, military vehicles stood parked in farmyards and in some places on the road itself. Civilians and French troops, their faces distorted with terror, lay huddled in the ditches, alongside hedges and in every hollow beside the road. We passed refugee columns, the carts abandoned by their owners, who had fled in panic into the fields. On we went, at a steady speed, towards our objective. (23)

By the time 7th Panzer had broken through the second fortified line the objective, by all the canons of orthodoxy, should have been to batten down the turret hatches for the night. Tank advances in darkness were considered too risky, even by such as Guderian, and would not become an accepted part of panzer doctrine for another three years. Rommel, though, was not one to let the darkness come between him and a few more miles. He sent the Panzer Regiment rumbling on towards Avesnes, through roads choked with abandoned military vehicles and fleeing refugees.

The tanks circled around Avesnes and came to a halt on the high ground to the west of the town. A POW cage was constructed in a field for the French troops retreating into their arms. Inside Avesnes itself a tank battle raged between the panzers and some stray French tanks until 4 a.m. Rommel did not stay to watch; he was already moving west again, towards Landrecies, with a small battle-group.

There was no doubt that at this point – around 3 a.m. on the morning of 17 May – Rommel had very little idea as to the whereabouts of his division. True to the spirit of panzer doctrine he was charging forward without adequate intelligence of his own forces; a risk justified by the more than commensurate chaos he was spreading among the French forces. Hoping (one suspects 'hope' is the operative word) that the division was following up behind him at a similar speed Rommel lanced his battle-group through Landrecies and headed on for Le Cateau, another eight miles down the road. Here at last, on a hill east of the town, he stopped the advance at 6.15 a.m., fifty miles on from the previous afternoon's starting-line. With grandiose understatement he now decided that 'it was high time that the country we had overrun was secured by the division, and the enormous number of prisoners – approximately two mechanised divisions – was collected'. (24)

This was no simple matter. The rest of 7th Panzer was much further behind than its commander thought, and the French had reoccupied parts of the road Rommel's force had advanced along. Retracing his steps with the object of hurrying the division forward, Rommel had to make a dash through one small town under heavy enemy fire. Leaving one lonely Panzer IV to hold the hill east of that town he then ran into a French column, from which encounter another *Boy's Own* episode evolved:

At our shouts it halted and a French officer got out and surrendered. Behind the car there was a whole convoy of lorries approaching in a great cloud of dust. Acting quickly, I had the convoy turned off towards Avesnes. Hanke swung himself up on the first lorry while I stayed on the crossroads for a while, shouting and signalling to the French troops that they should lay down their arms – the war was over for them. Several of the lorries had machine-guns mounted and manned against air attack. It was impossible to see through the dust how long the convoy was, and so after 10 or 15 vehicles had passed, I put myself at the head of the column and drove on to Avesnes . . . At length we arrived at the south-west entrance . . . without halting, Hanke led the lorry convoy on to a parking place and there disarmed the enemy troops. We now found that we had no less than forty lorries, many of them carrying troops, behind us. (25)

By now it was morning, and the division beginning to catch up. The remaining panzers and the Armoured Reconnaissance Battalion were sent on to clear the road and reinforce the detachment at Le Cateau. The advance had been secured, the risks vindicated.

VIII

Rommel was rather fortunate to be occupying what seemed to most a subsidiary sector. Gratifying though his success must have been to the High Command, its eyes were primarily fixed on the debouching of Guderian's spearhead from its Meuse bridgeheads. This was the *Schwerpunkt* of *Schwerpunkt*, the principle force. Here the greatest risk was being taken, the un-rolling of a flank from the river to the sea. Already one of Guderian's three panzer divisions – the 10th – was on blocking duty, standing sentry around Stonne to meet the expected French counter-blow. By the evening of 15 May it was being joined by 29th Motorised; the General Staff was not about to abandon orthodoxy, even amidst the breathlessness of *Blitzkrieg*.

Guderian thought these forces would more than suffice, and had thus set his other two panzer divisions loose in a westerly direction. His superiors were not so sure. On the evening of the 15th, von Kleist halted the advance, to Guderian's amazement and disgust. 'I neither would nor could agree to these orders, which involved the sacrifice of the element of surprise we had gained . . . ' (26) he wrote, in a tone that would become all too familiar in the years to come. This time he had his way, talking Kleist into allowing him another twenty-four hours foreward movement.

With this temporary reprieve Guderian restarted the advance. The shoulder was holding firm at Stonne; his other two panzer divisions met 6th Panzer in Montcornet and had to bargain for roadspace. Soon all three were threading through the town and fanning out for the drive west. By nightfall 1st and 2nd Panzer were at Marle and Dercy, fifty-five miles from Sedan, a third of the way to the Channel. By the morning of the 17th 1st Panzer had reached the Oise. But Guderian's twenty-four hours had been spent. He attempted to ignore this unpleasant fact, rather in the manner of a boating lake customer sailing on in blissful disregard of the owner screaming that his time was up. The owner was not amused. A message arrived from Panzer Group HQ, swiftly followed by Kleist himself, who strongly took Guderian to task for disobeying orders. The latter, with the sole justification of being right, threw a prima donna fit and asked to be relieved of his command. Kleist consented, probably to Guderian's annoyance. The panzer leader immediately invoked higher authority, informing Army Group HQ of the situation with the transparent motive of having the decision reversed. Rundstedt quickly asked Colonel-General List, commander of Twelfth Army, to settle the affair. List arrived, told Guderian that he would not resign, and that the order came from neither Kleist nor Army Group but from O.K.H. Having thus explained the impossibility of having the order revoked, List, with the Army Group's prior blessing, proceeded to do just that, granting Guderian the latitude of a 'reconnaissance in force'. Joining in the spirit of the thing Guderian promptly had a wire laid between his Corps HQ and his forward HQ so that O.K.H. could not listen in to his orders on their wireless intercept service. The Army's command structure was already showing signs of strain. For the moment success would be its own justification. But later . . .

The tightening hold on the reins was not O.K.H.'s, but Hitler's. The Führer had prophesied that the French would swiftly crack up; now that they seemed to be doing so he found it impossible to believe. Of the many persona jostling in his psyche, the intuitive genius of the political seer was already losing precedence to the 'iron-willed' infantryman who had endured four years of bloody stalemate in the Flanders battles of the First World War. Halder noted in his diary:

Führer is terribly nervous. Frightened by his own success, he is afraid to take any chance and so would rather pull the reins on us . . . Führer keeps worrying about south flank. He rages and screams that we are on the way to ruin the whole campaign. He won't have any part in continuing the operation in a westward direction. (27)

Halder was here being somewhat ingenuous. Hitler was not the only nervous man in the German Army. The key truth in this situation, as in many to come, was the distance between the cloistered HQs far behind the front, hung with maps and deluged with cold facts, and the commanders in the field. Neither Hitler nor Halder could see for themselves the roads clogged by refugees, the looks in the eyes of the French prisoners, could *feel* the defeat of France. To them the French Armies were flags on their maps; their paper strength, as far as they knew, was their real strength. To Halder this impression was partly compensated for by his long experience as a soldier and by his ability to read between the lines. To Hitler it was not. Throughout the war he would make the same error, confusing paper strength with real strength, potential with efficacy. For the moment it was the French Army to whom he attributed the impossible; later it would be his own.

To Guderian and Rommel it was a different matter. The possibility of an armoured counter-attack was not ignored, but neither would they allow it to paralyse them. They did not know that the French 1st Armoured Division had run out of fuel just as it had been about to counter-attack Rommel's Meuse bridgehead on 14 May, nor that the 2nd and 3rd Armoured Divisions were motoring this way and that, in a labyrinth of confusion emanating from higher quarters. Guderian knew that De Gaulle's 4th Armoured Division was trailing him westward along his southern flank; he also knew that the French had failed to grasp the concept of all-arms warfare, that his own Stukas controlled the skies, and that consequently the threat was not serious enough for him to take the bigger risk of standing still, of abandoning the surge to the sea.

But this was to consider negatives. In the heady days of mid-May Guderian was wallowing in positives. The scenes confronting him were living proof of all that he had ever claimed for panzer warfare. The deep penetrations were causing a total dislocation of the French command, of French formations down to the tactical level, of the French will to resist. Every mile further that the sword was sent into the body of France would accelerate this process. As in many games of patience, the further you get the more likely you are to win. Guderian was riding an armoured snowball. To ride on was to grow.

Looking down from his reconnaissance plane, the French novelist and aviator Saint-Exupery saw more clearly than either High Command what was happening below. One passage in *Flight To Arras* is as lucid an appreciation of panzer warfare as Guderian could have wished for:

One fact the enemy grasped and exploited – that men fill small space in the earth's immensity. A continuous wall of men along our front would require a hundred million soldiers. Necessarily there were always gaps between the French units. In theory, these gaps are cancelled by the mobility of the units. Not, however, in the theory of the armoured division, for which an almost unmotorised army is as good as unmanoeuvrable. The gaps are real gaps. Whence this simple tactical rule: 'An armoured division should move against the enemy like water. It should bear lightly against the enemy's wall of defence and advance only at the point where it meets with no resistance.' The tanks operate by this rule, bear against the wall, and never fail to break through. They move as they please for want of French tanks to set against them; and though the damage they do is superficial – capture of unit staffs, cutting of telephone cables, burning of villages – the consequences of their raids are irreparable. In every region through which they make their lightning sweep, a French army, even though it seems to be virtually intact, has ceased to be an army. It has been transformed into clotted segments. It has, so to say, coagulated. The armoured divisions play the part of a chemical agent precipitating a colloidal solution. Where once an organism existed they leave a mere sum of organs whose unity has been destroyed. Between the clots – however combative the clots may have remained – the enemy moves at will. An army, if it is to be effective, must be something more than a numerical sum of soldiers. (28)

Guderian's 'reconnaissance in force' motored west. On the evening of 17 May a bridgehead was secured across the Oise; on the 18th the tanks clattered into St Quentin. Next day the Somme was crossed, and the old battlefield of the First World War. De Gaulle made his move with 4th Armoured Division, causing Guderian a 'few uncomfortable hours'. The panzers were now forty-five miles from the sea. As a reward O.K.H. restored their freedom of movement!

In the north Rommel had also been halted for a while, after taking Cambrai on 18 May. The right wing of the panzer advance, of which 7th Panzer was a prime component, was being slowed for the wheel northward, so that the left wing, with further to travel, could keep pace. Rommel's troops rested, refitted, and brought their supplies forward during the 19th. At 1.40 a.m. the following morning they moved forward again through the darkness; by dawn the leading elements had reached the southern outskirts of Arras. The rest of the division was strung out behind them on the road from Cambrai. On the 21st the tanks and armoured reconnaissance vehicles were sent around the southern edge of the town, and at this point the enemy attempted to counter-attack.

The stroke delivered against Rommel at Arras was intended as the northern prong of an offensive aimed at cutting through the panzer corridor, behind the tanks and in front of the following infantry. It did not succeed. The southern prong never got started; the northern was weaker than intended and was lacking in adequate infantry support. In view of the consternation that even this limited force caused the Germans it was fortunate for them that it was no stronger. Their troops, unused to being attacked, let alone attacked by tanks, fell into confusion and started tangling up their lines of vehicles. A whiff of panic started to spread. Rommel, with characteristic resolution, strode purposefully up a nearby hill, acquainted himself with the general picture, and then swept like a storm through his troops.

I brought every available gun into action at top speed against the tanks. Every gun, both anti-tank and anti-aircraft, was ordered to open rapid fire immediately and I personally gave each gun its target. With the enemy tanks so perilously close, only rapid fire from every gun could save the situation. We ran from gun to gun. The objections of gun commanders that the range was still too great to engage the tanks effectively, were overruled. All I cared about was to halt the enemy tanks by heavy gunfire. Soon we succeeded in putting the leading tanks out of action. (29)

The battle continued into evening, causing the Germans no little anxiety, before 7th Panzer's tanks fell on the enemy rear, and, with significant losses of their own, forced him to retire.

The action at Arras had more serious long-term consequences.

It introduced the British to the 88mm anti-aircraft gun, first used here in an anti-tank capacity, which would cause them such problems in the desert. For the French it signalled the abandonment of the armies trapped north of the panzer corridor, and hence the virtual certainty of defeat. For the Germans the consequences were less obvious but of immeasurable scope. The panic experienced by certain units (notably SS *Totenkopf* on Rommel's left flank), the shock-effect of an attack delivered with little artillery or infantry, and no air support, sent a shiver running down the German spine, leading them to overestimate the forces trapped in the north, and to exercise an exaggerated caution. The group and army commanders – like Kleist and Kluge, the Army Group commander Rundstedt, the leaders at O.K.H. and Hitler – each suddenly became aware of the knife's edge which *Sichelschnitt* would have been against a more resolute opponent. The effect of such nervousness would soon be decisively felt.

On the day that Rommel ran into trouble Guderian was watching 1st Panzer attack Amiens. On the way he had spoken to the 10th Panzer commander in Peronne, to find that Balck had moved his own troops out for Amiens before 10th Panzer arrived to relieve them. The relief commander was not amused, particularly in view of Balck's answer: 'If we lose it you can always take it again. I had to capture it in the first place, didn't I?' (30) Had the French Army possessed such an *esprit de corps* who knows what grief *Sichelschnitt* might have come to? But by 20 May there was little evidence of it, and, in fairness to Manstein and Guderian, it should be remembered that *Sichelschnitt*, as a blow against the enemy's nervous system, was designed to shatter any *esprit* there was.

On the evening of 20 May 2nd Panzer entered Abbeville. During the night one of its battalions reached the coast. Since no one had decided what to do with the panzers once this magic stretch of shoreline was reached, the 21st was spent in waiting for orders. They arrived that evening. Guderian was to capture the Channel ports and trap the British Expeditionary Force. He swiftly decided to allot the three panzer divisions one port each: Calais for the 1st, Boulogne the 2nd, Dunkirk the 10th. But no sooner had this decision been taken than 10th Panzer was removed from his command, and placed in O.K.H. reserve. Dunkirk would have to wait a little longer.

On 22 May the attack began, 1st and 2nd Panzer driving across the Authie, the former on a straight line for Calais, the latter to force its way through into Boulogne. In the afternoon 10th Panzer was mysteriously returned to Guderian, after thirty-six wasted hours in reserve. Guderian now decided to push the advanced 1st Panzer on to Dunkirk, and leave Calais to the 10th. The indecisiveness of the direction from above must have irritated him, but there was still plenty of time. His panzers were considerably nearer to Dunkirk than the mass of the British forces striving to escape.

But now other influences began to force their way into the situation with disastrous results. Both Kleist and Kluge had been shaken by the Arras attack; now Kluge, on the 23rd, with that timidity which would cost the Germans dear in France and Russia, suggested to Rundstedt that the armour should 'halt and close up'. Rundstedt agreed. Brauchitsch and Halder emphatically did not. Their plan, noted by Halder in his diary, was for 'Army Group B by heavy frontal attacks merely to hold the enemy who is making a planned withdrawal, while Army Group A, dealing with an enemy already whipped, cuts into his rear and strikes the decisive blow'. (31) This made considerable sense, in that Bock's Army Group B was still some thirty-five miles from Dunkirk, while the more powerful armoured divisions under Rundstedt's Army Group A were a bare fifteen.

Here Hitler re-entered the picture. The battlefield in question was Flanders which, as he never tired of repeating, was the arena of his First World War career. It was, he claimed, unsuitable for tanks. They would be halted, as Kluge had suggested and Rundstedt concurred in, on the Aa Canal line; and rested and refitted for the Battle of France still to come. Dunkirk would be dealt with by the Luftwaffe, paragons of the National Socialist destiny. The Army had had its share of the glory; now it was the Air Force's turn. For two whole days, while the Luftwaffe, in face of stiff RAF resistance, struggled to make good Goring's promises, the panzer divisions watched the British strengthen the pocket's southern flank against them. By the time the halt order was rescinded on the afternoon of 26 May, the resistance was more formidable and the Luftwaffe had been grounded by the weather. The tanks inched forward without reward. The BEF had been saved, and with this salvation vanished any remote possibility that Britain would settle for a compromise peace.

IX

The panzers were taken out of the line, rested and re-deployed on the new front line of the rivers Somme and Aisne. South of this line the remaining bulk of the French Army, shorn of its finest formations and most of its British support, awaited the fresh onslaught. The Panzer groups of Hoth and Kleist, on the lower and upper Somme, would attack first, as Guderian's group on the Aisne needed more time to assemble.

Rommel's 7th Panzer, under Hoth's group, struck across the Somme on the morning of 5 June. Railway bridges had been left standing by the French; a vigorous seizure by Rommel's infantry followed; the engineers ripped up the rails and the tanks clattered across. Despite this oversight the French offered stiff resistance, pouring artillery fire into the bridgehead and defending the villages nearby with a tenacity not encountered by 7th Panzer during its drive on Arras. But little remained to stop the Panzer Regiment once it had burst out into open country, firing continuous salvoes into any suspicious-looking woods, advancing steadily through the cornfields. Be-

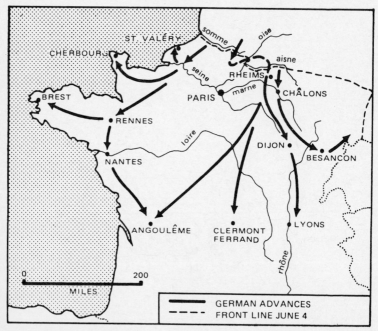

3 FRANCE: PHASE 2

hind the tanks the troop carriers of the rifle regiments mopped up the isolated pockets of French élan; ahead the fire of the divisional artillery cleared the division's path. Rommel's description of this day's advance is almost poetic:

> Over to our left, a giant pillar of smoke belched up from a burning enemy tanker and numerous saddled horses stampeded riderless across the plain. Then heavy enemy artillery fire from the south-west crashed into the division, but was unable to halt its attack. Over a broad front and in great depth, tanks, anti-aircraft guns, field guns, all with infantry mounted on them, raced across country east of the road. Vast clouds of dust rose high into the evening sky over the flat plain. (32)

By nightfall 7th Panzer had penetrated six miles.

During the next two days the enemy forces were pushed back to left and right as Rommel drove his division towards the Seine. The tanks avoided main roads and the barricaded villages, moving straight across country wherever it was possible for the wheeled vehicles to follow. A brigade of the British 1st Armoured Division held the Andelle river; it possessed ninety tanks but no artillery and few anti-tank guns. 7th Panzer lanced through its centre, forcing a retreat back towards the Seine. Now that river was only thirty miles away, and Rommel decided to attempt a *coup de main* seizure of the bridges at Elbeuf. As darkness fell on 8 June the Panzer Regiment and Motorcycle Battalion set off, hindered more by the combination of inadequate maps and lack of light than by the enemy. As they drove through villages the people rushed out to welcome their British deliverers. They were not the only ones surprised. 'We drove past an enemy anti-aircraft battery. There was still light in the guardroom and the sentries paid us honours as we passed.' (33) By midnight the battle-group had reached the Seine, nine miles from the Elbeuf bridges. The motorcyclists and five tanks were sent ahead, but were seemingly over-cautious. On arriving three hours later Rommel found the storming parties still forming up. Minutes later loud explosions heralded the French destruction of the bridges. Rommel was 'extremely angry'. The night, however, was still young. Fearing the efficacy of the French batteries on the far shore once it became light, Rommel hurried his tanks back downstream, through the enemy-held villages and early morning mist.

9 June found Rommel locating the rest of his division once more, and consolidating the vast hole it had torn in the French left flank. Two hundred miles to the east Guderian's group went over to the attack on the Aisne. In Paris Weygand was trying to persuade the French cabinet to sue for an armistice. 7th Panzer was ordered to turn north, to prevent the escape of the divisions it had thrown towards the sea during its advance from the Somme. On the morning of the 10th it assembled north of Rouen and drove for the Channel. By late afternoon the thirty miles had been covered. It was an emotional moment.

> The sight of the sea with the cliffs on either side thrilled and stirred every man of us; also the thought that we had reached the coast of France. We climbed out of our vehicles and walked down the shingle beach to the water's edge until the water lapped over our boots. Several dispatch riders in long waterproof coats walked straight out until the water was over their knees, and I had to call them back. Close behind us Rothenburg came up in his command tank, crashed through the beach wall, and drove down to the water. (34)

There was no time for bathing or building sandcastles. A strong enemy force was in Fécamp, so Rommel wheeled part of his force around the town, cutting off the potential escape route to Le Havre. He next turned his attention to St Valéry, where a sizable part of the 51st Highland Division was waiting to embark for England. Leaving 7th Rifle Regiment east of Fécamp, he took 6th Rifle Regiment and the mass of his tanks west. The British fortified line south of St Valéry, with strong anti-tank and artillery elements, held up the motorised infantry, but Rothenburg's tanks skirted around to the high ground overlooking the port from the north-west. The town was requested to surrender; refusal was answered by the concentrated fire of Rommel's armour. The raging fires and incessant harassing fire by the arriving infantry prevented embarkation during the night. The next morning the tanks, after engaging British warships in a long-range gun battle, rolled into the streets of the town and down to the docks. The defenders, out of ammunition, surrendered. Twelve thousand prisoners were taken, including twelve generals.

In the preceding two days Guderian had been slowly prising apart the French defences on the Aisne. By 12 June his leading units were on and across the Marne, the fortified villages behind them, a virtually open country spread about before their lines of advance. Kleist's forces, which had met strong resistance on the upper Somme, were switched west to exploit Guderian's breach. They broke through west of Rheims and plunged south towards the Loire. The French Government had already evacuated Paris, caught in a vicious squabble between their obligations to the British alliance and the plight of the broken French Army.

All around them the panzers advanced. The rush of vandal grace swept on; towards Cherbourg, Rennes, Dijon, the Swiss frontier. On 14 June Reichenau's Sixth Army entered Paris, the swastika floated from the Eiffel Tower, the goose-step resounded down the Champs d'Elysée. Across France chaos reigned, the roads jammed with refugees, village squares crammed with soldiers not knowing if the war was over. Some offered resistance, no matter how hopeless; others merely stared as the armoured columns swept past. *Sichelschnitt* had succeeded. Manstein's claims for it had been proven. The scythe had taken its harvest. France was beaten and Germany rejoiced. The Reich waited for the British to accept terms.

X

Herein lay the major flaw, not in what *Sichelschnitt* had done, but in what it had failed to do. Manstein's plan had been designed to eliminate the French and British armies in continental Europe, to do what Imperial Germany had failed to do twenty-five years before. In 1914, thrown back from the Marne and unable to finish France, the German General Staff had acquired a fixation on crossing the Marne, on finishing France. As in September 1914 they had not faced the Channel with a beaten foe behind them, the question of crossing twenty miles of sea had not arisen. When it did arise in June 1940 there was no answer to hand.

If the original oversight was the Army's, the responsibility for correcting it rested with the Supreme Command. Hitler had unleashed the war; he had expected the easy victory over France. The next step should have been thought out in advance. It had not been. Neither would this lack of foresight appear rare in retrospect. Rather it was the first solid evidence of the extemporary manner in which Hitler would conduct his war. The man who never tired of 'destiny' had no conception of temporal depth. Decisions would be taken on the spur of the moment, with little proper planning or consideration for the implications arising thereof. The problem of Britain would be tackled when it arose. That it was basic to the problem of waging war in Europe was no more appreciated by Hitler than it had been by the Kaiser. When this became apparent in June 1940 it was already too late. Doenitz, in charge of U boats, told Hitler that he would need three hundred to mount sufficient pressure on Britain. He had fifty-seven, of which only twelve were ocean-worthy. Goring was more optimistic, but he too had insufficient machines of the type required. The Luftwaffe had been created primarily as an Army support-arm, only secondarily as a strategic bombing force. The oil situation, which effected both submarine and plane, was also unfavourable. The synthetic production programme and the planned exploitation of Germany's own limited supplies would not bear sufficient fruit until 1942, the same year, ironically, as Hitler could expect to possess sufficient air and naval strength. In 1940 the blockading of Britain was beyond the Wehrmacht's strength.

Invasion? This was the possibility that forced itself to the fore. But invasion too was impractical. Even should the Luftwaffe secure the sky above the English Channel the Navy could only muster sufficient forces to protect a narrow corridor between the two coasts. Neither were there enough craft, certainly none designed specifically for the purpose as the Japanese were doing. The Army, offered this option of landing a few divisions on an open coast with dubious air cover, was not enthusiastic. Halder noted sarcastically that he might as well put the troops through a 'sausage machine'.

So what was to be done about Britain? Hitler's offer of peace produced only a growl of defiance. Clearly a tiger had been taken by the tail. For the moment it was as unable to strike out from its island cage as the German Army was to strike in. Hitler thought he had time to spare. In this he was correct, in his use of it mistaken. He saw the Channel as Britain's salvation, not his own failure to plan for a long war or adapt his approach to the enemy. His impotence before a stretch of water only assured him of his potency on land. If *Blitzkrieg* was inapplicable to Britain it was applicable anywhere on the European continent.

Herein lay a major legacy of *Sichelschnitt*. Victory had been so swift and so apparently effortless that the German leaders began to believe themselves infallible and their Army invincible. In such a frame of mind it was difficult to perceive the factors qualifying their French success, and hence to examine their victory in its proper perspective. That they did not is hardly surprising. It is always the losers that learn; the German triumph of 1940 had grown from the defeat in 1918. Now they would suffer for their own success.

If they had looked back over the campaign with a more sombre and self-critical eye they could have learnt much, seen many pointers to the future. The dominating factor throughout the campaign had been the absence of Clausewitz's friction: the factors of uncertainty and chance which separate conception from execution. This notion must have been central to the German General Staff's understanding of warfare; they should have reminded themselves and stressed its significance to their Führer. For France had been an ideal environment for panzer warfare. The distances short, the roads good and profuse, the weather kind. The panzers had no shortage of channels to flow along; the speed and depth of their penetrations were thus increased. French morale, already low, was lowered further. Speed increased further. And so on. The war was consequently short, the casualties low. Because the French supply system was ruptured so fast, there was no time for a strain to make itself felt on the German. Likewise the command structure. In short, everything went so closely according to plan that friction was minimal. Such success should not have been expected again. Surprise is a coin spent with rapidly diminishing returns. Not many countries had the road network or the political vulnerability that France had in 1940. Had this been fully appreciated the German Army could have been considerably improved. There were instances of friction in the French campaign; they should have been studied in the knowledge that they could only intensify in effect in future campaigns.

For one thing the low firepower of the German tanks and anti-tank guns had been thoroughly exposed. Guderian had practised with a captured French heavy tank, and watched the German shells bounce off its thick armour. If French tactical awareness had matched the quality of their equipment the German advance would have suffered more nasty shocks than it did. As it was Arras had been a nasty enough moment. For another thing the problem of moving across open country, when roads were jammed with civilians or blocked by fortified villages, had raised the need for putting tracks on all motorised vehicles, not just the tanks. In other countries, where road surfaces would differ little from those of an average French field, this might prove decisive.

The command structure had creaked in the rare moments of stress. The new approach might have succeeded, but its exponents were little more popular with the hierachy's traditionalists than they had been before. Some opponents, like Halder, had been conclusively won over; others, like Rundstedt and Kluge, had acquired only a superficial conviction. The habits of a lifetime did not die overnight. A strong hand would be needed to hold these factions together. And, for future success, it would have to be a wise hand, one that had learnt the barely visible lessons of France. Yet, fatally for the Wehrmacht, the hand that emerged belonged to he who had learnt least. And it was too strong.

Hitler had already forgotten that Manstein had devised the plan; *Sichelschnitt* had been his personal triumph, over the French, over his own General Staff. The latter had been timid, lacking in imagination and resolve. They had created difficulties where none existed. He had said it would be easy, and easy it had been. The vindication of victory took away any remaining inclination to listen to his professional advisers, made him more inclined to assume the right of continual interference in the military conduct of war. From such a position he would dismiss the real difficulties of the future as rooted in that same lack of imagination and resolve, not in his own inadequacies as a military commander and statesman.

XI

The flaws in the masterpiece took time to manifest themselves. In the summer of 1940 German doubts were rare. France had been blown out of the war in six weeks, the trauma of Sedan repeated, the frustration of the Marne avenged. From the Pyrenees to the Bug the Wehrmacht held sway over the continent of Europe. Britain nursed her pride and prepared for the Luftwaffe's onslaught; on the other side of Europe the Soviet Union held its breath and hurried more troops into the riven body of Poland. Both prepared for a war whose length could not be foreseen. As if to clear the decks Stalin sent the long hand of the Comintern as far afield as Mexico to remove the living ghost of Leon Trotsky, creator of the Red Army.

In the meantime the French settled down to occupation and the drums went rat-a-tat-tat through the streets of delirious Berlin.

The credit could be widely shared. To Manstein for the plan, the last great triumph of the General Staff's eternal obsession with operational strategy. To Guderian for the armoured force, which had made it possible and which carried it through. Both had needed to fight hard for acceptance, both had Hitler to thank for his encouragement, and for the decisive weight of his support in their battle with the traditionalist upper echelons of the German Army. To Hitler then goes the credit he would squander in the years to come. He forced through the plan he intuited was correct; he interfered little in its execution, and then sometimes for the better, as in the employment of airborne troops. O.K.H. also deserves some credit. Reluctant to accept an offensive in the West, reluctant to accept Manstein's plan, nevertheless, once these options became unavoidable, it translated a vision into a scheme with all the skills of its accumulated experience.

And finally those who fought *Sichelschnitt*: the driving commanders, the individual soldiers. Manstein wrote that in Hitler's time, up to and including 1940, the German Army was united as never before. There is little reason to disbelieve it. Nazi authoritarianism had only just begun to trickle down through the military hierarchy; in 1940 democracy still flourished within the German Army, bearing as fruit the priceless combination of discipline and initiative.

In 1940 all worked together: Führer, O.K.H., generals, soldiers. The result was triumph. It was the last time they all worked in harmony. The result, not surprisingly, would be tragedy.

References (Chapter 1)

1. Paget, *Manstein*, 2
2. M. Howard, *The Franco-Prussian War* (Rupert Hart-Davis, 1961), 53
3. Clark, *Barbarossa*, 9
4. Guderian, *Panzer Leader*, 24
5. Ibid, 25

6. Ibid, 30
7. Sun Tzu, *The Art of War* (OUP, 1963), 96
8. Manstein, *Lost Victories*, 118
9. Guderian, *Panzer Leader*, 90
10. Ibid, 91
11. Ibid, 92
12. quoted in Young, *Rommel*, 55
13. *The Rommel Papers*, 6
14. Ibid, 7
15. Guderian, *Panzer Leader*, 99
16. *The Rommel Papers*, 7
17. Guderian, *Panzer Leader*, 102
18. quoted in Williams, *France*, 44
19. Guderian, *Panzer Leader*, 105
20. *The Rommel Papers*, 12
21. Ibid, 14
22. Ibid, 16
23. Ibid, 19
24. Ibid, 24
25. Ibid, 25–6
26. Guderian, *Panzer Leader*, 107
27. quoted in Strawson, *Hitler*, 110
28. Saint-Exupéry, A. de, *Flight of Arras* (Penguin, 1966), 64–5
29. *The Rommel Papers*, 32
30. Guderian, *Panzer Leader*, 112
31. quoted in Wilmot, *Struggle for Europe*, 19
32. *The Rommel Papers*, 49
33. Ibid, 56
34. Ibid, 60

Chapter 2

BARBAROSSA –
THE ARROGANT FOLLY

There is no crime greater than having too many desires.
(Lao Tzu)

From France Hitler turned to the Soviet Union. Not so quickly
as these chapters might indicate, but neither so slowly as the
twelve-month lapse between campaigns might suggest. Before
France had been brought to the carriage at Compiègne, before
Britain had been tested in the skies, Hitler had resolved to move
East, to pit his victorious army against its seemingly predeter-
mined foe. The conquest of Soviet Russia would give Nazi
Germany undisputed sway over the European continent, im-
munity from outside attack, and the chance of contesting world
hegemony with the Atlantic powers and Japan. The failure
to subdue the Soviet *Untermenschen* (sub-humans) would provide the enemy with a similar position of power. In a sense
realised only later by the statesmen of Western Europe, the
old continent, shrunk by a global technology, had peaceful
room for only one political force. *Barbarossa* would decide
which it was to be: Slav or Teuton, state capitalist or fascist
(masquerading as international socialism and the New Order),
Stalin or Hitler, twisted reason or twisted romanticism. The
two crippled children of a senile capitalism would fight for its
inheritance.

The German General Staff, who pursued thought along
narrower channels, was at no stage a party to the original
decision. The world had left it behind; its Kaiser-given right
to choose suitable targets for the German war-machine on
military grounds was in abeyance. They were informed later
than the service or Party chiefs; theirs was to plan and execute,
not to question the destiny of the Reich.

The first people to know were Hitler's immediate entourage

at O.K.W.: Jodl, Keitel, Goring and Raeder. On 31 July he told them

> if Russia drops out of the picture, America, too, is lost for Britain, because the elimination of Russia would greatly increase Japan's power in the Far East . . . Decision: Russia's destruction must therefore be made part of this struggle . . . The sooner Russia is crushed the better. The attack will achieve its purpose only if the Russian state can be shattered to its roots with one blow . . . if we start in May 1941, we will have five months in which to finish the job. (1)

This strategic summary was rather simplistic, even to the hand-picked yes-men of O.K.W. It sounds remarkably like someone grasping for acceptable reasons to do something he wanted to do for other reasons. These other reasons we shall come to. But first, let us look at the strategic rationale, the errors involved, and the possible alternatives.

France had been beaten, Britain had not. The spectre of a two-front war on *land* had been, for an indefinite period, removed. To Hitler, who only understood land warfare – albeit with a rare appreciation of the possibilities inherent in air and naval support of ground operations – this meant that a two-front situation had been removed, period. And even if it had not, the argument ran on, destroying the Red Army on land was the quickest way to make sure. Like a juggler with two balls in the air, knowing that only one needed to be caught, Hitler decided to catch the one that looked easier, that fitted better into his hand.. He chose the wrong one. In asserting that the conquest of the Soviet Union would be easier than the defeat of Britain he made his one all-encompassing blunder of the war. He was really saying two things: the army was invincible; it could only be turned against Russia. In both cases he was mistaken. It could not be turned successfully against Russia; it could have been turned indirectly against Britain.

In the familiar pattern of land warfare, air and naval forces serve as auxiliaries, tuned as they are to speed the annihilative strategy pursued on the ground. Thus the German Navy and Air Force were supposed to clear the path for 'Sea Lion's' annihilation of the British Army on British soil. In the Soviet Union they would play a similar role, assisting the Army in delivering the one pulverising blow that would, hopefully, drive Russia out of the war. But there are other ways of utilising naval and air strength, and Britain above all demanded that they be so used. In this case it would be the Army who would play the auxiliary role, for if Britain was to be beaten it had to be by attrition, carried through by the Navy in the Atlantic, the Air Force in British skies, all three forces in the Middle East. Britain had to be strangled; she could not be run through. Yet Hitler only ever understood the sword.

Raeder and Göring, chiefs of the Navy and Air Force, naturally had other opinions. Both produced plans for continuance of the war against Britain. Raeder saw Hitler twice, on 6 and 26 September 1940 when he outlined to him the opportunities beckoning in the Mediterranean area. Spain should be brought into the war, he urged; Gibraltar and the Canaries taken as cover against a possible Anglo-American landing in north-west Africa; Malta should be taken, and, in collaboration with the as-yet-undefeated Italians, a strong force should be sent across Egypt and into the Persian Gulf area. Turkey would be brought into the war, Britain's lifeline to the East cut, Soviet Russia kept quiescent by the southern threat to her Caucasus oil. Göring's plan differed little, envisaging a strong armoured thrust through the Balkans, Turkey and Syria to similar destinations in Egypt and the Persian Gulf. Throughout the unwinding of the campaign, both agreed, all German war production should be geared to increasing the naval and air strength such a strategy required.

This 'Mediterranean option' offered a high probability of success. Even two years later, in the summer of 1942, another two panzer divisions in North Africa might well have toppled the precarious British position in the Middle East. In late 1940 the British were far weaker, the Italians had not had their confidence irreparably shattered, and the Russian campaign was not absorbing ninety per cent of the Reich's energies. Even Guderian, arch-exponent of *Blitzkrieg*, saw the soundness of such a strategy. Later he was to write that at his Besancon HQ in July 1940 he had reached the conclusion that

. . . we could ensure peace in the near future by, first of all, advancing at once to the mouth of the Rhone: then, having captured the French Mediterranean bases in conjunction with the Italians, by landing in Africa, while the Luftwaffe's first-class parachute troops seized Malta . . . The weakness of the British in Egypt at that time was known to us. The Italians still had strong forces in Abyssinia. The defences of Malta against air attack were inadequate. Everything seemed to be in favour of further operations along these lines, and I could see no disadvantages ... (2)

Whether Guderian really did see things so clearly in 1940 is, of course, open to doubt. But if Raeder and Göring could, then it should not have been beyond a man of Guderian's perspicacity. What might seem surprising is that it seems to have been beyond Hitler's.

It does not in the light of Hitler's assumptions about the Soviet Union. His assertion that continued British resistance made elimination of Russia a strategic imperative was mere gloss, designed to quiet his generals, perhaps even to quiet himself. The inverse urged by Göring and Raeder – that the defeat of Britain would leave Germany in a stronger position *vis-à-vis* the Soviet Union – made far greater strategic sense. The other argument he urged upon his generals – that Russia was preparing to attack Germany – was equally specious. Stalin was certainly preparing for war, but with the greatest reluctance. No, Hitler was not about to attack the Soviet Union on strategic grounds; he was about to do so because he believed that Russia *should* and *could* be defeated. The 'should' sprang from his most deeply-felt political desires; living-space for the *Herrenvolk*, the subjugation of 'inferior' races. The latter provided the 'could'. Communism was merely a social system devised for and by the corrupt and the primitive. 'We have only to kick in the door and the whole rotten structure will come crashing down.' (3)

Here we come once more upon Hitler's extraordinarily one-sided intelligence. He had grasped the idea of *Blitzkrieg* as no other politican and few other soldiers had; grasped its potential but not its limited applicability. He had grasped intuitively the importance of the air and naval arms in land warfare, yet not their applicability outside the confines of *Blitzkrieg*. He had grasped, as he never tired of telling his generals, the economic dimension of warfare, yet insisted on reducing it to flags on maps, static production centres. He never understood interdiction, only seizure. The importance of the Caucasus oil rightly obsessed him, the importance of Suez forever eluded him. And, above all, he played like a maestro on the fears and uncertainties of his opponents, yet never grasped the art of playing on their strengths. France in 1940 was easy prey; Britain's stance confused and angered him; Soviet tenacity would have the same effect. Unlike his generals he had not overestimated Poland or France; also unlike them he did underestimate Britain, Russia, and the United States. Particularly Russia. The Soviet Empire could be beaten, should be beaten, would be beaten. After that the rest would take care of itself. Who would stand against the master of Europe from Bordeaux to Archangel?

The underestimate of Soviet strength – military, economic, socio-political – would seep like woodworm through German planning, through the conduct of operations, through occupation policy, through armaments production. Until, as Hitler had so prophetically stated, the whole rotten structure came crashing down. His own.

II

In autumn 1940, beyond the higher echelons of O.K.W. and O.K.H., the Wehrmacht as yet knew nothing of the task ahead. Bock, transferred east in August, had guessed in his diary that he was expected to act as a 'kind of scarecrow to the Russians'. (4) Army or Group commanders like he and Guderian did not learn of *Barbarossa* before the onset of winter. By then the planning was at an advanced stage, both O.K.W. and O.K.H., true to Hitler's policy of divide-to-rule, having prepared detailed operational studies. O.K.W.'s showed a singular lack of imagination, envisaging a three-pronged attack, each prong carrying roughly equal weight, against Leningrad, Moscow and Kiev. The O.K.H. version, begun by Marcks and carried on by the then Quartermaster-General, the ill-fated Friedrich von Paulus, displayed rather more subtlety. Marcks and Paulus envisaged two strong forces advancing from Poland towards Moscow and Kiev, with an eye to an eventual super-Cannae in the Kharkov area. Two minor forces would advance on the extreme flanks, one from East Prussia aimed at Leningrad, the other from Rumania aimed at Kiev. This plan was submitted to a war-game at Zossen in early December; its outcome suggested a synthesis of the O.K.H. and O.K.W. plans – the four O.K.H. prongs with the three O.K.W. objectives, priority accorded the central Moscow axis. This synthesis was presented to Hitler in early December; it re-emerged, decisively but not too visibly altered, as Führer Directive 21 on 18 December. Hitler had maintained the strength of the Moscow prong, but for reasons of his own. He intended it to provide support to the two flanking prongs in achievement of their own objectives. This apparently minor shift of emphasis presaged the major, and crucial, division of opinon in August 1941.

On 2 January 1941 the Army Group Chiefs of Staff were let into the act, instructed to prepare their own plans for *Barbarossa*. Bock and his Chief of Staff Salmuth submitted a highly Moscocentric plan, practically ignoring Kiev and Leningrad. This was most uncharacteristic of the conservative Bock, and highly significant. If such a respected member of the old school should believe that an armoured surge towards Moscow, with all the attendant risks, offered the *only* real chance of success, then *Barbarossa* was going to be a frightful gamble. O.K.H. was unconvinced. Army Group Centre's plan was rejected.

At the end of the month there was a further conference, this time for the Army Group and Army commanders. Bock recalled an atmosphere of scarcely-concealed pessimism.

> Brauchitsch discussed in details the forthcoming operations against Russia, and stressed the importance of annihilating Russian forces in the border zones so that German forces could rapidly gain freedom of movement. I asked Halder, sitting next to me: 'What assurance do we have that the Russians will sit still in front of the Dvina-Dnieper while we destroy them?' Halder smiled wanly ... (5)

What assurance indeed? The General Staff's guru, the late von Schlieffen, had considered decisive success impossible in Russia. That country's armies, he argued, were too large to encircle; the countryside itself devoid of obstacles against which they could be pinned. The result would be a continual pushing of the enemy back towards his supply bases, and the consequent pulling of the German forces away from theirs. Space would grow in relation to usable force, the climate would take its toll, supplies would dwindle. German strength would slowly be sapped away.

Schlieffen had not lived to see the era of *Blitzkrieg*. The speed of the panzer forces in getting behind the Russian armies would prevent their withdrawal. So ran the counter-argument. The vastness of the spaces involved was not comprehended; the difficulties of encirclement on such terrain and against a resolute defence were discounted. 'We have only to kick in the door.' The physical reality of European Russia was under-

estimated as disastrously as the Soviet will to resist. The two
delusions were mutually supportive. As for the climate, well, it
would all be over in six to eight weeks. Each truth supported
another. They all rested on the one fallacy, that it would be
easy.

The preparations continued. More conferences, more war
games. The operation orders were signed, the troops and equipment moved slowly east. Air reconnaissance intensified. The
generals, absorbed in the how, stopped worrying for the
moment about the whys and the whethers, and reactivated the
arguments of the French campaign. Bock's Army Group Centre,
comprising Fourth and Ninth Armies in the centre, Second
and Third Panzer Groups on the flanks, and Second Army in
reserve, was to advance on Moscow via Minsk and Smolensk.
At the 27 March O.K.H. conference Brauchitsch insisted that
the two panzer groups should 'turn in' to form a pocket in the
vicinity of Minsk. Bock vigorously protested; they should be
allowed to push on at speed for Smolensk. Safety above speed,
said Brauchitsch. Speed was the only safety, said Bock. The
argument was not resolved, never would be. A clear decision
one way or the other at this stage would have spared the
Germans priceless time which was soon to be wasted in argument. And it would have prevented, or at least alleviated, the
chronic souring of personal relationships which did such
irredeemable harm to their direction of the war.

While they were arguing, disturbing intelligence was coming
in of the actual Soviet strength. In the spring of 1941 a visiting
Russian military commission was given, on Hitler's orders, a
guided tour of the German armaments centres. These Russians,
with an ingenuousness that matched Hitler's, refused to believe
that the Panzer IV was the Germans' heaviest tank, thus alert-
ing their guide, Guderian, to the probability that the Red Army
did have such a tank entering production.

The quality of armour was not the only source of concern.
In 1933 Guderian had visited a single Soviet tank factory producing over eight thousand tanks a year. In 1941 the entire
German armaments industry was delivering only one eighth of
that figure. Guderian had printed the Soviet figure in *Achtung!
Panzer!*, and had run into trouble with the censor. O.K.H. was
still loath to believe it, at least in public. In private they were
more circumspect. Paulus, receiving a friend in early June, confounded him by admitting that a map of Soviet armament
centres beyond the Urals, published as a subject of ridicule by a

Berlin newspaper, was in fact accurate. A studied blindness was becoming an integral feature of Wehrmacht planning. Inconvenient evidence was assumed to be a Soviet bluff.

Political decisions were also being avoided like the plague, though such avoidance was inexcusable even from the military point of view. The Army managed to prevent the S.S. securing a free hand behind their lines, but only to the benefit of the equally-detested Party. Hitler's demand for a war without chivalry, published via the notorious 'Commissar' and 'Treatment of Civilians and Prisoners' decrees, was not opposed at the source, merely expected to evaporate in practice through the workings of common Prussian decency. Doubtless in many cases it did, at least in the war's opening year, but with equal certainty in others it did not. This was besides the military point. Bock, after arguing about it with Brauchitsch, wrote in his diary that the Russians should be treated according to the normal rules of warfare, or 'we shall find them to be a rather tenacious enemy'. (6) If this was apparent to the narrow-minded Bock all the more reason why Hitler, arch-exponent of the psychological approach, should have realised it. It was he who expected the 'rotten structure' to collapse. What would make this less likely than an indiscriminate punishment of those who lived in it? Keitel's directive to the effect that anyone should be assumed to be a communist until proven otherwise has a familiar ring for all those who followed the American débâcle in Vietnam. Hitler, too, was turning a blind eye to the Wehrmacht's greatest potential asset: the discontent rife in Stalinist Russia, particularly among the non-Russian nationalities. This blindness, again, received encouragement from the fatal underestimation of Soviet strength. They were Slavs, *Untermenschen*. 'We'll supply the Ukrainians with scarves, glass beads and everything that colonial peoples like,' the Führer commented in a moment of generosity. (7)

On 14 June Hitler did not dispense sacks of beads for trading to his gathered generals. Nor did he justify the coming attack on grounds of the Aryan's burden, but on the strategic exigencies of the war. Little had changed in twelve months. With Britain undefeated, he argued, Germany's position could only be secured by total control of the European land-mass. The Soviets were in any case preparing to attack the Reich; in doing so they played into the hands of the German destiny. His detailed exposition, according to Guderian, was 'unconvincing'.

So long as the war in the West was still undecided, any new undertaking must result in a war on two fronts; and Adolf Hitler's Germany was even less capable of fighting such a war than had been the Germany of 1914. The assembled company listened to Hitler's speech in silence and then, since there was to be no discussion, dispersed, still in silence and with heavy hearts. (8)

Kesselring, visiting Bock a few days later, found him 'in contrast to the mood of previous campaigns, rather dispirited'. (9)

III

Delayed by the Balkan campaign and the late thaw in White Russia, *Barbarossa* began on 22 June 1941. At 3.15 a.m. the artillery opened fire; an hour later German troops crossed the frontier. South of Brest-Litovsk those of Guderian's tanks that had been waterproofed for 'Sea Lion' drove across the shallow bed of the river Bug. Moscow was six hundred miles in front of them. Guderian, across two hours later in his armoured wireless truck, followed 18th Panzer's tracks eastward. Overtaking the armour he reached the Desna bridge to find a few Russian pickets 'who took to their heels' when they saw his vehicle. Throughout the morning the Red Army High Command was forbidding its troops to violate the frontier without authorisation! Guderian would have smiled had he known. More than three years separated the Red Army from their next sight of the frontier.

As the armoured columns plunged forward through the bewildered Soviet defences the Luftwaffe crowded the skies above. By the end of 23 June it had destroyed over one-and-a-half thousand planes on the ground, and decimated the reserves flown hastily and piecemeal from Central Russia. Its mastery in the air undisputed, the Luftwaffe could devote all its attention to the ground, to breaking up enemy concentrations, interdicting the rail system, providing constant forward reconnaissance. In short, clearing the path of the long columns of German armour advancing below.

Through these first few days the ill-prepared Red Army, deprived of its experienced leaders by recent purges, broke before the onslaught. *Blitzkrieg* seemed irresistible; its sharpness and speed only thrown into greater relief by the ponderous enormity of its latest victim. The Italian journalist and writer Curzio Malaparte, travelling with the Eleventh Army in the far south, observed the Wehrmacht in motion.

> The exhausts of the panzers belched out blue tongues of smoke. The air is filled with a pungent, bluish vapour that mingles with the damp green of the grass and with the golden reflection of the corn. Beneath the screaming arch of Stukas the mobile columns of tanks resemble thin lines drawn with a pencil on the vast green slate of the Moldavian plain. (10)

The romance of this picture! With the clarity of a Japanese painting Malaparte catches the Wehrmacht at its moment of destiny, drawing graceful lines of death across the canvas of nature. Only the pregnant juxtaposition of two words – thin and vast – tells a different story, looks forward fifteen months to the inevitable end of this great adventure in a frozen city by a distant river. For the moment all is confidence; doubts must fight to be heard. Take Malaparte's description of a German camp:

> Strictly speaking, it is not a camp but a bivouac, inasmuch as it consists merely of a fleet of vehicles . . . As soon as they were awake the German soldiers got to work on their engines with pliers, pincers, screwdrivers, spanners and hammers . . . A smell of burning oil, carbonic acid, petrol, and white-hot metal recreates in the wood the characteristic atmosphere of a smithy . . . I watch them working; I note the way they use their hands, the way they hold things, the way they bend their heads over their implements . . . Rather than soldiers intent on fighting they look like artisans at work, like mechanics busying themselves about a complex, delicate machine . . . Their very gait, their very manner of speech, their very gestures are those of workmen, not of soldiers. The wounded have that tight-lipped, slightly angry air of workmen injured in an industrial accident. Their discipline has about it the same flexibility and informality as the discipline maintained by a gang of workmen. Their *esprit de corps* is an *esprit d'équipe*, a team spirit, and at the same time it is an *esprit de métier*. (11)

This picture of an Army fully involved in the day-to-day chores of waging war has a daunting 'suchness' about it. Yet in painting it, in concentrating simply on what is happening, Malaparte contrives to say much of the strengths and weaknesses of the German Army, the reasons for its successes and ultimate failure in Russia.

The 'flexibility and informality' of discipline confirms the democratic spirit of the Army at its lower levels, provides ample reason for the initiative displayed at those levels throughout the war. In its long and bitterly-contested fall from power the German Army will prove again and again that a discipline born of 'team spirit' is infinitely stronger than a discipline imposed formally from above. And the overpowering emphasis on machinery. In 1941 no other army so fully understood the power of mechanisation. The engine of the tank, as Guderian was fond of saying, was no less a weapon than its gun. Speed, surprise, concentration; they all came out of the panzers' exhaust pipes, these panzers attended to with such diligence.

But each of these facets had another face. The clinical, detached state of mind of these artisans – how will they react to opposition neither clinical nor detached? On the very first day of *Barbarossa*, in the far north, some of Manstein's troops came across a 'German patrol which had been cut off by the enemy . . . All its members were dead and gruesomely mutilated.' (12) The Russians were not intending to fight by the rules, any more than Hitler. Resistance was to be implacable, possessed of an emotional resonance and indifference to human life that these worker-soldiers tending their beloved engines would never understand. They would react with shock, eventually with a barbarism of their own, appearing all the more cruel for its mechanised veneer, so cold and precise. The machines too would need their diligent attention, for only that would carry them across a country without autobahns or good roads of any sort, where supplies would be to all intents and purposes what they carried with them. For the first few weeks these factors would remain largely dormant, veiled by the Wehrmacht's paralysing speed and the Soviet Command's ineptitude. But they were implicit in the venture itself, requiring only time to make themselves felt, visible, and finally decisive.

Those responsible for perceiving these trends were they who sat behind the desks and pored over the maps and statistics in command posts far behind the fronts. The individual soldiers, feeling the first stirrings of Soviet resilience, could only fight on, tend their equipment, trust to fate. The commanders like Guderian might have an inkling of the problems mounting ahead, but they too were so busy as to allow little time or energy for such anxieties. Their days were spent in whirlwind tours of their formations:

On 24 June I left my headquarters at 08.25 hrs and drove towards Slonim. The 17th Panzer Division had meanwhile arrived at this town. Between Rozana and Slonim I ran into Russian infantry which was laying down fire on the main road. A battery of the 17th Panzer Division and dismounted motorcyclists were returning the enemy fire without any particular success. I joined in this action and by firing the machine-gun in my armoured command vehicle succeeded in dislodging the enemy from his position; I was then able to drive on. At 11.30 hrs I arrived at the headquarters of 17th Panzer Division, at that time located in the western outskirts of Slonim, where I found not only the divisional commander, General von Arnim, but also the corps commander, General Lemelsen. While we were discussing the situation there was a sudden outburst of lively rifle and machine-gun fire in our rear; our view of the road from Bialystok was blocked by a burning lorry, so that we were in ignorance of what was going on until two Russian tanks appeared out of the smoke. They were attempting to force their way into Slonim, with cannons and machine-guns blazing, and were heavily pursued by German Panzer Mark IVs which were also firing heavily. The Russian tanks noticed the group of officers, of which I was one, and we were immediately subjected to a rain of shells, which, fired at such extremely close range, both deafened and blinded us for a few moments. Being old soldiers we had immediately thrown ourselves to the ground; only poor Lieutenant-Colonel Feller, who had come to us on a mission from the Commander of the Training Army, and was unaccustomed to active service, was too slow and suffered a very painful wound in consequence. Also the commander of an anti-tank battalion, Lieutenant-Colonel Dallmer-Zerbe, received a severe wound from which, I regret to say, he died a few days later. The Russian tanks succeeded in forcing their way into the town where they were eventually put out of action.

I next visited the front line in Slonim and then drove in a

Panzer IV through no-man's-land to the 18th Panzer Division. At 15.30 hrs I was back in Slonim, having ordered the 18th Panzer Division to push on in the direction of Baranovicze, while the 29th (Motorised) Infantry Division was instructed to hasten its advance toward Slonim. I then returned to my Group Command post. This drive took me unexpectedly through the middle of Russian infantry, which had come up in lorries to the very outskirts of Slonim and was on the point of dismounting. I ordered my driver, who was next to me, to go full speed ahead and we drove straight through the Russians; they were so surprised by this unexpected encounter that they did not even have time to fire their guns. All the same they must have recognised me, because the Russian press later announced my death; I felt bound to inform them of their mistake by means of the German wireless.

I rejoined my staff at 20.15 hrs. There I found messages waiting for me concerning fierce fighting on our deep right flank, where LIII Army Corps had been successfully defeating Russian attacks in the Maloryta area since 23 June. Between the XXIV and XLVII Panzer Corps elements of the XII Army Corps had managed to establish loose contact. The left flank of the Panzer Group was seriously threatened by an intensification of the attacks on the part of the Russian forces pouring back from Bialystok. To secure this rapid flank commitment of the 29th (Motorised) Infantry Division and of the XLVI Panzer Corps was necessary. (13)

As the campaign's first week unrolled the panzers continued their advance. By 27 June 17th Panzer had reached Minsk, two hundred miles from the Bug, and linked hands with Hoth's in-wheeling Third Panzer Group. In two pockets around Bialystok and Volkovsk six Russian divisions were trapped; now, west of Minsk, another fifteen felt the panzer ring tighten around them. Guderian had orders to swing in again on Smolensk, a further two hundred miles east, as fast as tank engines, opposition, and the security of the pockets behind him allowed.

These last two factors were already becoming a thorn in the side of success. Opposition was badly-directed from above; it nevertheless had a daunting quality, even in those first days. A captain in one of Guderian's panzer divisions wrote that 'there was no feeling, as there had been in France, of entry into a defeated nation'. (14)

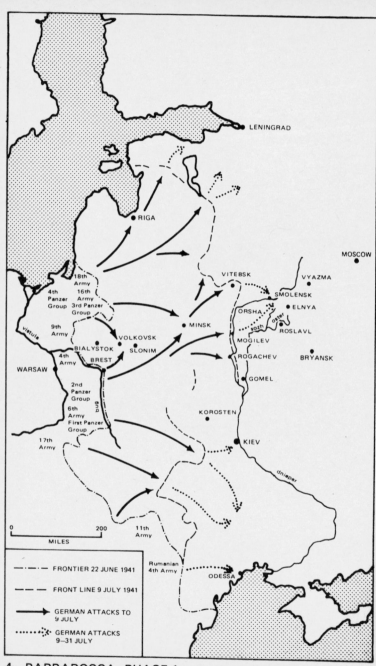

LENINGRAD

MOSCOW

RIGA

VITEBSK
VYAZMA
SMOLENSK

18th
Army
16th
Army
3rd Panzer
Group

4th
Panzer
Group

9th
Army

ORSHA
ELNYA

oster

sozh
ROSLAVL

MINSK

MOGILEV

VOLKOVSK
SLONIM

BIALYSTOK
BREST

ROGACHEV
BRYANSK

4th Army

WARSAW

GOMEL

2nd
Panzer
Group

6th
Army
First Panzer
Group

KOROSTEN

17th
Army

KIEV

dnieper

| 0 | 200 |

MILES

11th
Army

Rumanian
4th Army

ODESSA

— · — · —   FRONTIER 22 JUNE 1941

— — —   FRONT LINE 9 JULY 1941

➤   GERMAN ATTACKS TO
9 JULY

·····✕·····   GERMAN ATTACKS
9–31 JULY

4   BARBAROSSA: PHASE 1

If this was but a fleeting thought to the panzer commanders, to the hard-pressed infantry around the pockets that refused to surrender, it was a matter of continuing concern. Guderian, true to his code, preferred to solve the problem obliquely, by motoring further and further into Russia. Why waste time reducing pockets by direct confrontation when the sweep of advance would eventually render them irrelevant? Time, after all, was not on the Wehrmacht's side. Unfortunately for Guderian his use of infantry divisions for the assault on Brest had caused him to be placed temporarily under von Kluge's Fourth Army, and Kluge was not of the same mind. Neither was the Führer.

Hitler, during the first week, had almost forgotten about the advance, obsessing himself instead with Soviet attempts to break free of the Bialystok pocket. Consequently a continual battle was being fought in the higher reaches of command between Hitler and O.K.H. Bock's dispute with Brauchitsch in March had been a precursor of this dispute, Guderian's with Kluge was its practical expression. The real problem for the Germans, as yet unrealised, was that both schools of thought were essentially correct and mutually exclusive. The risks involved in leaving large bodies of Russians across their communication and supply lines were obvious. So were the risks of advancing in insufficient strength into the heart of Russia, with minimal flank guard and uncertain supply routes. Guderian's argument that a 'minimum amount of the Panzer Group' could be left to secure the pockets begged the obvious question. What if the 'minimum amount' necessary was too much for the continuation of his advance? Similarly the proponents of the opposite view had no answer to Guderian's pleas; that a postponement of the advance in strength would allow the Red Army time to strengthen its defensive line, and so make even the minimum amount he proposed to leave behind necessary to the success of the spearhead. Yet, if both schools of thought were correct, the inescapable deduction to be drawn was that the Germans had, literally, bitten off more than they could chew. There were not enough teeth for the amount of enemy and space. And if the only solution to this was to reduce the enemy and space without weakening the teeth, thus creating a more favourable balance, the argument still held. To take large uncertain bites and save time, or to take small certain bites and lose time. Advance or secure the pockets. One or the other. The Wehrmacht could not decide, and indecision would prove the most fatal thing of all.

For the moment he who had the stronger will decided. Bock, firmly convinced that watertight pockets were impossible on account of the terrain, vast space, and bad roads, was all for letting the armour loose. On 24 June, deciding to send Hoth ahead at full steam, he gained permission from Brauchitsch and Halder, only to have his orders reversed by Hitler. Fuming at this, as he believed, incorrect decision, Bock attempted to persuade Kluge and Strauss to close the pockets without armoured assistance, and thus prove his point. Kluge replied that it couldn't be done. 'Whose side are you on?' Bock asked him deprecatingly. That evening he noted in his diary that 'we are permitting our greatest chance of success to escape by this restriction placed upon my armour'. (15)

Guderian showed a more wilful turn of insubordination. Receiving an order to his distaste from Kluge, ordering 17th Panzer to prevent an enemy break-out rather than advance eastwards, he lightheartedly confessed the next day that a 'mishap had occurred in the transmission of orders', and that 'it was too late to do anything about it'. Kluge, with anything but a light heart, summoned Guderian and Hoth – to whose Panzer Group the same mishap had occurred – and accused them of mounting a generals' conspiracy. The generals talked themselves out of it. 'At least I could put his mind at rest on that score,' wrote Guderian contemptuously. Malaparte's *esprit de corps* was wearing perilously thin in the higher echelons of the German Army. (16)

Kluge and Guderian were not the only two whose relationship grated as June turned into July. Halder, sitting at the centre of the web, was beset from both sides. He gave his views to Brauchitsch, who took them to Hitler and came back looking like he'd been put through a mangle. In the other direction Bock was lying low, passing on O.K.H.'s instructions to his commanders with as little personal ratification as possible. So Halder, undecided himself, and anyway in no position to force through a decision, committed to his diary, in Alan Clark's words, 'one of the most craven admissions of executive incompetence that can ever have been uttered by a member of the General Staff: "Let us hope that the Commanding Generals of Corps and Armies will do the right thing without express instructions, which we are not allowed to issue because of the Führer's instructions to Brauchitsch." ' (17)

By 7 July Guderian was faced with such a decision. Should he attempt to seize crossings over the Dnieper with the forces he had, knowing that the infantry was a fortnight behind him, knowing also that the Russian defences were daily growing stronger? He had already suffered severe pressure against his spearheads, and attempts to seize the crossings at Rogachev and Mogilev by *coups de main* had failed with heavy losses. Guderian was not one to be put off. Reasoning with characteristic cheek – if Soviet pressure was strong now, then how much stronger it would be in a fortnight – he deployed his divisions for the seizure of bridgeheads across the river. He informed none of his superiors of this decision until, once again, 'it was too late to do anything about it'. The angry Kluge, descending on Guderian's headquarters, was, according to Guderian, 'clearly impressed by my objective explanation' that this operation 'would decide the Russian campaign in this very year, if such a decision was at all possible'. Whether this or the statement that 'my preparations had already gone too far to be cancelled' proved decisive in impressing Kluge is somewhat doubtful. In any case the Field-Marshal uttered his famous 'your operations always hang by a thread' and departed. This one, as it happened, did not. The Dnieper was crossed with only minor losses on 10 and 11 July. (18)

While Guderian and Kluge were deciding the course of the campaign O.K.H. was indulging its fantasies. A drive through Turkey and Syria was discussed, presumably to rendezvous with Rommel on the Suez Canal. Another force would then proceed through the Caucasus to the Persian Gulf. The Russians, apparently, had already been beaten. This achievement, it was hinted, had followed the postponement of the drive on Moscow and diversion of Guderian's Panzer Group southwards. Leaving this fatal seed to flourish O.K.H. next turned its attention to the occupation of defeated Russia. The number of troops required and the consequent number to be demobilised were carefully totted up. 'Such trains of thought,' Guderian wrote pithily, 'take a man far from reality.' (19)

O.K.H. had not taken complete leave of its collective senses. There were excuses for optimism. Guderian's forces, and Hoth's further north, were now over three hundred miles from the Bug, over half-way to the Soviet capital. Five armoured corps, long thin phalanxes separated by up to twenty miles of open ground, were pushing towards Smolensk, scattering the Red Army to right and left and into the spaces between. At this point, with the campaign only three weeks old, the romantic invincibility of the Wehrmacht still intact and eating space, it is as well to remember that look of 'eaten' space.

We are near a level-crossing, at the end of a goods platform. On the twisted rails lie enormous heaps of iron blackened by smoke of explosions, scored by overturned wagons and the remains of a locomotive shattered by a heavy bomb from a Stuka. The locomotive is standing on end, it appears to be emerging from beneath the ground, like some Plutonic chariot . . .

I drive along the main street of the town, which has been destroyed by bombs, exploding mines, fires, and the ceaseless pounding of the German artillery. Skeletons of houses tower precariously into the blue sky. Groups of wretched people rummage among the ruins, collecting fragments of treasured possessions, strips of scorched mattresses, empty bottles. Gangs of bearded Jews, supervised by soldiers of the S.S., are busy pulling down the tottering walls with the help of ropes, steel hawsers and long poles. Here and there in the dead city one hears the sound of falling bricks and stones. Troops of starving dogs or cats scuffle among the ruins. This, then, is Beltsy, once a prosperous township nestling in an extremely fertile valley golden with ears of corn. Over towards the airfield, on the road that leads to Soroki, a number of houses are still burning. A solitary anti-aircraft machine-gun is firing in the distance. The tracer-bullets disappear into a snow-white cloud resembling a cloud of flour. An old Jew, seated in the doorway of a fruit-shop, calls out to me in German: 'Alles gut, alles gut!' – All's well, all's well! (20)

IV

Far though the Wehrmacht had travelled in those first few weeks the cost had been commensurate. Casualties among the troops had been initially light, but by the end of July were beginning to climb appreciably. The damage done to the vehicles was more immediately apparent. The Germans had not been prepared for the state of the Russian roads. Those 'marked good on the maps did not in fact exist'. (21) The first formations to suffer were the newly-raised motorised divisions which, because of limited German industrial capacity, had been equipped with captured French trucks. These, on the dry and uneven road surfaces, simply began to break up. And there were next to no spare parts. The German tanks, swishing through deep dust, began to clog up; their engines wore out at an abnormal rate. Rain solved these problems but created another. The columns stopped. One shower turned the roads into long channels of mud, into which the wheeled vehicles sank with a resigned squelch. The Army was paying for its omission in not tracking all the vehicles.

The losses in men and motors were all the more serious in view of the fact that the Army had started *Barbarossa* with virtually no operational reserve and an underdeveloped armaments industry working at full stretch. Replacements for men and machines would be hard to find; the ever-lengthening supply lines and dearth of transport would make it difficult to bring even those that could be found forward. And while the ebb of irreplaceable German strength began to cause concern, reappraisals of Soviet strength were sending shivers up O.K.H.'s collective spine. On 8 July Halder reported that only forty-six of the 164 known Soviet divisions retained combat-worthiness; by the 23rd he had conjured ninety-three such divisions out of the air. Fifteen days of German attack had seen an apparent doubling of Soviet strength. Three weeks later he told his diary, with a tone so phlegmatic as to whisk the breath away: 'We reckoned with 200 Russian divisions. Now we have already counted 360.' (22) Given that during the month's campaign the three German army groups had been advancing on divergent axes, fanning out to north-east, east, and south-east, Halder was not exaggerating when he added that 'our front on this broad expanse is too thin'. A major strategic crisis was brewing.

It had been foreseen by the Zossen war game, held under Paulus's supervision the previous December. On the twentieth day of the offensive (D + 20), the gamers reckoned, both Army Groups North and South would be asking for an armoured 'loan' from Army Group Centre, the one to establish a solid front, the other to take Kiev. Such developments were certainly desirable in themselves. They would also safeguard Army Group Centre's flanks during its own march on Moscow. But, despite this, the gamers found that such 'loans' were not justifiable. 'In view of the paramount importance of preserving [Army Group Centre's] resources,' wrote Paulus, 'for the final, ultimate onslaught on Moscow, they felt that the other two Army Groups should carry out these operations with their own forces ... ' (23)

By mid-July, as Guderian and Hoth's panzer groups were

closing the ring around Smolensk, Army Groups North and South were indeed demanding additional armour, and for the reasons prophesied. But contrary to the gamers' recommendation Hitler decided to give it to them. Führer Directive 33 detached Second and Third Panzer Groups for operations in the south and north. That this decision, whether right or wrong, took two months to implement could be said to have lost Germany the war. That it did take so long is attributable to so many thinking it was the wrong decision, and to even Hitler not being convinced that it was the right one.

The position in mid-July was as follows: Army Group Centre had flung the Red Army back across the Dnieper, trapping large numbers of troops in a large pocket around Smolensk and a subsidiary one around Mogilev. In so doing they had thrust the remaining Russians back to left and right, north into the gap between Army Groups Centre and North, and south to the Sozh-Oster river-line. In front of Army Group Centre there was stubborn resistance around Elnya, but only in so far as the mass of the German force had not yet crossed the Dnieper. Hoth and Guderian's panzer spearhead was doomed to a period of waiting. In the north and south Soviet resistance had held up the advance. Leeb's lunge for Leningrad had been slowed in the Narva valley; the push of Rundstedt's armies in the south had been halted before Kiev and hung threatened by the Soviet Fifth Army lurking south of the Pripet Marshes around Korosten. In short: Army Group Centre could continue its advance once its full force had been brought to bear; the other two Army Groups were unlikely to be able to make much more progress without the use of Army Group Centre's armour. It was an either-or problem.

The 'either' demanded a gradualist strategy. The Germans would chew up the Soviet forces piece by piece, concentrating on small-scale encirclements in which seepage could be held to a minimum. In this way they could steadily destroy the Russian armies, slowly advancing on a broad front towards the three objectives laid down in *Barbarossa*. The armoured forces would be shuffled from wing to wing as required. Army Groups North and South would get their loans; Army Group Centre would wait before pursuing its attack on Moscow.

Given the alarming number of Soviet divisions that had escaped from the Smolensk pocket, and given the problem of the two flanking Army Groups, this sounded a reasonable enough strategy to Hitler. Halder disagreed.

Such a plan implies a shift of our strategy from the operational to the tactical level. If striking at small local enemy concentrations becomes our sole objective, the campaign will resolve itself into a series of minor successes which will advance our front only by inches. Pursuing such a policy eliminates all tactical risks and enables us to gradually close the gaps between the fronts of the Army Groups, but the result will be that we feed all our strength into a front expanding in width at the sacrifice of depth and end up in position warfare! (24)

For Halder, Brauchitsch, Bock, Guderian and Hoth, the alternative – the 'or' – offered far more. A straight drive for Moscow. Risky indeed, but no more so than the inevitable winter campaign promised by Hitler's solution. Halder and Brauchitsch wrote a memo to Hitler expressing their displeasure. A delay in Army Group Centre's advance, inevitable without its armour, would, they argued, give the Soviets ample time to deepen their defences. The Red Army was placing all its hopes in a winter campaign; they would avoid fighting whenever possible with this in view. In front of Moscow they would have to stand and fight. The fall of Moscow – the seat of government, a major industrial centre, and, most crucial of all, the hub of the railway system – would cut Russia in two. Such a possibility must take precedence over mopping-up operations.

The memo was not delivered for the moment, although its contents would hang in the air for another month. The actual situation intervened, in the form of a Soviet counter-attack around Elnya on 25 July. An Army Group Conference was called for the 27th to discuss future operations. Guderian, blissfully unaware of Hitler's new conservatism, arrived expecting 'to be told to push on to Moscow, or at least Bryansk . . . ' (25) He was soon disillusioned, receiving orders to move *south-west* against eight–ten Soviet divisions in the Gomel area. The reason given was Hitler's new policy of small encirclements and safety-first. One can imagine Bock and Guderian sitting together, sharing their disgust at this development. Not that they were resigned to accept it, rather colluding in that calculated insubordination for which Halder had begged his diary a month earlier. 'This order, Field-Marshal . . . of course I shall carry it out, but, first, don't you agree that the threat to the south-east, around Roslavl, has to be dealt with first?' 'Yes, that definitely does require your prior attention, Herr General

. . . and with any luck the Gomel situation will take care of itself in the meantime. We don't want to lose sight of which way Moscow is, eh?' So having received orders to attack Gomel, Guderian flew back to his Panzer Group to organise an attack on Roslavl, additionally cheered by being no longer subordinate to Kluge.

Hitler was less certain of himself, on 30 July issuing another Führer Directive (34) which effectively announced a period of procrastination. Army Group Centre would go over to the offensive, but its armoured groups would be withdrawn for rehabilitation rather than loaned out. Guderian had already been appraised of this indecision by Hitler's adjutant, who had visited him the day before. Schmundt told him that Hitler was still undecided as to where to make the next major effort. Guderian urged him to plead the case for Moscow on his behalf, and to argue 'against the undertaking of any operations that must involve us in losses without being decisive'. (26) On the 31st the O.K.H. Liaison Officer arrived at 2nd Panzer Group H.Q. He told Guderian that O.K.H. was prevented from, and Hitler proving incapable of, taking any decisions. Halder was still hoping that Guderian would force the Führer's hand.

One sign of creeping paralysis in any operation, military or otherwise, is a plethora of conferences. Barely a week after Army Group Centre's Novy Borissov meeting Hitler's private plane touched down at the airstrip. He interviewed Bock, Guderian and Hoth in turn. All apparently pressed for a resumption of the march on Moscow, but disagreed as to when they could resume. Bock said immediately, Guderian in two weeks, Hoth in three. Hitler then brought them all together and announced that he had decided to give Leningrad first priority. He had not yet firmly decided on the second, but was inclined to favour the Ukraine. So much for consulting the professionals.

The most interesting statement made by Hitler was to the effect that he would never have started the war (against Russia) had he believed Guderian's statistics for Soviet tank strength, printed in *Achtung! Panzer!* This breathtaking admission of political and military irresponsibility characterises as well as anything the gigantic gamble that *Barbarossa* had been from the beginning. The indecision of the German Supreme Command throughout August must be seen in this light, in the shock of discovering something that they should have known from the beginning. Suddenly their decisions spelt success or failure, not merely the speed of success.

Guderian's attack towards Roslavl was proceeding smoothly, and by 8 August had achieved its objectives. A huge gap had been torn in the Soviet front, through which the way to Moscow seemed tantalisingly open. Now, surely, was the moment. Bock sent Kesselring's planes forward to spy out the land; they reported that between Moscow and their front defences the Russians had virtually nothing. Kesselring said later that in his opinion

if the offensive against Moscow had been continued . . . [the city] would have fallen into our hands before the winter and before the arrival of the Siberian divisions . . . The capture of Moscow would have been decisive, in that the whole of Russia in Europe would have been cut off from its Asiatic potential and the seizure of the vital economic centres of Leningrad, the Donetz basin and the Maikop oilfields in 1942 would have been no insoluble task. (17)

Hitler would not see it, and by this time some of Hoth's divisions were en route for Leningrad. How could his mind be changed? Even Jodl was convinced, and together with Brauchitsch succeeded in dragging a compromise out of the Führer, by which Army Group Centre's two Panzer Groups would operate on the flanks for only two weeks, before returning to resume the march on the capital at the end of August. In the meantime the Army Group was allowed to 'improve its position for subsequent operations'. The possibilities open to the likes of Guderian were spelt out by Halder.

In themselves these decisions represent a cheering progress, but they still fall short of the clear-cut operational objectives essential to a sound basis for future developments. With these tactical reasonings as a staring-point, the Führer was deftly steered towards our viewpoint on operational objectives. For the moment this is a relief. A radical improvement is not to be hoped for unless operations become so fluid that his tactical thinking cannot keep pace with developments. (28)

This patronising hope was not to be fulfilled. The man most likely to speed matters beyond Hitler's comprehension and control, had, during the laborious construction of the compromise, tendered a plan for exploiting the Roslavl gap through an advance along the Vyazma axis. This, in the prevailing indecision at O.K.H., had been rejected as totally unsatisfactory. By the time Hitler had been persuaded of such possibilities, a temporarily resigned Guderian had decided to obey the order to attack Gomel which O.K.H. had been repeating for the previous three weeks. One of his panzer corps was consequently moving south-westward, unavailable for speeding up matters in the decisive sector.

Indeed, indecision seemed to be escalating rather than diminishing. Guderian's forces, en route for Gomel, asked Army Group for Second Army support on their right flank. This granted, Guderian was somewhat surprised to see strong units of Second Army moving north-eastward behind his own front. On enquiring of Second Army as to whether they had received the relevant orders he was informed that 'on the contrary it was Army Group itself which had ordered the formations to the north-east'. (29) It is not beyond the bounds of probability that Second Army's movements were the result of deliberate sabotage by Bock, eager to re-open the advance on Moscow.

Hitler's resolve, meanwhile, was hardening towards that peak of rigidity which his acolytes liked to call 'unalterable'. While Army Group Centre had dithered August away with insubordinations never insubordinate enough to achieve their cherished goal, Army Groups North and South had made minimal progress. The Soviets still held Leningrad and Kiev. So Hitler, despite a last plea from Brauchitsch on 18 August, returned to the letter and spirit of Directive 33, a wasted month behind him. For all the talk of the panzer groups needing rehabilitation they had received none, as Guderian had been too busy trying to stack the cards and Hoth loaning his out piecemeal to Leeb. Now they were to be sent north and south in toto and in earnest, further aggravating their perilous condition. By the time the Moscow offensive would be resumed this condition would be critical. As, of course, would be the time of year.

This time Hitler did not call on his commanders with the news, sending Halder instead. The Chief of the General Staff arrived at Novy Borissov with the gloomy tidings on 23 August; he, Bock and Guderian then discussed what could be done to alter the Führer's unalterable resolve. Guderian, as the only one who seemed capable of standing up to the Führer in person, was selected to visit him in a last desperate attempt to argue the Moscow option.

He arrived at Lotzen in East Prussia that evening and was ushered into Hitler's presence by Brauchitsch with the words, 'I forbid you to mention Moscow.' This was hardly auspicious. Neither was the speedy disappearance of Brauchitsch and the absence of Halder. Guderian found himself alone, confronting Hitler and his O.K.W. team. During the ensuing discussion he noted that 'all those present nodded in agreement with every sentence that Hitler uttered, while I was left alone with my point of view'. The Führer's rationale for the Ukrainian venture had gathered subtlety over the preceding month. It was now a primarily economic argument, centred around the Reich's need for Ukrainian raw materials for continued prosecution of the war. 'My generals,' he stated, not for the last time, 'know nothing about the economic aspects of war.' On purely military grounds Hitler justified his decision with the now-familiar argument that the central thrust could not be continued without prior safeguarding of its northern and southern flanks, that the Red Army must be destroyed piece by piece, methodically. The Crimea, he added, must be taken, and the Soviet air threat to the Rumanian oilfields neutralised. (30)

Guderian's counter-argument was equally familiar. Defeat of the enemy *forces* would prove decisive; these stood before Moscow. The troops were mentally and physically deployed for an assault on the capital; a successful attack would exert an enormous psychological effect on both Russia and the world, it would wreck the Soviet transport system and fatally disrupt the war effort. To move south instead would wear out the equipment and lose vital time; it would involve the Wehrmacht in a winter campaign for which it was not prepared.

But, as Brauchitsch had warned him, discussion was pointless. The Führer's resolve was indeed unalterable. Never one to do things by halves, Guderian asked that his entire group be sent south, to speed matters up. This last twist of logic sent Halder to bed with a minor nervous breakdown, perhaps pondering Paulus's report on the Zossen war game: 'Should Moscow not be attained, they foresaw a long-drawn-out war beyond the capacity of the German Armed Forces to wage.' (31)

V

The Kiev campaign was a great tactical success. Guderian's two panzer corps motored south, crossing the Desna on 25 August, the Seim on 7 September, finally reaching Lokhvitsa on 16 September. There they joined hands with Kleist's First Panzer Group, which had surged across the middle Dnieper on a wide front and wheeled north. In the gigantic ring forged by these two panzer groups and Rundstedt's infantry to the west of Kiev over 600,000 Russians were trapped. It was the single biggest haul of the war. And, according to Halder, 'the greatest strategic blunder of the eastern campaign'. (32)

September was three weeks old before Guderian could take his tanks out of the ring, give them an inadequate three days for rest and refitting, and send them back northwards. They had covered another four hundred miles on their own tracks since turning south in late August, and the effect was noticeable. Guderian, visiting 3rd Panzer on 15 September, found that one panzer regiment had only ten tanks still running.

Time too was growing visibly short. The *rasputitsa*, the rainy

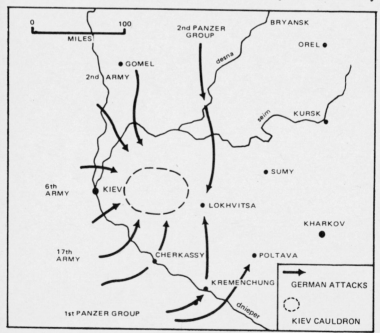

5   KIEV

season, had set in, slowing all movement, turning roads into canals. Guderian's account of the Kiev operation gives the impression that the seasonal conditions offered more resistance than the enemy. They would worsen. It had not been speed for speed's sake that had induced the Zossen war-gamers to insist on the drive from Smolensk to Moscow beginning not later than D + 40. That, on their assumed starting-date, of 15 May, meant 24 June. It was now 24 September, three months further into winter.

In its boxing bout with the Red Army the Wehrmacht was decidedly behind on points, and likely to be more so as the bout continued. So, having pleased the crowd with the grace of yet another immaculate Cannae, Guderian's panzers wearily filtered back across the Seim for their assembly area around Glukhov. This time it had to be the knockout. The troops, awed and depressed by the endless sameness of the ground rolling away beneath their tracks, were prepared for the one final effort that would crown their resilience with its due reward. It couldn't be too late.

At O.K.H. too the ebullience of the moment shrouded the deeper pessimism. Their sights were set on the paramount objective. Hitler was still thinking of Leningrad and the Ukraine, the Army's striking power still spread too wide, but Moscow at last had the priority it deserved and a force concentrated of commensurate strength. It must have been obvious to many by late September that the risks of *Barbarossa* had been high as their wilder fears, that at the political level the campaign had been riddled with misjudgements. The door had come crashing in, but the resilience of the Soviet structure had grown rather than diminished as summer gave way to autumn. In the background, still dim and indistinct, lurked the nightmare possibility of a long war, and defeat. For the moment such thoughts could be shrugged aside. The Wehrmacht could still win a short war. It had two months at most in which to take Moscow. Man against man, tank against tank. It must succeed. Failure would raise questions that could not be answered.

There were sound reasons for expecting success. Since 22 June the Soviet losses in men, tanks, guns and aircraft equalled the German intelligence estimates of those in existence. The Soviets must, *must*, be scraping the barrel. The Wehrmacht, though greatly weakened by the campaign's exertions, could still assemble a force on the upper Dnieper whose paper

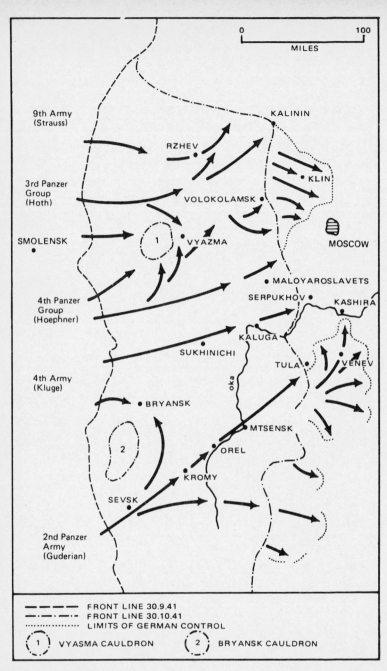

9th Army
(Strauss)

3rd Panzer
Group
(Hoth)

SMOLENSK

4th Panzer
Group
(Hoephner)

4th Army
(Kluge)

2nd Panzer
Army
(Guderian)

RZHEV

KALININ

KLIN

VOLOKOLAMSK

VYAZMA

MOSCOW

MALOYAROSLAVETS

SERPUKHOV

KASHIRA

KALUGA

SUKHINICHI

TULA

VENEV

oka

BRYANSK

MTSENSK

OREL

KROMY

SEVSK

0   100
MILES

– – – – –   FRONT LINE 30.9.41
– · – · –   FRONT LINE 30.10.41
· · · · · ·   LIMITS OF GERMAN CONTROL

(1)   VYASMA CAULDRON   (2)   BRYANSK CAULDRON

6   MOSCOW:
AUTUMN/WINTER 1941

strength came close to that assembled in June for the entire front. Hoeppner's Fourth Panzer Group had been brought down from the north and placed in the centre of the attack frontage, to pierce the Soviet line and send their armies falling back to right and left, into the arms of Hoth and Guderian's two panzer groups, moving in from the flanks like avenging jaws. Between these knives three infantry armies – Fourth, Ninth, Second – would advance steadily, picking up the pieces, tying down the ground.

Army Group Centre's commanders, whatever their forebodings, threw themselves wholeheartedly into the operation they had been championing, till now in vain, since the end of July. Only von Rundstedt, away in the south with orders to penetrate the Caucasus, gave way to realism. 'We laughed out loud when we received these orders,' he told his interrogators after the war. But Rundstedt's alternative – withdrawal to the Dnieper, or even the Polish frontier – had little more to commend it. The Wehrmacht had the tiger by the tail and at least half of its paws; the chance to finish it off was unlikely to recur.

The tiger was in not much better shape than the Germans expected. Stavka, the Soviet O.K.W. equivalent, had been given time to reinforce the central sector, to bring the T-34s and Katyushas past the teething stage. On all routes to Moscow tanks and guns had been dug in, surrounded by minefields, shielded by barricades of wood, wire and concrete. Those who manned the line knew the penalties for desertion, meted out with no compunction by the N.K.V.D. 'rear detachment squads'. Fight they would, how well was another question. The experienced core of the Red Army was all but gone; in its place untrained recruits, thrown into the front line with a rifle and little else, ordered to stem the advance of the most powerful army the world had ever seen.

It couldn't be done. The German offensive, code-named 'Typhoon', burst through the Soviet defences with hardly a sideways glance. Guderian, starting two days early on 30 September, sent his tanks through Sevsk on 1 October, Kromy on the 2nd. On 3 October they rolled into Orel to find the trams still running, industrial equipment bound for the Urals stacked in piles by the railway station.

In the centre Fourth Panzer Group accomplished its severance of the Soviet front. In the north Third Panzer Group cruised eastward north of Vyazma. By 4 October units from both Hoth and Guderian's groups were wheeling inwards as

Hoeppner's Group and Fourth Army wheeled outwards to meet them. Around Vyazma and Bryansk over half a million Red Army soldiers were caught in two cauldrons. It seemed like the penultimate triumph.

The commanders were involved in their usual argument. Hitler and O.K.H. insisted that the armour be used to seal the pockets; Bock demanded that Guderian be allowed to continue his advance on Tula while opposition remained weak. Bock was overruled. Guderian, unaware of Bock's espousal of his cause, added insult to injury. 'In which direction is Moscow?', he enquired sarcastically of the Field-Marshal.

Geography was not his only problem. Partisan activity – the fruit of German occupation policies – was now becoming noticeable in the rear. At the front Model's 3rd Panzer, attempting to force a way through Mtsensk, ran into the Soviets' only sizeable mobile unit, Katukov's T-34-equipped armoured brigade. The German division was thrown back with heavy losses. And on that evening of 6 October the first snow came down.

> It did not lie for long and, as usual, the roads rapidly became nothing but canals of bottomless mud, along which our vehicles could only advance at a snail's pace and with great wear to the engines. We asked for winter clothing but were informed we would receive it in due course and were instructed not to make any further unnecessary requests of this sort ... (33)

This rapid reversal of the 'beautiful autumn weather' (so described by an O.K.H. report of 'Typhoon's commencement) caused a ripple of concern in far-off East Prussia. O.K.H. asked Bock if he considered continuance of the offensive a feasible proposition. Bock, hopeful of a clear frosty November and reluctant to face the implications of abandoning the attempt, answered that it was. This seemed to satisfy Halder. 'With reasonably good direction of the battle and moderately good weather,' he wrote, 'we cannot but succeed in encircling Moscow.' (34) For the next few days this optimism seemed justified. Between 12 and 14 October the Third and Fourth Panzer Groups scored dramatic successes. Hoth broke through to the Kalinin-Klin highway only forty miles from Moscow; Hoeppner to Kaluga and Maloyaroslavets. Only Guderian, again assailed by Katukov's T–34s on the 11th, was making slow progress.

In Germany the fall of Moscow was expected any hour.
Radio stations interrupted their programmes to announce a
'special bulletin in a short time'. And while the Reich held its
breath panic swept through the Soviet capital. The old and
young were being evacuated, the government apparatus moving east to Kuybyshev on the Volga. German reconnaissance
planes flying over the city saw government officials feeding
archives and other documents into hundreds of street corner
fires. Looting began as law and order slipped away; it was
swiftly followed by street executions. Stalin remained, summoning Zhukov in haste from Leningrad. On the other side
Brauchitsch was phoning Bock for his opinion as to when the
city would be sufficiently secure for Hitler to make a triumphant
entry. Bock's reply is not on record.

This sudden flash of light at the end of a grim tunnel
flickered out as suddenly as it had appeared. The weather took
another turn for the worse, immobilising the panzer groups.
The tracked vehicles were used to drag the wheeled; an
increased strain on vehicles already worn down to far below
optimum performance. Many more were left useless in the
knee-deep mud. O.K.H. seemed determined to ignore such
difficulties. Guderian was inundated with instructions. Capture
Kursk, take Tula, close the pocket. Requests for an attachment
of priorities went unanswered. No anti-freeze arrived. No warm
clothes arrived. The snow kept falling, turning to slush, turning
to mud.

In the third week of October the Bryansk and Vyazma
cauldrons surrendered. Could this victory still be exploited?
Many Soviet troops had slipped through the thin screen to
join the stiffening Soviet line, drawn in a thin arc fifty miles
to the west of Moscow. The Third Panzer Group was prised
bloodily out of Kalinin. Around Mtsensk Guderian's troops
witnessed the galling sight of the new wide-tracked T-34s
careering over the mud into which their panzers sank and
settled. That the *Untermenschen* should have more tanks was
one thing; that they should have better tanks was a psychological blow, especially to badly-fed and inadequately-clothed
troops. The weather was playing havoc with German logistics.
Supplies reaching the front lines were down to twenty-five per
cent of the minimum requirements.

Still the advance went on. Finally taking Mtsensk, Guderian's
panzers crawled along the corduroy carpet they had laid on
the road to Tula. Petrol was desperately short. Hitler demanded

of Guderian that 'fast-moving units' should seize the Oka
bridges between Kashira and Serpukhov. Motoring along the
Tula road at the dizzy speed of 12 m.p.h. Guderian had time to
reflect on the credibility gap growing between reality and
orders. 'There were no fast-moving units anymore,' he wrote
later, 'Hitler was living in a world of fantasy.' (35)

At such a speed the prospects for surprise were minimal.
The attempt to take Tula by a *coup de main* failed; the town
was by-passed, left like a thorn in Guderian's side. Cold now
began to replace mud as the prime hazard. By 3 November it
had solidified the ground; in a matter of days it was causing
the first serious cases of frostbite.

On 12 November a conference was called by O.K.H. in
Orsha. Halder presided. Should the advance go on? Hitler said
yes, Bock said yes, Halder was inclined to say yes, Guderian
thought there was still a slight chance. The next day Guderian
received his orders for the sublimely-titled 'Autumn Offensive
1941': he was to take Gorky, a mere 180 miles east of Moscow!
The condition of his troops promised little hope of reaching
the Oka, some thirty miles distant. The supply situation was
chaotic. In the now sub-zero (Fahrenheit) temperatures many
of his men were still clad in denims. Their machines were in
little better shape.

> Ice was causing a lot of trouble, since the calks for the
> tracks had not yet arrived. The cold made the telescopic
> sights useless; the salve which was supposed to prevent this
> had also not arrived. In order to start the engines of the
> tanks, fires had to be lit beneath them. Fuel was freezing on
> occasions and oil became viscous. (36)

There were only fifty usable tanks left to Guderian's Panzer
Group out of a supposed six hundred.

Zhukov's line was holding, despite having been breached in
several places. The Germans had the strength to reach through
the screen, but not enough either to encircle it or push it back.
With the last reserves committed by 17 November one of Hoth's
divisions, the famed 7th Panzer, clawed its way into the northern outskirts of Moscow. But it could get no further on its own.
Units of Hoeppner's group reached the western suburbs on
29 November. They too could move no further. Guderian's
group was still held at arm's length to the south-west. The
pincers would not close.

The temperature was plummeting deeper each day. By 30 November there were 45 degrees of frost. To Hitler in the warmth of his bunker this was merely a statistic. Standing half-hypnotised before his giant map he saw the little flags inching towards and around Moscow. So little distance to go! He wanted to know when. Brauchitsch was sent to the phone.

Brauchitsch: The Führer is convinced that the Russians are on the verge of collapse. He desires a definite commitment from you, Field-Marshal von Bock, as to when this collapse will become a reality.
Bock: O.K.H. has falsely estimated the situation here. I have reported dozens of times during the past few days that the army group no longer commands the strength to force a decision. (37)

In front of Moscow the infantry made their final assault. On 4 December Second Army units penetrated the south-east suburbs, claiming to have glimpsed the towers of the Kremlin flashing in the sunset. They were thrown back.

The next day there were 68 degrees of frost. The Red Army, refuelled by the divisions arriving from Siberia that had been freed by Sorge's advanced intelligence of the Japanese attack on America, was poised to begin a counter-offensive. Guderian was already withdrawing, without orders. On 6 December the other two panzer groups were forced back. The German troops staggered westwards, leaving guns, tanks and comrades in the snow. There was not enough energy for a rout; merely a bitter struggle mile by mile away from the city of decision, away from an end to the war.

Rather than ending it was spreading. As the Wehrmacht began its ghastly retreat the Japanese carrier fleet, sailing unobserved out of the vast North Pacific, was reaching its pre-arranged positions north of Hawaii. The planes were leaving the decks, raining bombs down on Pearl Harbour, bringing America into the war. 'How different things would be if the Japanese had attacked the Russians,' Bock noted pathetically in his diary on 8 December. (38)

Guderian was less fatalistic. 'I would never have believed that a really brilliant military position could be so b———d up in two months,' he wrote home. (39) Neither would Hitler. The first reaction of the Army élite, tumbled from the hyper-tension of imminent victory into sudden unexpected catastrophe, was to begin a shouting match amongst themselves. And as it served no purpose to disagree as to how they had got into the mess, they began fervently disputing the best way to get out of it.

For the commanders in the front line it was an appalling situation. The Red Army was forcing huge holes in a 'line' already sundered by the blizzards and the over-stretching of the attacking formations. These forces, no longer attacking, were crippled by frostbite, intestinal disorders, and equipment which refused to cooperate with the men. The guns would not fire, the tanks would not start. By Christmas Eve Guderian's 'Panzer Army' had less than forty tanks; Hoeppner's four divisions had an average of under fifteen. No replacements were arriving; supplies, particularly medical, were as scarce as warmth.

Two imperatives dominated the situation. The armies had to fall back, and they had to do so in good order. Clearly the first priority was to cushion the shock of the Soviet offensive, the trauma of warmly-clad Siberian troops gleefully biting chunks out of an army that had believed itself on the eve of its greatest victory. On 14 December Guderian asked permission of Brauchitsch to withdraw his army to the partially prepared fortifications along the line of the Susha and Oka rivers. Barely had this been granted and the troops set in motion than Hitler's voice came crackling over the telephone from East Prussia refusing any withdrawal whatever. The troops were to stand and, if necessary, die where they were.

It seems to be almost an article of faith among military historians that this was Hitler's finest hour, the one enduring testament to the power of the 'will' over and above mere strategic considerations. (40) They proceed to justify this with an admiring summary of the 'nets of defended localities' system which was subsequently put into practice. It consisted of fortifying the towns on the railway spokes radiating out of the Moscow hub, and on the lateral Velikiye Luki–Smolensk–Orel–Taganrog line. Each of these towns offered supplies and shelter, the former if necessary by air. The Soviet waves could lap between them to their heart's content; the Army could wait, in relative warmth, for spring. The soundness of this strategy was evidenced by the fact that only Kaluga of the major 'hedgehogs' fell to the Russians, for which the strain involved on the Luftwaffe was a small price to pay. The point, however, and an obvious point at that, is that the Germans were not in these towns when they received Hitler's orders to stand fast. They had to withdraw to them. The dispute which cost five army commanders and thirty-five corps commanders their positions appears more of an excuse than a reason. Certainly in Guderian's account of his conversation with Hitler on 20 December there is no mention of 'hedgehogs'. The General informed his Führer that there were no defensible positions short of the Susha-Oka line.

Hitler: If that is the case they must dig into the ground where they are and hold every square yard of land.
Guderian: Digging into the ground is no longer feasible in most places, since it is frozen to a depth of five feet and our wretched entrenching tools won't go through it.
Hitler: In that case they must blast craters with heavy howitzers. We had to do that in the First World War in Flanders.
Guderian: In the First World War our divisions in Flanders held, on the average, sectors two to three miles wide and were supported in the defence by two or three battalions of heavy howitzers per division with proportionately abundant supplies of ammunition. My divisions have to defend fronts of 25 to 35 miles and in each of my divisions there are four heavy howitzers and approximately 50 shells per gun. If I use these shells to make craters I shall have fifty hollows in the ground, each about the width and depth of a washtub with a large black circle around it. I shall not have a crater position. In Flanders there was never such cold as we are now experiencing. And apart from that I need my ammunition to fire at the Russians. (41)

Hitler was no more impressed by Guderian's encyclopaedic memories of the First World War than Guderian was by Hitler's. To Guderian's anecdotes of the Russian winter, he replied that Guderian was 'seeing events at too close a range. You have been too deeply impressed by the suffering of the soldiers. You feel too much pity for them. You should stand back more. Believe me, things appear clearer when examined at long range.' Not so the winter clothing which Guderian, with a foresight bordering on malice, had tracked down to a number of railway sidings in Warsaw. Informed of this Hitler ranted and raged before summoning the unfortunate Quartermaster-General to find it was true. Guderian continued to push his advantage and later in the conversation went so far as to suggest the restaffing of O.K.W. with officers who had seen action in the front line. He was 'gruffly refused', and leaving the meeting heard Hitler mutter to Keitel: 'I haven't convinced that man!'

One thing they had convinced each other of, judging from the tone of the conversation, was their deep mutual contempt. It was this contempt, one suspects, that lay behind the wholesale dismissals and resignations of the year's end. The liaison between the Nazi Party and the traditionally-minded officer élite of the Army had always been a reluctant and suspicious one, and if success had papered over the cracks then failure had once more exposed them to the harsh light. Hitler and his staff could have shown more understanding of the difficulties experienced by the commanders in the field; they perhaps, with more trust and tact, could have achieved the withdrawal of their troops into the bastions without arousing his ire. But understanding, trust and act were not part of the ethos dominating the German conduct of the war. Mutual contempt was, and it would not be the last time that Germany suffered from the consequences.

Among the officers cast aside were Brauchitsch, Leeb, Bock, Rundstedt, Guderian and Hoeppner including all three Army Group commanders and two of the four Panzer Group leaders. Hitler's assumption for Brauchitsch's post as Army Commander-in-Chief merely put the gloss on his de facto assumption of dictatorial powers over all vital levels of the Army's activities. This, rather than the salvation of the armies broken before Moscow, was the real inheritance of December 1941. The mutually supportive skills of the German military leadership – the Führer's intuition and boldness in following it, the drive and intelligence of the field commanders, the thoroughness and experience of those behind the desks of O.K.H. and O.K.W. – which had given each its soil in which to flower, which had made the most of that peculiar German genius for waging war; all were now cast aside, replaced in the agony of defeat by a hierarchy whose rigidity would only grow with subsequent setbacks, which would bring out the worst in Hitler and generals alike. Rather than pushing each other up they would pull each other down. Hitler's intuition would wither in the rarified air of solitary control; the generals, denied any initiative, would be unable to wield their skills. Caught between them the once-omnipotent General Staff would become little more than a glorified military signal box.

Ironically enough Halder's protégé, Paulus, would be transferred to the front line and play a role of tragic prominence in 1942. As a last comment on the 1941 campaign, and on O.K.H.'s schizophrenic role in its conduct, one could do no better than quote Paulus's remark to a fellow officer at the end of December. Telling him about the previous year's war game he admits to having 'jotted down on paper what I thought would happen'. And, sure enough, 'everything has occurred exactly as I foretold'. (42)

The other tiger had been taken firmly by the tail. The Wehrmacht's hands were full.

References (Chapter 2)

1. quoted in Wilmot, *Struggle for Europe*, 56
2. Guderian, *Panzer Leader*, 136–7
3. quoted in Strawson, *Hitler*, 132
4. quoted in Turney, *Moscow*, 16
5. Ibid, 28–9
6. Ibid, 37
7. Hitler, *Table Talk*, 34
8. Guderian, *Panzer Leader*, 150
9. Kesselring, *Memoirs*, 88
10. Malaparte, *Volga Rises*, 25
11. Ibid, 29–32
12. Manstein, *Lost Victories*, 180
13. Guderian, *Panzer Leader*, 154–7
14. quoted in Clark, *Barbarossa*, 48
15. quoted in Tuney, *Moscow*, 55
16. Guderian, *Panzer Leader*, 162
17. quoted in Clark, *Barbarossa*, 61
18. Guderian, *Panzer Leader*, 169
19. Ibid, 175
20. Malaparte, *Volga Rises*, 84–5
21. Guderian, *Panzer Leader*, 180
22. quoted in Clark, *Barbarossa*, 96
23. quoted in Goerlitz, *Paulus*, 117–8
24. quoted in Fuller, *Decisive Battles*, 470
25. Guderian, *Panzer Leader*, 182
26. Ibid, 185

27. Kesselring, *Memoirs*, 98
28. quoted in Clark, *Barbarossa*, 91
29. Guderian, *Panzer Leader*, 196
30. Ibid, 200
31. quoted in Goerlitz, *Paulus*, 107
32. quoted in Fuller, *Decisive Battles*, 473
33. Guderian, *Panzer Leader*, 234
34. quoted in Fuller, *Decisive Battles*, 479
35. Guderian, *Panzer Leader*, 244
36. Ibid, 248
37. quoted in Turney, *Moscow*, 146
38. Ibid, 149
39. Guderian, *Panzer Leader*, 261
40. see Clark, Fuller, Liddell Hart, etc.
41. Guderian, *Panzer Leader*, 265
42. quoted in Goerlitz, *Paulus*, 43

Chapter 3

NILE AND VOLGA –
THE END OF THE LEASH

The concentration of effort in the defence of Stalingrad is a grave mistake on the part of the Russians.

(Hitler, 6 September 1942) (1)

The German Army survived the winter of 1941; the remains of its tradition of independence died in the snow before Moscow. The Führer was now at the helm, assuming even that little power that had eluded him over the previous decade. The last ballast had been thrown overboard; the ship moved to his will. 'This little matter of operational command,' as he told Halder, 'is something anyone can do'. (2) So perished three hundred years of accumulated experience.

The winter had left its scars on Hitler. The generals, whom he had mistrusted before France, had now shown their true colours and proved him right. They had lost him *Barbarossa* with their obstructionism, their outdated ideas, their wilful disobedience. But at last he was free of their interference. Henceforward they would do what, and only what, they were told. They would be good servants of the Reich and the Nazi ideal, as expressed, of course, in the unfolding of his own personal destiny.

Few men can have held such power, or wielded such intuitive gifts, yet been so totally devoid of the self-critical faculties that make such power occasionally excusable or such gifts utilisable. Defeat, rather than forcing Hitler to search himself, only drove him to seek out any hints of weakness in others. He became less self-critical, in so far as it was possible. Always inclined to counter facts with the mystique of the will, he now took to discounting them altogether. Figures for Russian tank production provided by his own intelligence services he greeted with shouts of scorn and attacks on the furniture. It was as if a child of four had been denied the sweets in an empty

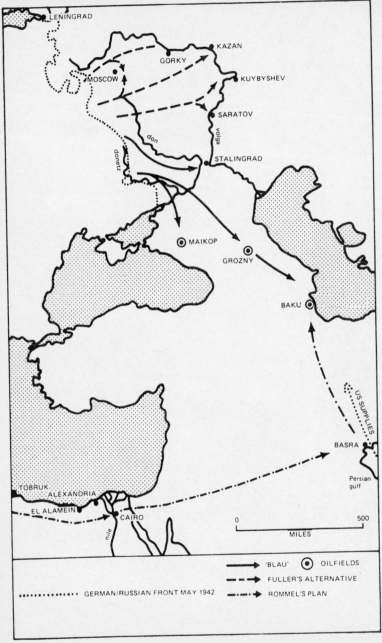

7 SUMMER 1942: OPTIONS

box. Unlike most such children, Hitler wielded an egotism not in the least attractive. And he wielded it over a continent.

The coincidence of his rise to supreme command and slide into these depths of childishness was not fortuitous for the German war effort. Since his division of strategic control – O.K.H., the war with Russia; O.K.W., the remainder – Hitler alone had access to the whole picture. If he was not to perceive the war clearly, then no other German was likely to. By January 1942 it was becoming more and more essential that somebody did.

The war was now global; a situation created by Japan's Pearl Harbour attack and wilfully compounded by Hitler's declaration of war on the United States. Having spent some months attempting to persuade the Japanese to attack either the British at Singapore or Russia in the Far East it would have seemed more prudent at this juncture to forsake the Rising Sun. Hitler, though, was not in awe of U.S. power, considering Roosevelt a decadent expression of a decadent nation. In any case, he argued, the U.S. was already a belligerent in all but name.

This casual globalisation of the war was not accompanied by a global strategy, let alone a thorough expansion of the German Army and its industrial support. The one inspired step taken by Hitler at this juncture was the appointment of Speer as overseer of armament production, an appointment occasioned by Todt's death and partially crippled by Hitler's refusal to clear the new man's path through the jungle of Reich baronies. That Speer achieved so much was a tribute to his own efforts. They were sorely necessary.

The Army itself had suffered grievously through the winter. Casualties for the East were in excess of a million; they inevitably included a heavy toll of the Army's experienced troops. Equipment was in no better state. The sixteen panzer divisions in Russia possessed an average of less than ten tanks each by March 1942. No matter how great Speer's efforts in his first months in office would be, the striking power of the Wehrmacht in 1942 would not be such as to allow for extravagance. This time there could be no mistake; the objectives had to be chosen with unerring accuracy and pursued with vigour. And this time it would be Hitler's choice and Hitler's responsibility. The scapegoats were all gone.

None of the options were very attractive, but not all were hopeless. In the Mediterranean opportunities still beckoned.

With a minimal force Rommel had inflicted several crushing victories on the British. His main problems were insufficient supplies and inadequate force. Solve these two problems – by the taking of Malta and the dispatch of another two panzer divisions – and Rommel could break through to Suez. Then, Raeder argued with Hitler, the Middle East was wide open; for a southerly attack on Russia or a grandiose link up with the Japanese somewhere on the Punjabi plains. Britain would be thrown out of Asia, locked into her islands, surrounded by U boats. The menace of a two-front war would be obviated, at least for the time it took to deal with Russia.

The first part of this plan appealed to Hitler; the consequent suspending or weakening of operations against the Red Army did not. As so often before and after he chose to pursue both to the detriment of each. His main priority never wavered: defeat of the Soviet Union. Britain, he thought, would find it as hard to attack Germany as Germany found it to attack Britain. There was time here to spare. But not in Russia; the Red Army had to be dealt with now, before it recovered from the winter campaign, which had, he opined, consumed the last of its strength. One more kick at the door and . . . Goebbels saw him in March and noted in his diary that 'the Führer again has a perfectly clear plan of campaign for the coming spring and summer'. The 'again' was ominous. Goebbels's added comment that 'this may mean a hundred years war in the East' was unduly optimistic. (3)

II

This plan of campaign was outlined in Führer Directive 41, issued in April. Clear it might have been; it was also, according to Fuller, 'radically unsound'. (4) This time Hitler had determined not to encircle and destroy the Red Army but to deprive it of its mobility. The seizure of the Caucasus oil would stop every Soviet tank in its tracks; it would also allay the Reich's own oil shortage, the implications of which had been impressed on Hitler by his economic wizards. Such an objective had been considered before. As long ago as November 1941 Halder had recommended, when weather conditions permitted, 'an all-out thrust in the south towards Stalingrad in order to occupy the Maikop-Grozny area at an early date'. (5) Halder had only been thinking of the Reich's oil shortage; Hitler was thinking

Dummy tanks on manoeuvre in the early years.

of winning the war. That Germany needed the oil to continue prosecution of the war was disproved in succeeding years; that the Caucasus oil was vital to the Red Army is probable. Its capture might conceivably have won the war. But was it likely? Six months had passed since Halder's recommendation, made at a time when the fall of Moscow appeared imminent. Those six months had instead witnessed a major catastrophe, a weakening of the Wehrmacht and a strengthening of the Red Army. The Caucasus was further away than it had been in November. Was there no option that offered victory at less cost and with greater certainty?

Fuller thinks there was. A further all-out drive in the centre, he argues, towards the line of the Upper and Middle Volga, would have produced the same, if not better results, than Hitler's *Fall Blau* (Case Blue). By seizing the string of towns along that river – Saratov, Kubyshev, Kazan, Gorky – the German Army could have severed European Russia, the Caucasus and Siberia, each from the other. The advance required was of a similar magnitude to *Blau*, some four hundred miles. This was not inconsiderable and it could be argued that, like *Blau*, it was beyond the Wehrmacht's capacity. But if the possibilities of success were about equal the risks involved in failure were not. An eastward drive would not have appreciably lengthened the overall front, merely the supply lines. The German forces would not have been spread to the extent that vulnerable stretches became inevitable. Hitler's south-eastward drive, in contrast, almost doubled the length of front the German forces had to hold. Vulnerable stretches were inevitable. And given that the *Schwerpunkt* was heading south-east, those stretches would be behind them, along the Don, in an area made easy for Soviet concentration by the configuration of the railway network. This last point was apparently made to Hitler, who flew at the unfortunate man reciting statistics of what the Red Army could bring to bear in this area, 'with clenched fists and foam in the corners of his mouth, and forbade him to read such idiotic twaddle'. (6)

Whatever the dubious merits of *Fall Blau* they were not added to by its practical elusiveness. As far as Halder was concerned Hitler had asked for an operational plan geared to the objective of Stalingrad. The Caucasus was to be masked with a strong mobile force centred on Armavir. This represented a virtual inversion of the plan to strike into the Caucasus with the masking force positioned at Stalingrad. To First

Panzer Army commander Kleist Hitler confided that Baku was his eventual objective; to his trusty early-hour co-revellers he stressed the possibility of surging north from Stalingrad along the Volga. This confusion was called flexibility. It was in fact confusion. It would be resolved in the manner peculiar to Hitler: on the spur of the moment, with little reference to the temporal depth of the campaign or the effect such off-the-cuff decisions had on other previously-made decisions.

This defect, which more and more characterised Hitler's control of his Army, was further exacerbated by his method of issuing orders. The positions of units at nightfall were forwarded to Supreme Headquarters for Hitler's morning perusal. Thence further orders were issued, which frequently failed to reach the troops before evening. In the twenty-four hours that had elapsed the position had as often as not changed beyond recognition and the orders were inoperable. Failure to operate them, however, was not an initiative taken lightly in the Wehrmacht in 1942.

Of course, all the objections that could and should have been raised in the spring of 1942 – blurred grand strategy, ambiguity of strategic objectives, tactical interference from the highest level, the inherent peril of the long exposed flank – they could all be shrugged aside if the intelligence figures really were twaddle, if the Russian really was at the end of his long and painful tether. The German force looked strong enough on paper: sixty German divisions (including ten panzer and six motorised) and forty-three Allied divisions. The further dilution of actual intra-divisional strength carried out in the winter had been all but forgotten. The *number* of divisions looked impressive, and doubtless Hitler did not fail to impress his generals with it when all were assembled at Poltava on 1 June, a few miles from the battlefield where Charles XII of Sweden lost his war in Russia. The planners and administrators were there: Halder, Keitel, Heusinger, Wagner. The commanders in the field dutifully listened to their tasks: Bock, Sodenstern, Kleist, Ruoff, Mackensen, Weichs, Hoth, Paulus and Richthofen. A list of impressive professionals, strong on Clausewitz but weak in insubordination. Those with such strength had disappeared during the winter. If such a thought crossed Hitler's mind with anything less than satisfaction, it would have been brushed aside. He needed no one now to do anything but follow. The war was going well, he told the assembled company. Four hundred thousand Russians had been captured in May during Manstein's conquest of the Crimea and Timoshenko's disastrous Kharkov offensive. In Africa Rommel was about to take the offensive. Tobruk would soon fall. The Battle of the Atlantic was going Germany's way. All that was required of those assembled here was this final decisive blow against the *Untermensch* goliath.

All this was true, but far from the whole truth. These successes marked the last spasms of German expansion, the last fruits of a fading initiative. Far more significant were the iceberg tips of the enemies' successes. Thirty-six hours before Hitler harangued his generals the Allies had delivered the first thousand-bomber raid on Cologne. Three days later, and ten thousand miles away, the back of the Japanese carrier fleet was broken in the Battle of Midway. The tide had not so much turned as somersaulted for Germany's ally, barely six months after Pearl Harbour.

June 1942 proved a decisive month for Nazi Germany. In the Mediterranean the last chance was created and then thrown aside. The Battle of Gazala had begun in the last week of May. After a shaky start Rommel's inspired handling of his armour, so in contrast with that of his opponents, destroyed the bulk of the British armour, forcing a general withdrawal eastward. By 21 June the Afrika Korps had taken Tobruk, captured a reasonable quantity of supplies, and was poised to pursue the British into Egypt.

Rommel now had a problem. Should he pause to take Malta or push forward towards the Nile? Reasoning, against Kesselring's advice, that the captured supplies made action against Malta for the moment unnecessary, that in any case speed was essential to prevent a British recovery, and that, in all probability, given the Reich's resources and the low importance attached to the African theatre at higher levels, it had always been a question of one or the other, he decided to press his slender advantage.

The tragedy of his situation was not of his own making. For eighteen months he had been bombarding his superiors with appreciations of the possibilities open to the Axis forces. Writing after injury in 1944 he listed what should and could have been done:

(a) The creation of an adequate air concentration in the Mediterranean area, by moving Luftwaffe formations from France, Norway and Denmark.

   (b) Transfer to the North African theatre of several of the armoured and motorised formations which were lying idle in France and Germany.

   (c) Malta should have been attacked and taken.

   (d) The appointment of one man to take charge of supplies, with full powers over all Wehrmacht authorities concerned in their handling and protection.

These measures had nothing extraordinary about them and would have been quite normal to take, yet they would have conclusively decided the war in Africa in our favour. (7)

And once the Canal was taken, the whole Mediterranean turned into an Axis lake, supplies could have been moved unmolested to Egypt for a thrust across Arabia to the Persian Gulf. Occupation of Mesopotamia would block the move of American aid to Russia through Basra, would threaten Russia from the south, and, most important of all, would have ended the Wehrmacht's chronic shortage of oil through seizure of the Gulf oilfields. This last point made ridiculous Hitler's assertion that the Caucasus oil was essential for prosecution of the war. If oil was that important to Germany, and this remains doubtful, the Middle East offered an easier option than the Caucasus. That the forces for such an operation could have been made available was proved, Rommel observed bitterly, by the relative ease with which 'it was found possible to ship anything up to 60,000 tons a month into Tunis', once it was too late. (8)

If such an effort could have been mounted in June 1942, if necessary at the cost of postponing the summer offensive in Russia, the consequences for the war as a whole would have been striking, if imponderable in the long term. It was not.

When I put this plan forward in its essential features, it was turned down by people of limited vision as a complete fantasy. But in no single point was it based on unfounded suppositions or unjustifiable hypotheses. It would have given the 100 per cent certainty which at other times they always demanded. Anyone who fights a whole world must think in continents. (9)

This was the rub. Hitler was still not thinking in continents. Many have taken Stalingrad as an example of a prestige battle, of the primacy of psychological over other strategic interests.

To Hitler the whole war in the East had such a value. All other theatres were subsidiary; the decisive blow would be that which beat the Russian. Rommel's success was satisfying no doubt. He made him a Field-Marshal, agreed that Malta could wait, and gave his blessing to a further advance. But no reinforcements, no supply priority. By the end of June Rommel had stretched his elastic to within sixty-five miles of Alexandria. He had twelve German tanks still running with which to reach the Nile.

III

Blau was to be conducted in four phases, but first a number of preliminary operations were called for. First, the Isyum salient had to be bitten off by Kleist's First Panzer Army; this was achieved late in May with the unwilling assistance of Timoshenko's offensive towards Kharkov. Second, Sixth Army attacked in the direction of Kupiansk and Volchansk, considerably shortening the German line during June. By the 28th *Blau* could begin. As Rommel moved up to the El Alamein line in Africa the offensive that was to finish off the Russian got underway on the plains of the Upper Don valley. Its execution would match its conception.

Phase One was to be executed by Bock's Army Group B, comprising Fourth Panzer Army under the ever-faithful Hoth, Sixth Army and Second Army. The Panzer Army, placed in the centre, was to drive due east from the Kursk region to Voronezh on the Don; Second Army to fill the northern shoulder, Sixth to move north-eastward and cut off any Soviet retreat to the south. This phase proceeded with the customary smoothness of *Blitzkrieg*; Hoth's panzers streaking across the high steppe at too great a pace for the bewildered Soviet infantry. Above them the Luftwaffe controlled the skies, spying out the land in front, rendering the Soviet forces blind. The Red Army's armoured reserve, advancing westward nevertheless, ran headlong into the Panzer Army's anti-tank guns southeast of Stary Oskol. Thus crippled they fell easy prey to flank and rear attacks by the marauding armour. Within ten days Hoth had reached the Don. Here the first problem arose.

Voronezh was to be the shoulder-pin of the Volga drive. Bock interpreted this as necessitating its capture. This would deprive the Red Army of railways for counter-concentration;

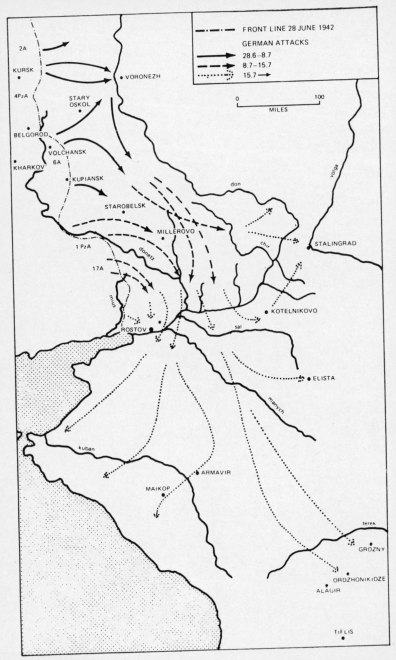

FRONT LINE 28 JUNE 1942
GERMAN ATTACKS
28.6—8.7
8.7—15.7
15.7 ——

0   100
MILES

2A

KURSK

VORONEZH

4P₂A

STARY
OSKOL

BELGOROD

VOLCHANSK
6A

KHARKOV

KUPIANSK

don

volga

STAROBELSK

MILLEROVO

STALINGRAD

1 P₂A

donetz

chir

17A

mius

KOTELNIKOVO

ROSTOV

sal

ELISTA

manych

kuban

ARMAVIR

MAIKOP

terek

GROZNY

ORDZHONIKIDZE

ALAGIR

TIFLIS

8 BLAU

it would help to exacerbate Soviet fears of a fresh German onslaught on Moscow. A sound strategy, it proved hard to carry through. For a week Fourth Panzer Army struggled, at cost and without success, to dislodge the Red Army from the eastern sections of the city. And while this battle continued large Soviet forces, which should by now have been in Hoth's bag, were trudging south towards sanctuaries across the Don. Hitler lost his patience, dismissed Bock, and set Fourth Panzer Army in motion once more for the south. The plan was already beginning to fray at the edges.

As Sixth Army, for the moment minus Fourth Panzer Army, turned south into the land corridor between Don and Donetz, First Panzer Army erupted from its Isyum bridgehead to begin Phase Two. Wheeling right to form Sixth Army's western flank (Fourth Panzer Army should have been the eastern flank), it contemptuously cast aside Soviet opposition, reaching Starobelsk by 11 July. The tanks sent up their tails of dust, gunfire resounded across the steppe, the villages went up in flames. Opposition, as a S.S. major noted, was considerably weaker than the year before. That this might denote intelligent movement of forces by Stavka rather than the lack of them occurred to few. 'The Russian is finished,' as Hitler commented in his celebrated exchange with Halder. The Chief of the General Staff, to his eternal discredit, replied: 'I must say it is beginning to look uncommonly like it.' (10)

The speed of the German advance notwithstanding, the number of prisoners and quantity of equipment captured was negligible when compared with the booty of previous years. This was taken as evidence that the Red Army was scraping the last barrels; in fact it merely indicated the speed and efficiency of their retreat. Still, as the offensive entered its third week it could not be denied that the Wehrmacht was once again in full flood. If the Red Army could not halt it then only Hitler could. There now followed a series of decisions which will forever haunt anyone seeking to hail Hitler as a competent strategist.

First he removed from the line, and transferred West against a possible Anglo-American landing in France, the two crack divisions *Leibstandarte* (later 1st S.S. Panzer) and *Grossdeutschland*. Second he moved two panzer divisions north to counter an imaginary threat to Army Group Centre. Third he suddenly ordered Manstein's Eleventh Army, *Blau*'s lone strategic reserve, north for an assault on Leningrad. Having with these three transfers reduced his force to the bare minimum he then proceeded to make the worst error of all.

Unfortunately for the Wehrmacht, Fourth Panzer Army had made such good progress since its Voronezh rebuff that by 13 July it had 'caught up' the main advance and was motoring south-eastward along Sixth Army's left flank. Phase Three called for these two armies to form a shoulder-pin for the Caucasus advance by taking Stalingrad. Hitler now had other ideas. The weakness of opposition suggested that Sixth Army could accomplish this task on its own; First Panzer Army's forcing of the lower Don might prove more problematic. He redirected Hoth southwards to help Kleist.

Initially this merely created two traffic jams. Fourth Panzer Army forced its way across Sixth Army's line of advance, a slow and tedious task, finally to reach the Lower Don and find the approach roads packed with Kleist's vehicles. Soviet opposition was negligible; Hoth's help, far from being necessary, merely impeded Kleist's advance into the Caucasus. Sixth Army meanwhile had reached the Don further up to find opposition far from negligible, and urgently needed Hoth's assistance.

Hitler, in typical fashion, proceeded to compound the error. The priority given to the two objectives, never clear, was abandoned in favour of a simultaneous pursuit of each. The objectives, moreover, were expanded. Kleist, who as far as O.K.H. was aware, had as his objectives the Maikop and Grozny oilfields, now received open instructions from Hitler to force the passes over the Caucasus Mountains and descend on Baku. Gone too was any ambiguity concerning Stalingrad. The city was not to be masked or brought within artillery range, it was to be taken in the fullest sense, street by street.

Kleist at least knew the nature of his task, no matter how impossible it might have seemed. Hoth was left hovering on the Don crossings for six days before he received fresh orders, for an advance north-east along the eastern bank of the Don, to aid Sixth Army in the capture of Stalingrad. Taking the route he would follow in less auspicious circumstances five months later he soon met stiff resistance. Stalingrad was no longer as ripe for the taking as it had been a fortnight before. Now it would require a fight, although exactly how critical a fight was still hidden from the Germans.

Hitler was as yet undeterred. The traffic jams on the Don, he screamed at the General Staff in a 23 July meeting, were their responsibility. Halder's patience with this sort of accusation was wearing thin.

The situation is getting more and more intolerable. There is no room for any serious work. This 'leadership', so-called, is characterised by a pathological reacting to the impressions of the moment and a total lack of any understanding of the command machinery and its possibilities. (11)

The so-called leadership had repeated the mistake of 1941: divergence of objectives creating an unfavourable ratio of force to space. The reverse of this had won the Battle of France, as much due to Hitler's enthusiastic espousal of panzer concentration as to anything else. Now for the second year running he had scattered his force across the depthless steppe. And two was all the chances he was going to get. The whirlwind had been sown. Only the reaping remained.

IV

The fate invited in summer was sealed in autumn. First the advance in the far south stalled beneath the snow-capped Caucasian peaks. One reason was lack of fuel, another was the slow draining off of Kleist's units to feed the new 'Verdun' five hundred miles north on the Volga. In July, First Panzer Army had been reinforced by Fourth Panzer Army when it needed no reinforcement. In September it was stripped of artillery, air support, troops and supply priority in favour of the seizure of Stalingrad, which could have been taken in July had Hoth not been diverted south to give Kleist that unnecessary help. Another vicious circle of incompetence on Hitler's part, further evidence of the unreality of those goals he refused to compromise.

Stalingrad had meanwhile been taken in the originally intended strategic sense. It no longer functioned as an armament production centre; the Volga was closed to shipping by the guns of 16th Panzer at Rynok. This was no longer sufficient for Hitler. He wanted the streets, the houses, the glory. From 15 September, for a month, Sixth Army and Fourth Panzer Army attempted to take the city by storm. Hindered by the destruction caused by the Luftwaffe's bombing offensive in late August, which had turned defensible positions into strongpoints and a city into a fortress, the German troops pressed slowly forwards, street by street and house by house, into the city of Stalin. Casualties were enormous, advances measured in yards. The German Army's greatest asset in Russia – mobility – counted for nothing in this sort of fighting. The Red Army's greatest assets – skill in camouflage and superhuman tenacity in defence – counted for everything. Hitler would not see it. Rather than abandon the city he drew more and more troops and equipment from Kleist's forces in the Caucasus and the already over-extended front on the Don running north to Voronezh. This was strategic suicide.

Halder, whose control of the campaign had passed from the nominal to the non-existent, grew more and more alarmed and exasperated as the errors multiplied and compounded themselves. On 30 July he had noted down that Hitler's decision to reinforce Sixth Army at Kleist's expense was the 'rankest nonsense'. In September, as the magnitude of the German peril, should Stalingrad not be taken swiftly, became clear to him, he made a series of strenuous efforts to dissuade Hitler from continuance of the folly.

The German front in Russia, he argued, was over two thousand miles long. In length it demanded an overstretching of the available forces that was far beyond the safety margin. That was not all. The very configuration of the front was an open invitation to disaster. South from Voronezh it hung in two large and unseemly bulges, one directed east on Stalingrad, the other south-east towards the Caucasus Mountains. And all the force in these bulges resided in the tips. Along the flanks of the northern bulge stood the make-believe armies of Germany's allies, strong in men but weak in everything else – armour, anti-tank weapons, artillery and, above all, morale – needed to face a Russian onslaught. Between the two bulges, covering a space three hundred miles wide and ideally suited for Soviet cavalry, there was only a solitary division, 16th Motorised at Elista.

The possibilities open to the Russians were numerous. They could break through the gap between the bulges and cut off Army Group A in the Caucasus; they could break through the Allied armies on the flanks of the Stalingrad bulge and encircle the German forces in and around the city; they could make for Rostov, from north or east, and cut off both bulges in one mighty swoop. Any or all of these they could only do, of course, if they had operational reserves available.

Paulus and Weichs, commanding Sixth Army and Army Group B respectively, went to see Hitler at Vinnitsa on 12 September, and drew attention to this threat to their flanks. Hitler probably waved the latest intelligence reports from 'Foreign Armies (East)' at them. It claimed that the Red Army had no significant operational reserve. All that was required of Weichs and Paulus, Hitler stated, was they take Stalingrad in the attack scheduled for 15 September. He would worry about the flanks.

So would Halder. As the assault broke down into isolated actions, and as it became obvious that Stalingrad was not going to fall without exacting an inordinate price, he once again urged Hitler to pull the armies back. The Führer, goaded into one more rage by this meticulous man's lack of faith in the *Volk* destiny, seized upon a flimsy excuse and sacked him. The logistics specialist Zeitzler took over. Hitler wanted someone to put his plans into practice, not someone to make plans that contradicted his own.

Halder was not the only one to object. Weichs and Sodenstern, his Chief of Staff at Army Group B, also saw the failure to take Stalingrad at the first assault as the signal for a withdrawal. They wanted to get their troops into suitable winter positions as soon as possible, and to prepare the armour for a mobile role behind the infantry. Above all, they wanted a strong tactical reserve behind the Allied armies. This could only come from Sixth Army. At the beginning of October they asked that Stalingrad should be masked rather than taken; the front transformed from a bulge into a line stretching from the Volga elbow south of the city north-west across the land-bridge to the Don. O.K.H. agreed. Hitler did not.

Not even ominous warnings of a Soviet build-up opposite the Rumanians on Sixth Army's northern and southern flanks would deter him from dominion over the ruins of Stalin's city. And as October moved into November, and fresh disasters accumulated on the fringes of his Empire, his resolve to take Stalingrad became fatally confused with his wish to demonstrate the continued virility of the Wehrmacht and his direction of its fortunes.

On 4 November Montgomery's Eighth Army broke through at El Alamein, and the Afrika Korps began its six-month retreat towards the prison cages in Tunis. On 8 November the Anglo-American force landed in Morocco. Three days later German and Italian troops occupied Vichy France in response.

These events were to tie down four of the Army's finest divisions – 7th Panzer, *Leibstandarte*, *Das Reich* and *Totenkopf* – while the war swung in the balance in the East.

On 11 November the fourth and final offensive began in Stalingrad. No longer did the combatants face each other on the surface. There only the tanks cautiously probed and edged their way through a wilderness of broken masonry. Beneath sheets of metal, underneath burned-out tanks, high in the empty façades of destroyed buildings, snipers lay in wait for the rash and the reckless. Under the ground the sappers furiously dug new tunnels, creating labyrinths of their own to connect the cellars and sewers of the city. Within forty-eight hours this last 'decisive' offensive had dissolved into the bitterness of isolated actions fought for insignificant pieces of wasteland. Not a few groups of Germans succeeded in clawing their way across the remaining three hundred yards to the banks of the Volga, to gaze out across the ice-flows of the freezing river, and the steppe beyond that they would only see as prisoners.

These small groups of exhausted soldiers marked the high tide of the Nazi Empire that had spread like a stain across Europe in the preceding three years, and of the ninety-year German struggle for European hegemony that had begun on the battlefields of Sadowa and Sedan. The leaders of the old Prussian Army would have been surprised to see them there, on a river fifteen hundred miles from Berlin. But a Prussian had not ordered them there. Neither had a soldier. An Austrian politician had. The once quasi-omnipotent German General Staff would have preferred that they had not been there. But now it was quasi-impotent.

Halder was gone; he lacked belief in the Nazi destiny. Guderian and Bock were gone. They had believed facts more solid than the Führer's genius. Rommel was far away in Africa, but even there the rain of senseless orders to win or die were causing him to doubt the Führer's sanity. The Nile, like Moscow, had proved a mirage. And now the Volga. There Hoth remained, but he had always taken orders. Of the architects of France's fall only Manstein still held the Führer's trust, with an ever-weakening reciprocation. It would be to him that Hitler turned when disaster struck.

The hour was fast approaching. The German groups who had reached the Volga turned to find their retreat cut by similar groups of Red Army soldiers. Stalingrad had become untakable by either side without outside aid. There was too little force for too many ruins. Their fate decided elsewhere, still the soldiers of both armies struggled for heaps of rubble that meant no more than a few extra bodies for the snow to preserve.

Outside the city the German Army had no more to expend. The operational reserve was virtually non-existent. The Red Army had been more thrifty. As dawn broke on 19 November, on the Don north and south of the city a massed barrage of artillery signalled the Soviet counter-offensive. To the Red Army it must have sounded like the ringing of bells, to the Germans a peal of doom. The subjugation of the *Untermenschen* had proved beyond them. The quest for victory was at an end.

References (Chapter 3)

1. Hitler, *Table Talk*, 694
2. quoted in Strawson, *Hitler*, 146
3. quoted in Fuller, *Decisive Battles*, 505
4. see Fuller, *Decisive Battles*, 505–6
5. quoted in Goerlitz, *Paulus*, 145
6. quoted in Fuller, *Decisive Battles*, 504
7. *The Rommel Papers*, 513
8. Ibid, 513
9. Ibid, 515
10. quoted in Clark, *Barbarossa*, 163
11. quoted in Fuller, *Decisive Battles*, 514

PART 2

The Struggle for Stalemate

Let me see
Can this be real?

Can this be real?
I shall know soon

Gods everywhere
Wherever you live,
Can this be real,
Living my life,
Loving my life,
To ride alone along
This lonely path
Toward war and death?

(Pawnee song)

Chapter 4

PERIL ON THE DON

*He whose generals are able and not interfered with by the
sovereign will be victorious.*

(Sun Tzu)

On the morning of 19 November 1942 Stuka ace Hans Rudel
was flying north towards the Don from Morosovsky.

The weather is bad, low-lying clouds, a light fall of snow,
the temperature probably 20 degrees below zero; we fly low.
What troops are those coming towards us? We have not gone
more than half-way: Masses in brown uniform – are they
Russians? No. Rumanians. Some of them are even throwing
away their rifles in order to be able to run faster: a shocking
sight, we are prepared for the worst. We fly the length of the
column heading north, we have now reached our allies'
artillery emplacements. The guns are abandoned, not
destroyed. Their ammunition lies beside them. We have
passed some distance beyond them before we sight the first
Soviet troops. (1)

Rudel may have been prepared for the worst, no one else
seemed to be. Paulus's half-hearted anxieties for his northern
flank along the Don were little more perceptive than O.K.H.'s
notion that the Soviets had no operational reserves. For over
two months Zhukov had been feeding troops and *matériel* into
the danger zone. Three armoured corps, four cavalry corps
and nineteen infantry divisions were pouring out of the Don
bridgeheads between Veshenskaya and Kremenskaya, their
Schwerpunkt aimed at Kalach, in Sixth Army's rear and astride
its solitary supply line. The following day another two armoured
corps and nine infantry divisions were to attack south of Stalingrad, break through the Rumanian Fourth Army and head

north-west for the same destination. The Soviet team of Zhukov and Vasilevsky had been anticipating the moment for months. Sixth Army, the cream of the German Army in Russia, was to be encircled and wiped off the map.

As news of the Soviet attacks percolated up through the rickety German command structure it became apparent that the German Army was as ill-placed to counter the blow as Halder had said it would be. The great majority of the armoured formations and the better infantry divisions were already fully engaged as spearheads of the two great advances, either beneath the Caucasus Mountains or enmeshed in the rubble of Stalingrad. To counter the blow with the forces not so engaged would not be easy. It would require clarity of thought and speed of action, strategic and tactical expertise of the highest order. As the first week of crisis unrolled it became clear that the German command structure was as ill-fitted to provide such a response as the forces were ill-placed to execute it.

Of all the armies fighting the Second World War the German should have been best-equipped to deal with such a situation. As Manstein wrote, somewhat wistfully, after the war:

It has always been the particular forte of German leadership to grant wide scope to the self-dependence of subordinate commanders – to allot them *tasks* which leave the method of execution to the discretion of the individual . . . the granting of such independence does of course ·presuppose that all members of the military hierarchy are imbued with certain tactical or operational axioms. Only the German General Staff can, I suppose, be said to have produced such a consistency of outlook. (2)

This 'consistency of outlook' was based on more than shared 'tactical or operational axioms'. It assumed an Army in which personal and political trust were the norm, and in which as a consequence all senior commanders had access to the available information. In 1942 these assumptions no longer held. Hitler had never trusted the Army for social and political reasons; they had no 'National Socialist spirit'. Their consistency of outlook he characterised as narrow, traditionalist and over-cautious, preferring his own proven military genius. So, distrusting their political reliability and disdainful of their professional expertise, he blocked the flow of information. Only those at the highest levels could now view the overall situation;

only they could act, only they were allowed to act. The rest of the command structure was rendered rigid, both by lack of authority and lack of information. In any crisis situation Hitler's speed of response would have to make up for the overall lack of flexibility.

This development had naturally not occurred overnight. But in 1940 its consequences had been averted by success, in 1941 partially obviated by subtle insubordinations. By 1942 the success and the insubordinate commanders had both disappeared, and nothing served to alleviate the workings of this grotesque structure save the persuasive powers of those who inhabited it.

At the summit were the man they had to persuade and his rubber-stamp O.K.W. The Führer paced up and down beneath his wall-maps, voicing his incredulity that the Army should have failed him so abysmally. Keitel and Jodl bowed and scraped and told him how right he was. In this campaign Hitler had taken a particular interest in Sixth Army, nominally under Army Group B, and the Army Group in the Caucasus. In both cases he exercised almost direct control, frequently ignoring the intermediate levels of command.

Just below the summit, as far as the war in the East was concerned, was O.K.H., the nominal Army High Command. It too was attempting to make reality out of Hitler's dreams, but constantly chafing at the interference from above. Here at least there were some operational intelligences, who had some idea of what advancing across an inch of the map really meant, who could see a campaign as possessed of temporal depth, not merely a chain of whims strung together by the inspiration of the moment. When asked, O.K.H. could provide sound advice, but it was not often asked. Hitler expected it to perform the logistics functions and leave the strategic thinking to him. Thus the appointment of Zeitzler.

The next level was that of the Army Group, in this case Army Group B. Weichs was the commander, Sodenstern his Chief of Staff; they nominally controlled, for the moment, four Allied armies (two Rumanian, one Italian, one Hungarian), the two armies about to be encircled (6th and 4th Panzer), and Second Army on the Upper Don adjoining Army Group Centre. Manstein, en route for his new appointment as commander of the newly-formed Army Group Don (itself carved out of Army Group B), found them both apathetically pessimistic. Their advice had been ignored in October; their forebodings had been amply fulfilled. Reduced to the status of executors of the Führer's mistakes they could hardly be expected to radiate enthusiasm. Theirs being not to reason why, they were prepared to do and die only with reluctance.

For their respective subordinates in Sixth Army – Paulus commanding, Schmidt his Chief of Staff – it was a matter of more immediacy. Yet they too had their hands tied, firstly by ignorance, soon after by orders. There were two equally unsavoury options open to Paulus and Schmidt. They could do what seemed, from their blinkered perspective, to need doing. Or they could wait for the time it took Hitler, who alone had an unblinkered perspective, to make up his mind. Both courses were fraught with peril. It often took the Führer an interminable time to take those decisions he wished to avoid (i.e. decisions forced on him by crises he neither expected nor wanted to accept responsibility for), and by the time he had made up his mind the situation was demanding another decision, the first having been rendered irrelevant by changing circumstances. Paulus and Schmidt, dashing hither and thither in the chaos of their Army's encirclement, knew in their bones that an immediate break-out was the best option available. But how could they press these views if the Supreme Command, with its more comprehensive information, disagreed? How were they to know whether the promises of relief and supply by air were reality or delusion? Manstein later wrote that Paulus, having personally served at the highest administrative levels, should have known better. But even he also admitted that Paulus was essentially in the dark, and that a break-out would 'momentarily have meant a bigger risk than forming a hedgehog position in Stalingrad'. (3)

Manstein himself had been ordered south from Vitebsk with the rest of his Eleventh Army HQ Staff to take command of Army Group Don, comprising Sixth Army, Fourth Panzer Army, and what remained of the Rumanians. He boarded a train on 21 November – weather having prohibited flying – and that evening chatted with a morose von Kluge on Orsha station. Kluge gave him the up-to-date news, and added as encouragement that Manstein would find movement of even a battalion impossible without the Führer's prior assent. Doubtless depressed by the news, which further emphasised the lunacy of the orders he had been given – to stop enemy attacks and *recapture lost ground* – Manstein journeyed on south at the snail's pace dictated by the interrelated problems of railway inefficiency and partisan activity, uncheered even by his aide's morale-boosting use of the Eleventh Army HQ gramophone.

Last in this list of the relevant sources of indecision came the Luftwaffe. Fourth Air Fleet was responsible for the Stalingrad sector, Richthofen its commander. From him the chain led up through Jeschonnek to Göring and Hitler. The weak link was Göring, more likely to be hunting art treasures in the West than wondering whether the Luftwaffe really could supply 'Fortress Stalingrad'.

For by the 21st, as Manstein learnt on arrival at Starobelsk, 'Fortress Stalingrad' was the official designation. The previous three days had been spent in a mad whirl of messages up and down and across the command structure, in which nearly everyone had done their best to convince Hitler that Sixth Army's only chance was a rapid break-out from its encirclement. Because by no stretch of the imagination, save perhaps Göring's, could it be adequately supplied by air. Hitler's resultant decision was that Sixth Army should stand fast in anticipation of relief and supply by air. Why?

II

'The terrain on both sides of the Don is one vast endless steppe, broken occasionally by deep valleys, in which villages are tucked away. The landscape recalled the North African desert, but with snow instead of sand.' (4) So wrote Mellenthin, appointed at this hour as Chief of Staff to 48th Panzer Corps, on 19 November the sole German operational reserve in the Don bend. Comprising 22nd Panzer and a Rumanian armoured division, this corps' condition offered ample opportunities for contrast with the Soviet forces it found itself engaging. While the Red Army's brand new T-34s rolled south by the hundred, and the mass-produced artillery pieces and katyusha rockets spread havoc ahead of them, 48th Panzer Corps was crippled by supply difficulties, obsolete equipment, and a recent encounter with mice. The Rumanians were equipped mostly with Czech armour, and virtually defenceless against the T-34. 22nd Panzer's problems were more unusual. In reserve behind the Italians on the Middle Don during the autumn the division, for lack of fuel to keep the engines running, had been forced to dig its tanks into the ground and cover them with straw as protection against the frost. The straw attracted mice, who then proceeded, with great if unconscious devotion to the Soviet cause, to nibble their way through the rubber insulation on all the electrical wiring. When the tanks were dug out preparatory to moving south thirty-one out of 104 were already *hors de combat*. The journey was no less ruinous, for somehow the snow-sleeves for the tank-tracks got mislaid. By the time 22nd Panzer reached the battlefield of Peschannyy in the late morning of 19 November there were only twenty tanks, slithering this way and that, to halt the rush of the 450 tanks of Soviet Fifth Tank Army. The Soviet forces, ever-mindful of German skill in handling even such a small unit, merely swerved past the obstacle and headed on south-east for Kalach.

On the southern flank of the Stalingrad bulge things went rather better for the Germans. The experienced 29th Motorised Division, which had led Guderian's charge across Russia in 1941, bottled up one avenue of Soviet penetration and was about to attempt the same with another when Paulus, displaying the blind orthodoxy typical of the General Staff at their worst, ordered it to stand fast as defensive cover for Sixth Army's southern flank. In this he was severely under-estimating Zhukov's strategic *savoir faire*. He, almost alone of the Soviet generals in the first two years of the war, had grasped the 'indirect approach' which his more imaginative German counterparts took as military gospel. The Soviet forces were not aimed directly at Sixth Army but, indirectly, at its lifeline. The southern prong of the offensive, with notable caution after its mauling by 29th Motorised, continued its march on Kalach and the bridge over the Don.

On the bridge itself a small German force waited with the demolition charges. As evening fell on 22 November they observed a column of tanks looming out of the western dusk. Whose were they? The first three were panzers – it was all right. The German force, refusing to be flattered by this Soviet imitation of one of their own favourite ruses, was swiftly overwhelmed. The next day the two Soviet spearheads met amidst great rejoicing east of the bridge. Stalingrad was cut off.

At all the various German H.Q.s such a probability had been anticipated for some hours. On 21 November the local Luftwaffe had been doing its best to convince Paulus and Schmidt that Sixth Army could not be supplied by air in the event of its encirclement. There were not the planes available. This opinion was also communicated to Göring, Hitler and Weichs.

The next day Paulus and Schmidt, as was common practice in the Army, took an hour each in separate rooms to consider the position and then compared notes. In the event they were in agreement. Sixth Army must break out as soon as possible, south-west to the line of the Chir and Lower Don. But not immediately, as Schmidt told Richthofen: 'We can't, because we haven't got the necessary fuel. And if we tried we should end up with a catastrophe like that of Napoleon.' (5) A year after the Moscow débâcle the fate of the Grand Armée continued to haunt the Wehrmacht.

Later the same day an order arrived from Hitler. To await orders, or, in other words – don't move. The Führer was thinking of denying the inevitable.

On the 23rd O.K.H. got into the act. As the pincers were closing east of Kalach an emissary from Zeitzler arrived in the pocket by plane to talk with Paulus and Schmidt. After these conversations, and telephone consultation with Zeitzler himself and Weichs, everyone agreed that a break-out was the best option still open. Zeitzler then attempted to convince Hitler, thought he had succeeded, and phoned Paulus with the good news that he could expect an order the next day. Preparations could then begin for action on the 27th. Paulus, thinking perhaps to push the opening door a bit faster, sent Hitler a signal that night –

Unless I concentrate every available man to inflict a decisive defeat on the enemy advancing from the south and west, my Army will be faced with imminent destruction.

. . . as it will not be possible to hold the eastern and northern fronts with the weak forces still available, I shall have no option but to fight my way out south-westwards.

We shall, it is true, suffer heavy material losses, but the majority of these fine fighting men and at least a portion of their arms and equipment will be saved.

Although my subordinate commanders, General Heitz, Strecker, Hube and Jaenecke, all agree with my views, I personally accept full responsibility for this grave communication.

In view of the situation, I request you to grant me complete freedom of action. (6)

What Paulus omitted to mention was that another of those subordinates, General Seydlitz, had already withdrawn his front some eight kilometres in the north, and in the process had seen one of his infantry divisions pinned down and destroyed by the Russians. It was an evil omen for the general withdrawal, one which doubtless preyed on Paulus's mind in later weeks. For the moment it mattered little, for Hitler would have none of it. The next day a Führer Directive arrived. Sixth Army was to hold its position. It would be supplied by air. A relief column would arrive in due time, though not to extricate it – to strengthen the occupation of Stalingrad!

And still the argument went on. Richthofen, contemplating on 25 November the previous day's Luftwaffe losses in the air-lift – forty-seven planes employed, twenty-two shot down – urged both Jeschonnek and Zeitzler to recommend that Sixth Army break out while it still had sufficient strength. He tried to contact Göring but the Reichmarschall was apparently in Paris.

Weichs was also trying, as were Paulus's subordinate commanders in the cauldron. Seydlitz submitted a memorandum on 25 November, telling Paulus that 'it is our inescapable duty before our own conscience, our duty to the Army and to the German people, to seize that freedom of action that we are being denied by the present order'. (7) Paulus could not agree. He would not disobey the Führer. And now Manstein had advised against breaking out.

The new commander of Army Group Don's collection of remnants had finally reached Novocherkassk on the 25th. He was a strategist of the old school. Not a crusader like Guderian; not an inspired leader like Rommel. A strategist. Someone who could look at the problem from all sides, weigh the component parts against each other, compute the optimum solution. And, on his endless train journey, Manstein had grasped the essence of the situation. Everyone was shouting about Sixth Army, pressing for 'break-out' or 'stand-fast', but more was at stake here than Sixth Army. The ludicrous disposition of the entire German southern wing invited a far more devastating fate than the loss of one army. The Soviet forces pushing slowly towards the Chir were about 180 miles from Rostov; Kleist's First Panzer Army in the Caucasus was more than twice that distance from this vital link in its supply line. And if anyone knew how fast armour could move it was Manstein. He had covered over a hundred miles in three days in June 1941. At present the Soviets were not making any strong push towards Rostov. But if Sixth Army broke out, those seven Soviet armies encircling it would pour down the Don valley like a tidal wave. If Sixth Army were to be extricated, it had to be brought out intact, and it had to continue to tie down those armies now encircling it. Otherwise the whole southern wing would be forfeit, and the Germans would have lost the war.

The chances of bringing out Sixth Army in one piece were not good. Break-out would have to be directed either west via Kalach or south-west via Kotelnikovo. In neither case would there be a substantial force to meet them. Sixth Army would have to fight its way alone, across at least a hundred miles of open steppe, in winter, defending itself on all four sides, carrying its wounded. All without adequate nourishment for either men or machines. On the morning of the 24th Manstein, breaking his train journey at Dnepropetrovsk, advised Zeitzler that it would be better to wait for an adequately mounted relief operation if – a strong if – the relief force would be strong enough for the job and Sixth Army could be supplied by air in the meantime. Hitler promised the former, Göring the latter. Most of the German generals subsequently blamed Göring for the disaster. Guderian talks of his incompetence and idleness, Rommel of his baleful influence. Manstein described his assurance that Sixth Army could be supplied by air as 'the supreme frivolity'. Doubtless Göring's dedication to the Russian venture, which he had opposed from the outset, was not what it should have been, but Hitler was only too eager to believe assurances that involved him in no sacrifice of the ruins won at such a cost by Sixth Army.

III

Manstein, confronted with the question of which route offered the best chance of relieving Stalingrad, began to assemble forces under the aegis of Fourth Panzer Army (some of which was trapped with Sixth Army in Stalingrad) around Kotelnikovo. A seventy-mile advance would be required from this direction, as opposed to forty from the still-desperately-held Don bridgehead at Nizhne Chirskaya, but the danger from the flanks was considerably less, as elements of 16th Motorised confirmed in a long reconnaissance sweep between Elista and the Volga elbow.

The forces available, despite Hitler's assurances, were minimal. The main weight would fall on 57th Panzer Corps, comprising a much-weakened 23rd Panzer from the Caucasus (which arrived late and minus its artillery) and the full-strength 6th Panzer, which had been en route from France since the crisis began. 17th Panzer was also due to appear, but due to dithering at Supreme Command level did not arrive until the operation was a week old. To start operations on 12 December Manstein had less than two hundred tanks, without their full-arms support, guarded on the flanks by two weak Rumanian corps.

The delays incurred and the weakness of the force were certainly the result of irresolution among Manstein's superiors, stemming from a fundamental indecision regarding the objective of the operation. Hitler had not yet, and in fact never would, bring himself to abandon Stalingrad. Manstein's orders were to relieve Sixth Army, not to extricate it. If Stalingrad was abandoned, Hitler argued, it would take a great deal of unnecessary effort to recapture it in the following spring. Neither had he accepted that the Caucasus was beyond the Army's present strength, and forces which Manstein desperately needed for the relief operation were not forthcoming. 16th Motorised was still sitting around Elista because Army Group A refused to relieve it. Once again strategic greed was leading to tactical starvation.

Hitler could not bring himself to believe in the extent of the Soviet strength gathering around the Don bend. If there were 143 formations, as Army Group Don insisted there were, then they had to be severely under-strength formations. The Red Army could not possibly have formed and equipped 143 strong formations! His own forces, which in contrast were under-strength, he persisted in treating as if they were not. A paper-strength ratio of 45 German to 143 Russian Hitler translated as 45 German to 70 Russian, and since the Germans were tactically superior fighters there was little cause for concern.

Manstein's appreciation of German strength was more accurate. With the exception of 6th and 11th Panzer the German forces had been in almost continual action since June. This, taken together with the chronic supply situation, had reduced corps to divisions, divisions to brigades, and brigades to battalions. Manstein's translation of the paper-strength ratio was more like 20 German to 120 Russian, or a one to six disadvantage. If the Germans were tactically superior they would need to be, as the crisis looming on the Chir would amply demonstrate.

Hoth's Fourth Panzer Army, advancing north-eastward from Kotelnikovo, was only the *principal* relief force. On reaching the Aksay river it was to receive assisting pressure from 48th Panzer Corps in the Nizhne Chirskaya region. This assistance was never to materialise. The Red Army struck first, on the Chir.

The motivation behind this timely Soviet offensive remains obscure. It is probably true that Zhukov and his team, as Alan Clark argues, were determined not to let their dreams of an advance on Rostov prejudice their grip on Sixth Army. This deliberate self-limitation made the most of Soviet troop qualities at this stage of the war: numerical superiority and great tenacity in the holding of fixed positions.

Zhukov knew that the standard of training, and the initiative of commanders at the lower level, would make too deep and ambitious penetration with their armour a risky affair. He knew, too, that many of the Corps or even Army commanders had neither the flexibility nor the imagination for a 'General Intention'. (8)

This notwithstanding, Zhukov found himself in early December in the enviable position of finding two goals – Stalingrad and Rostov – mutually supportive. The Germans had to hold the Chir line; for the Don–Chir bridgehead as a jumping-off point for the relief operation's support, for protection of the airfields at Tatsinskaya and Morosovsky which supplied the besieged army, and ultimately for the security of Rostov and the Donetz crossings. To the Soviets, pressure on the Chir not only promised a possible breakthrough towards Rostov, it also, by creating such a threat, obliged Manstein to reduce the forces engaged in the attempted relief of Sixth Army. So, in the first week of December, as Fourth Panzer Army sluggishly assembled across the Don, Zhukov threw what forces he could spare, tactical ineptitude and all, against 48th Panzer Corps on the Chir.

The Corps comprised two divisions at this time: 336th Infantry Division and the newly-arriving 11th Panzer Division from O.K.H. reserve. Both were in reasonably good shape, and commanded by men who understood the task in front of them, and who worked well together. 11th Panzer's commander, General Balck, whom we last encountered leading Guderian's spearhead regiment in France, was one of the finest panzer commanders of the war; resourceful, bold, an intuitive master

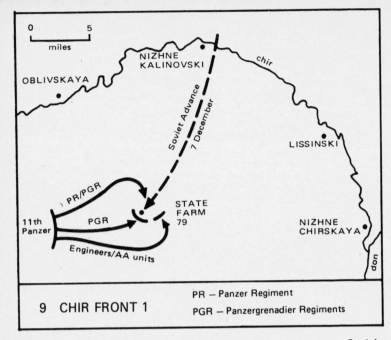

0 ────── 5
miles

NIZHNE
KALINOVSKI

chir

OBLIVSKAYA

Soviet Advance
7 December

LISSINSKI

PR/PGR

STATE
FARM
79

11th
Panzer

PGR

NIZHNE
CHIRSKAYA

Engineers/AA units

don

9   CHIR FRONT 1

PR — Panzer Regiment

PGR — Panzergrenadier Regiments

of panzer tactics. He was fortunate at this juncture to find in
General Lucht an infantry commander who understood well
the principles of panzer defence. The infantry would guard
the 'front-door', and if occasionally forced to admit an intruder,
would endeavour to shut the door behind him. Inside the house
11th Panzer would play the 'avenger' role, seeking out the
intruder and destroying or ejecting him.

The first 'break-in' was on 7 December, a Soviet armoured
corps breaking past 336th Infantry's left flank in the region of
Nizhne Kalinovski and motoring south towards State Farm 79.
11th Panzer, still in the act of arriving from Rostov, was
sent straight into action with a lesson for the Soviets in
armoured tactics. Advancing from the west, Balck sent his
engineer battalion and anti-aircraft units to hold the south-
eastern boundary of the penetration, and one panzergrenadier
regiment to deliver a holding attack from the south-west. The
majority of the tanks in the panzer regiment and the second
panzergrenadier regiment drove through the night in a long
arc north of the collective, to cut the Soviet line of retreat. En
route they fell upon a column of Soviet motorised infantry,
slicing through the lorries with machine-guns blazing. Leaving

the burning wreckage of the column scattered across the steppe, Balck turned the tanks south against the State Farm. At dawn the Soviet forces found themselves trapped in a ring of fire as Balck's three formations closed in from all sides. Fifty-three Red Army tanks were destroyed; the small remainder skulked off into hiding among the gullies that dissected the surrounding steppe.

Five days later the Soviets tried again. This time they sent two columns through the infantry-held front, one at Nizhne Kalinovski, the other north of Lissinski. Eleventh Panzer marched through the night to fall on the Lissinski force at dawn, then turned about and marched fifteen miles to the north-west to account for the other intruders in early afternoon. By 13 December the division had been on the move, virtually without rest, for eight days. Casualties were not high, but still more than could be shrugged aside. When the division could get any sleep, as Balck said after the war, was a question never clearly answered.

'As for the tactical incompetence of the Soviet commanders -- it confirmed Zhukov's forebodings.' Balck wrote:

The fighting on the Chir was made easier by the methods adopted by the command of the Russian Fifth Tank Army. They sent their various corps into battle without coordinating the timing of their attacks, and without the cooperation of the numerous infantry divisions. Thus 11th Panzer Division was enabled to smash one corps after another ... (9)

Mellenthin endorsed this opinion.

Russian tactics are a queer mixture in spite of their brilliance at infiltration and their exceptional mastery of field fortification, yet the rigidity of Russian attacks was proverbial. The foolish repetition of attacks on the same spot, the rigidity of Russian artillery fire and the selection of the terrain for the attack, all betrayed a total lack of imagination and mental mobility. Our Wireless Intercept Service heard many a time the frantic question: 'What are we to do now?' (10)

Nevertheless the strategic placing of these attacks (the Chir front) and the strategic timing (during the assembly of the relief operation) more than compensated for the lack of initiative displayed in their tactical conduct. They were keeping Manstein's forces stretched, and that for the moment was what mattered. For by 16 December Hoth's relief force had reached the Aksay and it was time for 11th Panzer to exert some flanking leverage across the Don at Nizhne Chirskaya. But the division was needed elsewhere; Balck had received news of yet another Soviet breakthrough higher up the Chir valley. Reluctantly he turned 11th Panzer north once more to administer a check to the advancing Soviet column. This achieved he heard of a further breakthrough at Nizhne Kalinovski. There was no time to help Hoth. Balck wheeled one panzergrenadier regiment north to plug the hole, the other west to stem the advance. Between them the panzer regiment rolled through the night to fall on the enemy at dawn. Its remaining twenty-five tanks advanced undetected into the rear of one Soviet column, dispatching forty-two Soviet tanks without loss. Further west, shielded from knowledge of the German presence by high ground, a second Soviet column met the same fate. Twenty-three more tanks were accounted for.

Despite this initial success 11th Panzer had to fight a bitter action to push all the Soviet forces back across the Chir. Two weeks of intensive combat had been slowly wearing the

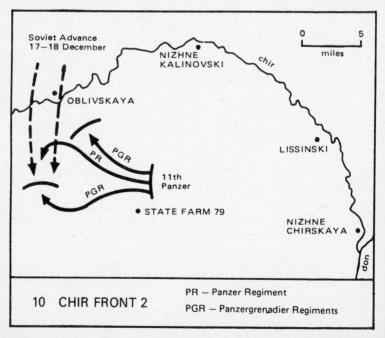

10　CHIR FRONT 2

PR — Panzer Regiment
PGR — Panzergrenadier Regiments

division away, and the Soviet forces seemed as limitless as ever. 'The German armoured units,' wrote Mellenthin, 'were like isolated rocks in a vast ocean, with the Russian masses rushing past to the right, the left, and far behind.' (11) As 11th Panzer wiped up the remains of this attack the front creaked and collapsed a hundred miles further to the north, on the Italian sector above Kazanskaya. Driving their armour across the frozen Don the Soviets emerged from dense fog into the positions of the startled Italians who, with few exceptions, broke and fled. Even should the Chir front continue to hold it had now been outflanked.

This last crisis found Manstein looking more and more like one of those figures in twenties' comedies, trying to plug three burst waterpipes with two hands. The Stalingrad relief force, skilfully led by Hoth and his panzer commanders, had forced a passage across the Aksay, and by 19 December had reached the Mishkova, only thirty miles from the siege perimeter. But with the Chir front shaking in the storm, and the Italians on the Middle Don having been blown away, it was only a matter of time before forces would have to be rushed west to stem a south-flowing flood; forces that would have to be taken, in lieu of any alternative, from Hoth's relief army. Time was running out all along the front. If Stalingrad were to be relieved it would have to be within days.

Manstein, without doubt anticipating the tussle about to take place, had submitted an 'appreciation' to Hitler as early as 9 December. It included the following passage:

One must allow for the possibility that the Russians will take the proper action and, while maintaining their encirclement of Stalingrad, launch strong attacks . . . with Rostov as their target. If this happens our most vital forces will be operationally immobilised in the fortress area or tied down to keeping the links with it open, whereas the Russians will have freedom of action along the whole of the Army Group's remaining front. To maintain this situation throughout the winter strikes me as inexpedient. (12)

The rampant sarcasm of the last line failed to move the Führer. The log-jam in the situation – the future of Sixth Army – remained unresolved.

In practical terms this came down to Sixth Army's role in its own relief. There were two phases to the operation: 'Winter

Tempest' and 'Thunderclap'. The former involved the establishment of a corridor through which Hoth's four hundred supply-laden lorries could be funnelled to Sixth Army. The latter involved the evacuation of the pocket. Both phases demanded action by Sixth Army; the first an exertion of pressure on the Soviet ring from inside as Hoth attacked from the outside, the second a phased withdrawal from the city. To Manstein these two phases were inseparable, rather like a man's left leg preceding his right leg through a door. Hitler, on the other hand, wanted Sixth Army to place one leg out whilst keeping the other firmly in position inside the house. Consequently Paulus, denied permission to move both legs, refused to move either. This vicious circle spun round and round for a week while Hoth clung precariously to the Mishkova line and the Don front to the west yawned wider and wider.

Everyone in the pocket, including Paulus and Schmidt, favoured a break-out.* But they were not prepared to order or even prepare for one without the Führer's permission. To Manstein's whispered pleas for a fait accompli to force Hitler's hand,† Paulus replied with a sad estimate of his Army's ability to cross the necessary thirty miles. There was insufficient fuel, the horses had mostly been eaten, it would take weeks to prepare. Hoth would have to come closer. Ah, but he can only do that, Manstein argued, if Sixth Army pushes from the other side against the Soviet forces holding him up. Ah, but we can't do that, retorted Paulus and Schmidt, without endangering the northern and eastern siege perimeters that the Führer has

* Paulus and Schmidt were not prepared to gamble with their Army or their careers. They wanted nothing short of a definitive order from Hitler, or one from Manstein sanctioned by Hitler, before they would prepare to move. As Schmidt said to Manstein's Chief of Staff on 20 December 1942:

In the event of major penetrations (by the Soviets), let alone break-throughs, our Army reserves, in particular the tanks, have to be employed if the fortress is to be held at all. The situation could be viewed somewhat differently if it were *certain* that 'Winter Tempest' will be followed immediately by 'Thunderclap'. In that event local penetrations on the remaining fronts could be accepted provided they did not jeopardise the withdrawal of the Army. (13)

† According to Manstein:
On express instructions from Hitler the Army was to continue to hold its existing positions within the pocket. That this would not be possible in practice when it broke out to the south-west to meet Fourth Panzer Army was perfectly obvious, for when the Soviets attacked on the northern or eastern fronts it would have to give way step by step. In the event, undoubtedly, Hitler would have had no choice but to accept this fact, as he did on later occasions. (14)

ordered us to hold at all costs. Manstein appealed to Hitler; the latter met him with a smug: 'I fail to see what you're getting at. Paulus has only enough petrol for fifteen to twenty miles at the most. He says himself he can't break out at present.' (15)

As this argument continued Zhukov's precisely-timed assault on the Middle Don was wreaking the intended havoc. Strong forces were advancing on the airfields from which Sixth Army's grossly inadequate air-lift was being conducted. There was no choice for Manstein. One of Hoth's panzer divisions had to be sent west. Hoth, who had probably come to realise that nothing short of armageddon would change Hitler's – and thus Paulus's – mind, gave him the best: 6th Panzer. It was the end of Stalingrad's chances of relief. Manstein, from the strategic point of view, was not altogether sorry. The most empathetic feelings for Sixth Army's long death agony could not hide the strategic fact that the Stalingrad siege was tying down over half the Soviet forces in the Don sector. The remainder were causing quite enough problems.

Nevertheless he asked Hitler for 3rd Panzer Corps from Army Group A for a final attempt. This could apparently not be spared. Hitler had another idea. The S.S. Panzer Corps, soon to assemble in the Kharkov area, would by mid-February be in a position to drive the 350 miles to Stalingrad's relief. This, to Manstein, must have been one of many final straws. Insanity seemed to be feeding on itself. Richthofen, complaining to Jeschonnek that Hoth's air support had been whisked away at the vital moment to bolster the collapsing Italians, was greeted with the idiotic rejoinder that he himself had constantly warned of the weakness of the Middle Don front. Indeed I did, Richthofen might have said to himself, but it was only too weak because all the strength was, and is, trapped in the city we are trying to relieve. With weakened air support. 'I told von Manstein all this,' Richthofen wrote in his diary; 'we both feel the same – that we're like a couple of attendants in a lunatic asylum.' (16)

IV

The Soviet forces which had broken through to Tatsinskaya airfield were summarily dealt with by the combined forces of 6th and 11th Panzer. The airfield had been taken on Christmas Eve, amidst an orgy of atrocities reminiscent of the Apaches.

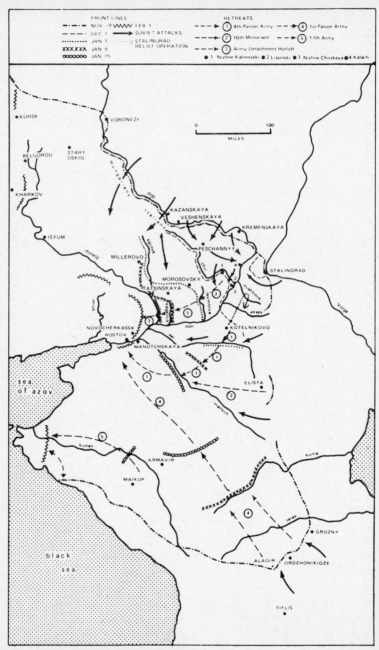

11   RETREAT: WINTER 1942-3

The Soviets too, it might be noted, were defending their home-land. On this occasion they met with little success. Sixth Panzer sealed off the northern exit to deny escape or potential rein-forcement; 11th Panzer, by the devilish light of Sixth Army's supplies burning on the runway, crushed the Soviet occupiers. A week later the two divisions staged a repeat performance at Maryevka, some ten miles to the east.

These successes in stemming the Red Army's advance on Rostov shone in an otherwise unmitigated gloom for the Ger-mans. They took place, after all, sixty miles behind the supposed 'front', now manned by formations grouped under the name of Army Detachment Hollidt. These were being slowly levered back by the incursions around their flanks towards the line of the Donetz. And just as surely, across the Don, Hoth's forces were being pushed back to their starting-line at Kotelnikovo.

In effect three huge gaps had opened in the German front. Gap One yawned west of Army Detachment Hollidt. There only a small force centred on Millerovo covered the rent torn in the Don front by the Italian collapse. Through this gap the Red Army could drive south towards Rostov, as the ill-starred Tatsinskaya force had been doing, or south-westwards towards the Sea of Azov. Either course would cut the Don–Dnieper railway, the sole supply-line for the entire southern wing. Gap Two had appeared in the Don valley as Army Detachment Hollidt and Fourth Panzer Army were pushed back along diverging lines, the one west, the other south-west. Soviet exploitation of this could involve flanking movements against the rear of either force or, again, a direct strike at Rostov and the lifelines of both Fourth and First Panzer Armies. Between these last two, plugged only by the eternal vigil of 16th Motorised, was Gap Three, threatening the rear of the German forces in the Caucasus.

The only real plug for any of these gaps was Sixth Army's continued pull on the mass of the Soviet forces. Inside Stalin-grad its position was passing from the critical to the pitiful as cold and hunger claimed their victims by the hundred each day. Yet it had to hold on, for its surrender would unleash the catastrophe. Written off as a positive force, the negative role of the trapped army remained crucial. It had to remain in being, no matter what the cost in suffering.

The solution to this situation, at least in the short term, was quite simple. Or at least it seemed so to Manstein, fuming over others' lack of ability to perceive the obvious. Since the German position in the Caucasus rested strategically on a strong German position in the Don bend – that had been the rationale for attempting to take Stalingrad in the first place – the Caucasus could no longer be held in the absence of such strength. Evacuation of forces there would automatically close Gap Three as they moved northwards and Gap Two as Hoth's forces followed them out through Rostov and Army Detachment Hollidt withdrew to the Donetz. Then the combined weight of the two Panzer Armies could be shifted further west to plug Gap One. It was as simple as that in outline, and the Army contained quite enough trained logisticians to work out the details and enough good commanders to execute them.

The prerequisite of this scheme's adoption was Hitler's early acceptance of the need for a swift contraction of the German front, including a swift withdrawal from the Caucasus. What Manstein feared most was the Führer's acquiescing in such a retreat only when its escape route was already blocked. Through the first half of January this grim likelihood increased as Soviet forces bit deeper into the spaces between the German forces, forcing them slowly back.

The Chir position was abandoned finally, Hollidt falling back steadily from river to river: Chir, Tsymbiya, Kagalnik. Behind the four infantry divisions 6th, 11th and 7th Panzer did their best to safeguard the flanks and check possible breakthroughs. Fourth Panzer Army was also retreating river by river: Sal, Kuberle, Manych. In constant danger of encirclement Hoth kept his force concentrated against Soviet incursions down the Don and Manych valleys. As Manstein wrote: 'A hard-and-fast line was likely to prove about as effective as a cobweb in Fourth Panzer Army's situation.' (17) But gathered in for self-preservation Hoth's force could do little to stop odd Soviet forces breaking past it to spread havoc on the Lower Don. One such force approached to within a mile of Manstein's H.Q. at Novocherkassk. The tank-repair shop next door provided an improvised defence as Manstein concentrated on bombarding Hitler and O.K.H. with urgent appeals.

As early as 20 December he had informed Zeitzler that Army Group A's position in the Caucasus was untenable. Nine days later Hitler finally sanctioned a withdrawal to the Kuma line, still over three hundred miles the wrong side of Rostov. Then, to add grist to Manstein's overtaxed mill, Kleist informed him on 2 January 1943 that it would take his forces twenty-five days to retreat even that short distance. Further, Hitler had by no means committed himself to giving Manstein the armour – First Panzer Army – he needed for his grand plan to stabilise the front. The Führer had come to accept the loss of *part* of the Caucasus, but a withdrawal of Army Group A into the Kuban bridgehead, he argued, would offer the chance to try again next spring. This piece of 'sheer wishful thinking', as Manstein characterised it, did contain an element of that lunatic logic that had so incensed Richthofen. Hitler had himself stated quite baldly that possession of the Caucasus oilfields spelt either victory or defeat for Germany, and it is possible that he was right. The catch came in the rigid polarisation of alternatives – victory or defeat. Manstein's plan was based on the supposition that the most Germany could now hope for was a tie. Hitler was still thinking of winning. And, as any football fan could have told him, what makes sense in the pursuit of victory makes little sense in pursuit of a draw.

This fundamental, and unspoken, difference of views created problems enough. O.K.H., attempting to disguise impotence as deep consideration, and Kleist, unwilling to surrender his armoured élite to Manstein, further delayed the process. By

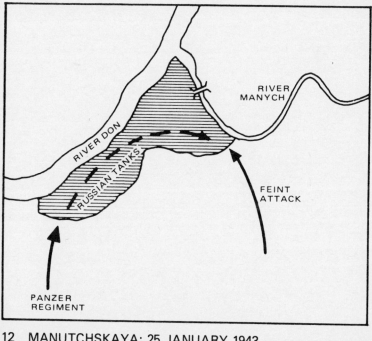

12   MANUTCHSKAYA: 25 JANUARY 1943

mid-January it had still not been decided whether Army Group A would retreat. In its rear, meanwhile, only a timely action by 16th Motorised, on the move at last, foiled a Soviet penetration across the Upper Manych.

The final act of the drama began with Soviet offensives 350 miles apart from each other. First the Hungarians, like the Italians before them, cracked on the Upper Don and more Soviet armour started to pour southwards into the virtually empty Don–Donetz corridor. Simultaneously in the south one Soviet force tied down Fourth Panzer Army as another slipped past, crossed the Manych where it joins the Don, and motored insolently west as far as Rostov airfield. These were concrete enough threats for anyone, and though the hastily summoned veterans of 11th Panzer quickly threw the Russians back into Manutchskaya, the latter managed to retain a bridgehead there for re-creation of the threat.

Hitler acted promptly, ordering the majority of First Panzer Army through Rostov. Five days later, on 27 January, he placed it under Manstein's command; the Field-Marshal could stop asking and start ordering the Army to get a move on. It says much for the Army's skill in logistics that not only was First Panzer Army brought safely through, but as many trains were kept flowing the other way to stock up Seventeenth Army in the Kuban bridgehead.

In the meantime the resourceful Balck was exercising his tactical expertise. Deciding to evict the Soviet force from Manutchskaya, and failing on 24 January with a frontal assault, he employed a faultless ruse on the following day. As the Soviet tanks were dug in around the south-western streets of the village Balck ordered heavy artillery fire on the north-eastern section, and followed it up with his armoured cars and half-tracks under a heavy smokescreen. The Soviets, imagining that the *tanks* were advancing into their rear, dug themselves up and turned to face the threat. Then the tanks, advancing unseen from the south-west, did hit them in the rear. Twenty Soviet tanks were knocked out, five or six hundred troops killed or wounded. The Germans lost one man. They even managed to take the Manych bridge intact.

V

As the tanks of First Panzer Army slowly rattled through Rostov on their flat-cars, bound for the deepening crisis on the Donetz, the army whose appalling ordeal had made their escape possible prepared to lay down its arms in the crumbling fortress of Stalingrad. If no one will ever know how many Germans were encircled by Zhukov's November attack – 220,000 is a relatively low estimate – the conditions they endured during the ten-week siege are common knowledge. In two stages, on 31 January and 2 February 1943, Sixth Army surrendered. Of those who formed the long columns trudging east through the snow towards Soviet imprisonment only six thousand would see Germany again.*

The effect of this disaster on the German war effort is hard to measure. The front, as we have seen, had been largely recreated in the time it took Sixth Army to die. The Soviets, as we shall soon see, had not felt the German Army's power for the last time. As Manstein wrote later: 'Stalingrad need not have meant that the war in the East – and *ipso facto* the war as a whole – was irretrievably lost. It would still have been possible to force a stalemate if Germany's policies and military leadership had been adapted to such a solution.' (18)

Stalingrad, like El Alamein and with more reason, has frequently been seen as the turning-point of the Second World War, the decisive defeat, from which the Wehrmacht could never recover. True, Stalingrad was dramatic, it came in the middle of the war, it marked the still-point between territorial ebb and flow. In the strictly military sense, however, Stalingrad was not an irredeemable disaster. An army had been lost; the Soviets had lost many armies. The strategic position of the German southern wing had been threatened, but it would recover. It did not deny the Germans victory; the Battles of Britain, Moscow, and the Atlantic had already achieved that much. Neither did it doom Germany to defeat. If any single battle could claim that distinction it would be Kursk, still six months and a number of German successes away.

Stalingrad was more of a signpost than a decision, evidence of the residual poison working in the veins of the German war machine, that would produce the convulsive spasm of *Zitadelle*. It had been the climax of Hitler's campaign, the fruit of *Bar-*

---

* It should be noted that throughout the war Soviet prisoners in German hands received no better, and frequently worse, treatment.

barossa's arrogant folly, of the greater arrogance and greater folly of *Blau*. The generals who had pledged themselves to Hitler had found few causes for doubt in the summer of 1940. The following year they had tried hard to convince themselves that his follies were the result of misinformation, Göring's ineptitude, Party influence, anything in fact but the Führer's own incapacities as a war leader. As 1942 turned to 1943 that faith had been destroyed; the pledge was now an empty, if still binding, totem. Guderian, drawn to Hitler by the latter's espousal of the panzer doctrines he had championed in vain against the Wehrmacht establishment through the thirties; Rommel, who had ridden to success in France and then found himself largely beyond interference in the far-off North African desert; Manstein, who had formed a high opinion of his Führer as the only man to understand the stunning grace of *Sichelschnitt* – all were now disillusioned. For the second winter in succession the pride of the Wehrmacht had been left scattered in the snow. They would all hold high positions in the last years; their professionalism and their mutually supportive love of country and fear of Bolshevism would see to that. But the tone of their obedience would be a different one. Each would work for Germany, either with or against its Führer as each saw fit. The identification of the two was gone, spread-eagled in death on the banks of the Volga, amidst the ruins of a city whose name would henceforward stand as a synonym for strategic incompetence, tactical ineptitude, blind inhuman pride and wasted heroism.

References (Chapter 4)

 1. Rudel, *Stuka Pilot*, 63–4
 2. Manstein, *Lost Victories*, 382–3
 3. Ibid, 303
 4. Mellenthin, *Panzer Battles*, 168
 5. quoted in Goerlitz, *Paulus*, 239
 6. Ibid, 233–4
 7. quoted in Carell, *Hitler's War on Russia*, 596
 8. Clark, *Barbarossa*, 227–8
 9. quoted in Mellenthin, *Panzer Battles*, 180
10. Ibid, 182

11. Ibid, 169
12. Manstein, *Lost Victories*, 559
13. quoted in Carell, *Hitler's War on Russia*, 610
14. Manstein, *Lost Victories*, 323
15. quoted in Manstein, *Lost Victories*, 340
16. quoted in Goerlitz, *Paulus*, 282
17. Manstein, *Lost Victories*, 386
18. Ibid, 290

Chapter 5

LAST DANCE OF THE MATADOR

For today the salvation of the Russian people and its revolutionary achievements is indispensable to the salvation of the world.

(Victor Serge, 1941)

At the beginning of February 1943 the Wehrmacht was stretched to the utmost, all its waning strength devoted to the freeing of its horns from those precarious positions to which Hitler had wilfully attached them. Army Detachment Hollidt was strung out along the Lower Donetz, forming a front of barely connected forces. First Panzer Army was deploying, at last, along the Middle Donetz. Fourth Panzer Army, facing enemy forces five times its strength, was still holding the door to the Caucasus at Rostov. These three armies, all grossly under-strength, exhausted and shaken by retreat, held an arc from the mouth of the Don, along the line of the Don–Donetz to the area of Lissichansk. Here the 'front' disappeared into a two-hundred-mile-wide chasm, to reappear with the also depleted Second Army around Kursk and Belgorod.

The 'proper' Soviet course, as Manstein might have said, was not hard to fathom. It was to drive, at speed and in strength, through that gap; to reach the Dnieper and cross it, and to wheel south against the Black Sea coast west of the isthmus leading to the Crimea. If such a move could be executed not only Manstein's forces, but also Kleist's in the Crimea and Kuban, would be cut off and deprived of supplies, subject to piecemeal destruction. And in that event Army Group Centre to the north would be left hanging in mid-air, and the whole German position in Russia would collapse like a line of dominoes.

The sheer apparent hopelessness of the situation would work in the Germans' favour, and in more ways than one. The spy network known as 'Lucy', which had forewarned Stavka of

Blau, became infected by the deep gloom prevailing at O.K.W. and O.K.H., and passed on information that tended to bolster already over-confident Soviet expectations. Of that more below. For now it is sufficient to note that Lucy's almost complete access to the Wehrmacht's higher commands availed it little in February 1943. For once these commands were not in control. Manstein was, and Lucy had no agents on his staff.

And the Field-Marshal was not feeling gloomy. Tense and nervous, perhaps. But this was no Stalingrad, with immovable pieces doomed to fight or fall where they stood. On the vast board he surveyed between Don and Dnieper the pieces were all moving. Skill was the primary factor here, not the mystique of the iron will. Movement implied the possibility of concentration against a dispersed enemy. It allowed for victory as well as defeat.

Just as Zhukov in the previous months had created a situation in which the Red Army's assets would prove decisive, so now Manstein was stacking the cards for the Wehrmacht. Defending fixed lines with such a numerical inferiority would be suicide; rather he would pit the initiative and resourcefulness of his panzer élite in a situation devoid of fixed lines, under the guiding hand of his own strategic grasp. For this brief period of weeks the Wehrmacht in the East would be guided by a professional strategist. Hitler was about to receive his final lesson in basic principles.

The strategic option which the Soviets were offering Manstein was clear enough. They would drive for the Dnieper bend; in doing so they would invite a counter-stroke against their flank. Manstein's first task was to assemble a force capable of launching such a thrust. Here lay the risk. In order to gather this force he would be obliged to denude the front of its armoured strength. In such an event minimum safety demanded that first the front be shortened. Army Detachment Hollidt would have to be withdrawn to the Mius and the eastern Don Basin abandoned to the enemy. Convincing Hitler of this would not be easy.

Manstein's chance to try came soon enough, for on 6 February Hitler's private plane arrived with a request for his presence at the Wolfsschanze. To the Field-Marshal's astonishment Hitler was sweet reason itself. Opening the conversation with an open-hearted admission of his own responsibility for Stalingrad, the Führer proceeded to argue fluently against the proposed withdrawal. The Don Basin was economically neces-

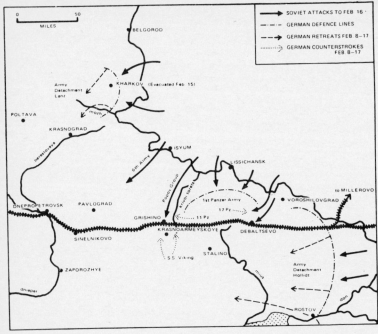

13   DONETZ 1

sary; it was politically inadvisable to give up territory. The Soviets could only be stopped by a bitter and resolute defence. The thaw was coming. The S.S. Panzer Corps was assembling in the Kharkov area and would restore the cohesion of the front.

Manstein, despite airing a rather deflationary opinion of the S.S. Panzer Corps's capacity for winning the war single-handedly, answered Hitler not with dire threats of what might happen if the withdrawal was delayed, but with the glittering promise of his proposed counter-stroke. This was a strategic withdrawal, he argued, voluntarily undertaken as a means to destroy Soviet armies, not a tactical withdrawal promising no more than less frontage to defend.

Hitler listened, and perhaps still depressingly aware of what strategic inflexibility had cost Sixth Army, agreed. Manstein, somewhat pressing his luck, then brought up the question of appointing a new supreme commander for the Eastern Theatre. Even this failed to arouse the Führer, who merely asked, rather irrelevantly, if Manstein thought Göring would fit the bill, since no one else could be appointed over his chosen successor.

Doubtless armed with the consolation that things could thus be worse Manstein dropped the subject and, armed with the requisite sanction, hurried back east to set in motion Army Detachment Hollidt's retreat to the Mius.

II

The rare moderation of Manstein's talk with Hitler was not being mirrored in Moscow. There the mood was one of unrestrained optimism. Reason was being carelessly thrown out of the Kremlin windows as exaggerated reports of the German difficulties came humming in on the telephone wires.

The basic reason for the Soviets' lack of justification in celebration was the inexperience of their commanders in planning and conducting armoured offensives. The Soviets still had not grasped, and ultimately never needed to grasp, the essence of the 'panzer idea': assemble a force strong enough to overcome any obstacle in its path, aim it decisively at a given point, and push it as fast and far as its infantry and supply support would allow. In February 1943 the Soviets assembled no such force for the simple reason that they recognised no decisive point of aim. Instead they created a number of forces, none of them strong enough to stand up on their own to a concentrated German response, aimed them at diverging objectives, and neglected to provide either air or infantry support on the scale required.

In the film *Northwest Passage* Spencer Tracy and his troop have to ford a swift-flowing river. The only way they can achieve this is by sending across a human chain, struggling all the way against the current, until the leading man is firmly anchored to the far shore. Then the rest of the troop can pass over this 'bridge', protected from the power of the current by the wall of men. In France the Wehrmacht pushed its chain to the Channel and anchored it fast. In Russia in 1941 space defeated such a grand objective, and the panzer groups had to restrict themselves to local Cannaes, concentric pincer attacks. In February 1943 the Soviets had such anchors at hand – the Dnieper, the Black Sea, the Sea of Azov – and a resolute lunge for any *one* of them could have proved decisive. But they aimed for all of them. As a result the chains were never strong or long enough to anchor themselves. And even worse, each chain, running out of men in midstream, was pushed forward until neither bank provided an anchor. The Soviet forces, like flotsam struggling up a beach against an ever-increasing undertow, would find themselves grounded and left by the tide, easy prey for the mobile groups concentrated against them.

In the first two weeks of February, as their forces pushed through the spaces gaping in the German front, this mistake was not apparent to the dreaming Stavka. On the contrary they believed a super-Stalingrad was at hand. The Germans were in full retreat, streaming for the shelter of the Dnieper. They would be cut off, destroyed, and the war won. As the Wehrmacht had dreamed of finishing the Red Army west of the Dnieper in 1941, so now the Russians dreamed of destroying the Wehrmacht east of that river.

By 10 February such a prize seemed within their grasp. A mechanised corps had broken through the newly-created Mius front in the east. A large force of cavalry, supported by armour, had broken through on the Middle Donetz east of Voroshilovgrad, and advanced forty miles to cut Army Detachment Hollidt's main rail supply link at Debaltsevo. This cavalry force intercepted two trains of reinforcements and dispatched them with their sabres. Fifty miles further west a large armoured group under Lieutenant-General Popov had pushed in First Panzer Army's left flank and motored up the frozen Krivoi Torets valley to bring the same railway into tank gun range at Grishino. Popov had upward of two hundred tanks in his command; his orders were to march on Mariupol on the Sea of Azov coastline. Further west still another large force from the Soviet Sixth Army, comprising two rifle corps, two tank corps and one cavalry corps, had crossed the Donetz near Isyum and was advancing steadily south-westwards towards the Dnieper bend. In the north Sixty-ninth Army and Third Tank Army were slowly squeezing the Germans out of Kharkov, fourth city of the Soviet Union. For the moment it was success all along the line. On 11 February South-Western Front received the ultimate green light: 'You are to prevent the enemy's withdrawal to Dnepropetrovsk and Zaporozhye, to throw back the enemy forces into the Crimea, block the approaches to the Crimea, and thus cut off the German Southern Group.' (1)

III

The forces Manstein needed to turn Stavka's celebrations into a wake were steadily becoming available. Fourth Panzer Army, unbeknown to the Soviets, had for a week been moving west through the slush and the snow, to an assembly area midway between Stalino and Zaporozhye, to the north the S.S. Panzer Corps, which formed the striking power of Army Detachment Lanz holding the Kharkov area, would soon be freed from defensive duties by the German abandonment of the city.

This last event was a piece of supreme good fortune for Manstein. It represented Hitler's one attempt to impose himself on the overall situation, which, if successful, might have wrecked the entire plan. But luckily for Manstein the commander of the S.S. Panzer Corps, Paul Hausser, was of stronger stuff than Paulus. Despite a direct and twice-given order to hold Kharkov to the last man – an order reinforced by his immediate superior Lanz – Hausser reacted to the quasi-encirclement of his forces in Kharkov with an order for immediate break-out by the one remaining exit.* On 15 February two of the Reich's finest divisions, *Das Reich* and *Grossdeutschland*, fought their way clear of the burning city, and were thus available to Manstein in the days to come.

This was not the only fruit of Hausser's insubordination. The Soviets, mindful of Hitler's views on withdrawal, could only assume that the abandonment of Kharkov formed part of that general retreat to the Dnieper they believed to be taking place. Such confirmation served to stifle doubts raised in the ensuing days by those on the spot.

The immediate effect of Kharkov's fall was less to Manstein's liking – a rapid descent on his Zaporozhye H.Q. by Hitler and his O.K.W. entourage. They arrived on the 17th and stayed for two days, during which time Manstein had to expend all his energy in fighting off an attempted subversion of his grand scheme. Hitler, though still mindful of the deficiencies Stalingrad had exposed in his insistence on rigid defence, was no longer so timid in questioning the efficiency of the elastic variety. 'Operations to my generals seem to imply only retreat,'

---

* Hitler's fury at this disobedience of the supposedly ultra-loyal SS was partly mollified by the obvious strategic advantages which accrued from it and which became almost immediately apparent. Nevertheless a head had to roll. It was Lanz's.

he repeated in a number of guises. He had given Manstein ground to trade, and what had happened? It had been given away. The eastern Don Basin, and now Kharkov. And for what return? Of course the Army was under strain at the decisive points, since he, Manstein, had only a third of his forces committed. What were the others doing? They must recapture Kharkov at once. The generals were always overestimating the enemy. Why, even at this moment Rommel was driving the Americans back into Algeria.* A similar note of emergency was needed in Russia, a similar resolution.

Manstein, with the highly-charged restraint of one who sees a careful plan threatened by last minute impetuosity, explained to his Führer and the wooden figures of Keitel and Jodl what was really happening. The Soviet forces were over-extending themselves, losing their momentum. A few days more and they would be ripe for dismemberment. Then, and only then, when the gap in the German front had become a gap in the Soviet front, would the panzers head north and retake Kharkov. It was a matter of timing, of patience and nerve. The matador must hold the cloak long enough for the bull's curiosity and ambition. After that the dance could begin.

Hitler was not impressed. Not until the next day could he be brought to believe in the Soviet forces trundling past Manstein's cape. Then, with their capture of Pavlograd, he reluctantly agreed to postpone Kharkov's recapture, especially since *Totenkopf*, the last third of his beloved S.S. Panzer Corps, was reported axle-deep in mud outside Poltava. On the 19th the Soviets were reported at Sinelnikovo, only twenty miles from the Dnieper, and only forty from Zaporozhye. As Hitler's plane disappeared into the western sky, flanked by its Messerschmitt escort, Manstein breathed a deep sigh of relief and hurried back to the operations room. 'What can we use against the force at Sinelnikovo?' he asked his Chief of Operations, General Busse. With the air of a successful conjuror Busse reported that the excellent 15th Division was in the process of arriving from France at Dnepropetrovsk. Hastily summoning the acting commander, Manstein and Busse ordered the train to continue on through to Sinelnikovo. In the early morning of 20 February, ten days after leaving the Atlantic coast, the troops of 15th

* The major German counter-offensive conducted in Tunisia began on 14 February, tore apart the US 1st Armoured Division on the 17th, and seemed on the brink of further successes as Manstein was talking to Hitler at Zaporozhye.

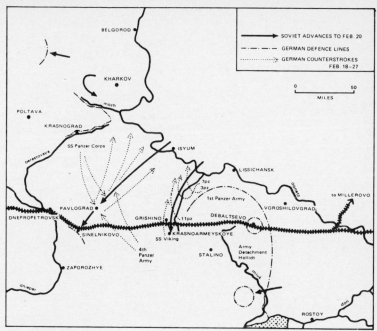

14   DONETZ 2

Division erupted from their wagons into the midst of the
startled Soviets.

Meanwhile the two pincers for the main operation were
assembling, the S.S. Panzer Corps around Krasnograd, the
Fourth Panzer Army south-east of Pavlograd. Once again the
panzer engines burst into life, and the two tank forces moved
across the snow-covered steppe for a rendezvous at Pavlograd.
By 23 February it was theirs, and the advance guard of Soviet
Sixth Army was helpless in their rear. Further north the Popov
group was faring no better. Halted by the S.S. 'Viking' Division
north of Krasnoarmeyskoye, it also had to contend with the
raiding activities of 7th and 11th Panzer in its rear. Already the
lack of experience in long advances and the consequent supply
turmoil had taken their toll of Popov's force. Now with the
enemy all around him Popov begged permission to retreat. All
he received from above was a bland assurance that the Germans
were in retreat themselves, and that he should continue his
march south with the utmost vigour.

In any case it was too late. The panzer divisions now had the
bit firmly between their teeth. Wheeling north in a concerted

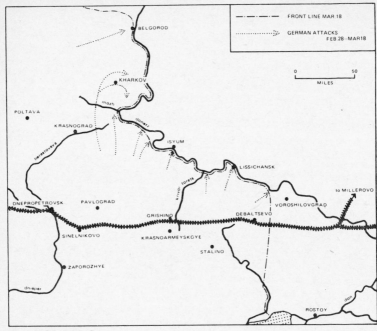

15   DONETZ 3

motion the S.S. and 48th Panzer Corps proceeded to slice the long
tail of Sixth Army into shreds, while 40th Panzer Corps performed a similar dissection on Popov. Around Debaltsevo the
cavalry penetration had been surrounded, worn down, forced
to surrender. By 27 February the Germans were everywhere
approaching the Donetz in strength, the Soviets falling back
over the melting river in disorder. Behind them they left 23,000
dead and 615 tanks.

All eyes were now on Kharkov, in which the red flag had
been hanging for only three weeks. The Soviet Sixty-ninth and
Third Tank Armies, which had been pushing west towards
Poltava, were precipitously drawn back, and large elements of
the latter were dispatched south into the space where Sixth
Army had been. The Soviet Command, who only a week before
had been praying for a late spring thaw, now implored Mother
Nature for an early one. Manstein, considering the question of
Kharkov, decided not to risk moving his force east of the
Donetz lest they be caught by such an eventuality. Instead he
sent the S.S. Panzer Corps in an arc to the west of the city,
Fourth Panzer Army in a flatter arc to the east between city

and river. The former enjoyed success while the latter met stiff Soviet resistance; this folded as the S.S. wheeled through the city and back southward into the Soviet rear. The swastika hung once more in Kharkov's Red Square, Hausser had atoned for his disobedience, Manstein was completely vindicated. On 18 March Belgorod fell to *Grossdeutschland* panzergrenadiers before the thaw wrote finis to the campaign. Only a large salient around Kursk remained to the Soviets as compensation for their shattered hopes. The Germans were back on the melted Donetz, back where they had been the previous spring. For them the tide seemed to have turned anew. Not towards victory, a best forgotten dream, but towards a possible stalemate, an end of the war with honour and without retribution. Manstein thought it possible.

By the end of the winter campaign the initiative was back in German hands, and the Russians had suffered two defeats. Though not decisive in character, these did lead to a stabilisation of the front and offer the German Command a prospect of fighting the war in the east to a draw. Nevertheless, we could clearly bury any hope of changing the course of the war by an offensive in the summer of 1943. Our loss of fighting power had already been too great for anything of that order.

The obvious inference for the Supreme Command to draw was that it must strive with every means at its disposal to come to terms with at least one of Germany's opponents. (2)

Manstein did not know his Supreme Command. Less than a month before the recapture of Kharkov, Goebbels spoke with the Führer's voice to the packed Sportpalast in Berlin. Stalingrad, he said, had 'purified' the German people to 'the depths of their being'. Total war was proclaimed amidst a frenzy of dedication to the 'hard and pitiless' struggle to come. Bourgeois scruples were to be thrown to the four winds. 'Now folk rise up,' he concluded in a paroxysm of emotion, 'and storm break loose.' (3)

Between the professional strategists and this Nazi hunger for extremes there seemed no meeting ground. So thought the generals, and they were wrong. The war was their meeting ground; it was no longer possible to pass by on the other side of the road. In total war all levels merge, and military skill is based upon political understanding. As this war totalised, the German generals' lack of understanding began to prejudice the application of their skills.

IV

Manstein's success was, in its way, almost as fatal to German war hopes as the triumph of 1940. These two campaigns were run almost exclusively by the military, the first because Hitler was still feeling his way, the second because he was suffering from a hangover after Stalingrad. In both cases the division between political and military authority – each to his own – which the German generals sought and recognised, was reasonably clear-cut. They thought this normal. This had happened for two hundred years. Hitler's interference was abnormal, not the way things should be.

In Nazi Germany the normal was abnormal and vice versa. This the German generals would not face. Hitler was vulgar, inept, hysterical . . . but they could not bring themselves to believe that he was mad, that they had been waging war for four years to the tune of a diseased brain. They preferred to see him as incompetent, his mistakes as aberrations. The failure of the armaments industry, the failure of Grand Strategy to avert a two-front war, the chaos of the command structure, the dubious treatment of prisoners and civilians, the general degeneracy of the regime – all aberrations, all deviations from the God-given norm learnt in the War Academies. If the generals could only be left alone to conduct *their* war, the war of lines and numbers and graceful coups. All the politicians had to do was to supply them with the troops, the materials, the national targets. Afterwards the politicians could make the peace, could make the most of victory, alleviate defeat. But the war was the generals', was the meaning of their lives, their skill, their art. Surely that was obvious. Surely the success of Manstein would make the Führer see sense.

But the war was not theirs, it was Hitler's. And as Hitler had spread his ideology across peacetime Germany so he spread it through the sinews of the nation at war. The roots of that ideology do not concern us here. It is enough to say that the tree of German romanticism found evil root in the soil of capitalism's deepest crisis. And as the branches of the state became the branches of the tree so all were infected without exception.

Armament production was a classic example. We have seen how unprepared German industry was to conduct a sea–air war against Great Britain. It was equally ill-prepared to face a long war of any sort. Fuel was a constant cause for concern throughout; its shortage a primary reason for the strategic errors of summer 1942. Germany was the last of the major warring states to be put on a full war footing, to employ women in industrial work, to gear the motor industry purely to vehicles usable in war. The solutions taken, when at last they became inevitable, were pure romanticism. Individuals were chosen to solve social problems. Directly responsible only to the Führer they possessed power limited only by the ambition of their fellow barons. With armament production Hitler was fortunate. He found Speer, the one man among the barons who could achieve the miracles for which Nazi inefficiency had created the need.

With armament design he was less fortunate. Here Hitler inherited the genius of Ferdinand Porsche: erratic, egotistical, intuitive. In short, Hitler himself dressed up as a mechanic. It was thought that the blessings of his genius more than made up for his lack of urgency. Quality would triumph over quantity in the end, particularly in view of the thousand-year timespan granted the Reich by destiny. So Porsche doodled on, devising giant tanks and miniature tanks, while the Soviet production figures soared above the German, and the troops at the front cried out for quantity as well as quality.

The divide-to-rule principle proved as disastrous for the Armed Forces as it did for armament production before Speer. Hitler had insisted upon creating a command structure within which only he would have access to the whole picture. The old Army Command (O.K.H.) were given Russia as their preserve, the O.K.W. all other theatres. Each could be fobbed off by Hitler with reasoned explanations of the other's predicament which they had no way of checking. Even inside their own theatres these organisations were subject to semi-constant direction from above, and to undercutting of their authority by Hitler's direct communication with their subordinate formations. As if this was not enough each was staffed by men who lacked the character to oppose Hitler, whose one qualification for their exalted offices was an ability to say yes to anything from strategic suicide to mass murder.

This was Hitler's leadership principle, the *Führerprinzip*, a medieval command archetype that was totally at variance with the complexity of the war it sought to direct. For such a war the German Army had been prepared as no other army in Europe. Initiative and discipline ran from top to bottom of the command structure; theory and practice were intimately linked. Democratic, flexible, ideally-equipped militarily to fight a war of such scope and complexity. And it was all thrown away, had to be thrown away, for political reasons. It was submerged beneath the Nazi *Führerprinzip*. A medieval mind directed a mechanical army. Like a peasant driving a particularly fine motor car, Hitler exhilarated himself with the speed attained and the distance covered. When the car broke down he kicked it. The car did not understand this treatment. It had been driven too fast and too far, along too many bad roads. Of course it would break down; didn't the driver realise this? He did not. The peasant was not interested in what made the car go, only in the fact that it did. This worked well while the car was going, and it was in fact the peasant's boldness as a driver that had so confounded those who found themselves in his line of travel. But once the car started to go wrong the relationship between it and the driver became problematic. Hitler was not a mechanic. He put in new carburettors, new sparking plugs, new everything. But no one dared to tell him that it was the big end that had gone. Because he was a very powerful peasant, he had a personal praetorian guard and, anyway, there had only ever been one big end to use.

National Socialism's peasant-like reaction to technology was well-matched by its attempt to create pseudo-scientific theories of racial hierarchies. These too cast a blight on the Wehrmacht's attempt to subdue the world, not so much in terms of their application *vis-à-vis* the 'final solution to the Jewish question' – that crime with few parallels had little effect on the conduct of the war in its crucial years – as in the tendency these theories created to underestimate an enemy whom they were simultaneously provoking to a greater effort.

This was particularly true of the war in the East. Fuller found it astonishing that Hitler, 'a man of exceptional political perspicacity . . . made no efforts to win over the subjugated peoples of Western Russia, but deliberately set out to antagonise them'. (4) Whether or not Hitler's ultimate aims in Russia prohibited him from utilising such political potential it is quite clear that he felt no need of doing so. No *Untermensch* army was going to stop the Wehrmacht, bearers of the Aryan destiny in the East.

The war in Russia in this respect brings to mind the only two defeats ever suffered by the United States Army, inflicted by the Sioux in 1867-8 and the Vietnamese in 1965-75. In all three cases the fatal underestimation of the enemy was grounded in racism. *Untermensch*, savages, gooks. Each war further-more was fought on the soil of these inferior beings, on the beloved plains of the Indian, in the jungle of the Vietnamese, on the endless steppe of the Russians with its climatic extremes. Each enemy was familiar with the environment, an advantage which tended to cancel out the invader's superior technology. Listening to the German commanders, and particularly to Hitler, one is reminded of Lieutenant Fetterman's boast that with eighty men he could ride through the whole Sioux nation. He had his chance; like many Germans he did not return.

Also in each war the overwhelming sense of superiority disdained any real psychological or political approach until it was too late. Such advantages as there were in this respect were wilfully spurned. The only good Indian is a dead Indian. The Germans and Americans had the same problem distinguishing communists from the rest; both decided to err on the side of butchery. Hitler would have appreciated the educated hypocrisy of a General Westmoreland: 'The Oriental doesn't put the same high price on life as does a westerner. Life is plentiful, life is cheap in the Orient. And as the philosophy of life expresses it, life is not important.' (5) Not that the Nazis ever subscribed the Russians with a philosophy. In moments of good cheer they saw them as helpless children; the German role would thus be 'analogous to that of England in India'. (6) In moments of adversity the Russian was merely an animal, with consequent strength and cunning, but apt to panic and completely without culture. The Russian was brave because he was stupid; the German because he was racially superior. This was after the first setbacks. When *Barbarossa* began there was no need to make such dubious distinctions. The Soviet Union was ripe for dissolution. Slav meant slave. So confident was Hitler of military victory that he tied his political hand behind his back. By the end of 1941, once it had become distressingly clear that *Barbarossa* was more than just a large-scale manoeuvre, that hand could no longer be untied. The Soviet Union was united as never before. The damage had been done.

One old Russian woman told a German soldier: 'I shall tell you a great truth; the Russian people will not be saved by the man with the bigger gun but by the man with the greater soul.' (7)

Old women should be listened to. Though both Hitler and
Stalin, their records suggest, had souls shrivelled below the
size normal for humans, Stalin had a revolution on his side,
one that had caused great miseries and hardship in the twenty
years of its youth, but that also had struck a new chord in the
history of the human species. The Russians were conscious of
this and Stalin, taking no chances, fused the revolutionary
destiny with eternal Mother Russia, thus creating a 'soul' of
inestimable power. Against it National Socialism offered nothing save empty and vicious tyranny. Victor Serge, exiled
Trotskyist, knew Russia. He saw clearer than German Intelligence the way things would go. He knew that the chaos of the
preceding years – the slaughter of the revolutionary generation
in Party and Army – would cost Russia dear. There would be a
'horribly successful advance'. But:

> Russia spells an end to the effortless victories, an end to the
> unchallenged butcheries like Rotterdam – the butchers are
> now being paid back in kind; an end to the conquests with
> immediate booty – real trouble is beginning; an end to the
> hope of peace in the near future, since nobody can really tell
> any longer when the fighting will end. There are so many
> factors tending to material and moral attrition . . . The Nazi
> Empire has been halted in its tracks. (8)

Serge wrote that in 1941; by 1943 it was incontrovertible truth.
The Nazi Empire had been halted, as much by its own inner
corruption as by the heroic resistance of the Red Army. The
German Army had been starved of equipment by the slave-
driven chaos of its armament production programme, mis-
directed by the ruthless incompetence of its Supreme Command, crippled by the petrification of its command structure,
blinded by racism to the reality of its enemy. Each stemmed
directly from the savage nonsense that was Nazi ideology; each
was militarily decisive.

Liddell Hart wrote that 'the German generals of this war
were the best-finished product of their profession – anywhere.
They could have been better if their outlook had been wider
and their understanding deeper. But if they had become philosophers they would have ceased to be soldiers.' (9) If, as seems
likely, the first two sentences are correct, then the third is
merely a truism. If the German generals had become a little
more philosophic they would have realised that wars are not

always won by military means alone, that military means in themselves exist at any time in relation to the society wielding them, and that German society in 1943 had already forfeited any chance of avoiding defeat.

But they were not philosophers. And they did not realise. As they travelled back and forth across the Empire they had won it seems unlikely that they looked down from their planes to see the smoke rising from the crematoria of occupied Europe. And if they did sometimes glimpse the wood around the trees, they still failed to bring the two together. Rather they indulged in a series of fantasies, whose realisation would gain them the war:

If German strategy could be committed to mobile defence . . .

If, as Guderian and Manstein urged, an operational brain could be appointed to head O.K.W., or at least an independent O.K.H. . . .

If that man had the strength of will to channel Hitler's whims into the sound strategy or the cul-de-sacs they might deserve . . .

If the clarification of German armaments production could take priority over the squabbling of the Reich barons . . .

If Göring could be retired . . .

If the generals themselves could maintain a modicum of mutual respect amidst their chronic personal differences . . .

If, if, if . . .

Then the winter of 1942-3 had demonstrated once more the individual resourcefulness of the German soldier, the initiative and discipline that characterised the Army from private to field-marshal, that together made the German Army a match even for the vast resource and numerical superiority of its opponents.

But none of these 'ifs' sustained. None could sustain. Both Rommel and Guderian, dreaming of peace in the West for a free hand in the East, were deluded in their appeals to rationality. That above all had no place in the cancerous state pulsing at the heart of Europe. The war, indeed, could not be won. For Hitler, the creator of extermination as a state policy, this could only mean that the war would be lost, with as romantically destructive a flourish as possible. For the Allies, too, there was no alternative. Those Germans who could not understand the bond between the Anglo-Americans and the Bolshevik hordes, only so failed because they saw not their own nation. Marxism was the last child of the European Enlightenment; Stalinism, no matter its bastard parentage, was the grandchild.

Reason, the European bond, held the Alliance together, as it would break it apart once the common foe – unreason – was swept into oblivion.

The generals did not see this. For them reason resounded only within the limits of their profession. Here they were masters, as the winter had proved. The dreaming went on through the spring of 1943. One last attempt to seize by purely military means what the other means would forever deny them.

If their awareness had been wider they would have known that purely military means were a thing of the past. Even in Clausewitz's time.

References (Chapter 5)

1. quoted in Carell, *Scorched Earth*, 178
2. Manstein, *Lost Victories*, 438
3. quoted in Heiber, H. *Goebbels* (Robert Hale, 1972), 289–90
4. Fuller, *Decisive Battles*, 473
5. quoted in *Radio Times*, 11.3.76
6. Hitler, *Table Talk*, 33
7. quoted in Fuller, *Decisive Battles*, 474
8. Serge, V. *Memoirs of a Revolutionary* (OUP, 1963), 368
9. quoted in Manstein, *Lost Victories*, 17

Chapter 6

PANZER HARI-KIRI

It seemed as if we were driving into a ring of flame.
(Tiger radio-operator on the first day of *Zitadelle*)

In the last two weeks of March the 1943 spring thaw spread northwards along the Eastern front. The Russian 'roads' disappeared. The two Supreme Commands, their armies immobilised for at least a month, had time to ponder in earnest the lessons of the winter and the coming summer campaign. Both had received some sharp shocks and disillusionments in the preceding months. The Wehrmacht had suffered as one of its best teeth – Sixth Army – had been wrenched slowly and painfully from its jaws; the Red Army, scenting victory beyond its wildest dreams, had discovered that those jaws contained not a few other cutting teeth. The air on the Eastern front was therefore one of cautious expectation. The Soviets believed that time was on their side, and that, provided they were careful, they would have a successful summer. The Germans were more divided. Hitler, never slow to find reasons for extreme optimism, began once more to dream of a decisive blow against the Red Army. Impressed by Manstein's success, and quickly forgetting the reasons for it; eager to pit his new tanks against the foe, and fearful of the political consequences likely to flow from a passive stance, he was ready to listen to ideas of how this hard-won initiative could be wielded in an offensive fashion.

His generals were less sure. Some, like the reinstated Guderian, would remain implacably opposed to further large-scale offensives in the East. They would rather the Russians bore the onus of attacking. Manstein was more ambivalent.

What did still seem possible – given proper leadership on the German side – was that the Soviet Union could be worn down to such an extent that it would tire of its already excessive sacrifice and be ready to accept a stalemate. At the time in question this was far from being wishful thinking. On the other hand, such an aim could not be realised by going over to purely defensive, static warfare. (1)

There were not enough divisions to man such a defence, not enough time before a second front was created in the West. Forcing a draw to the East was only possible if the Wehrmacht could succeed,

within the framework of a – now inevitable – *strategic defence*, in dealing the enemy powerful blows of a localised character, which would sap his strength to a decisive degree – first and foremost through losses in prisoners. This presupposed an operational elasticity on our part which would give maximum effect to the still-superior quality of the German command staff and fighting troops. (2)

Would the Soviet Government 'tire of its already excessive sacrifice' and settle for a compromise peace? This was strange reasoning from a rabid anti-communist like Manstein. He knew that Hitler cared not a jot for the already excessive sacrifice of the Wehrmacht; what led him to believe that Stalin would be any more concerned for the fate of his country? Nevertheless the reasoning seems to have been correct. Stalin, like the German generals, still believed that Hitler was amenable to compromise. And he was concerned. In June he dispatched Molotov to a meeting with Ribbentrop in occupied Russia, there to be disillusioned. His in-the-circumstances-generous offer of the pre-June 1941 frontiers was rejected out of hand. Hitler offered the Dnieper as their mutual border, nothing less. The issue was referred back to the field of battle.

What did Manstein's strategic recipe imply for the conduct of operations in the spring and summer of 1943? This was a question his training had fitted him to answer, and a plan had been forming in his mind prior even to the recapture of Kharkov. He first proposed it to Hitler on 10 March, and thereafter with diminishing faith in its acceptance until O.K.H. definitively rejected it in early April. Since it offered a superior chance of success than the plan eventually adopted it deserves perusal.

In essence it envisaged a repeat performance of his recent triumph, a luring of the enemy into position for the flashing

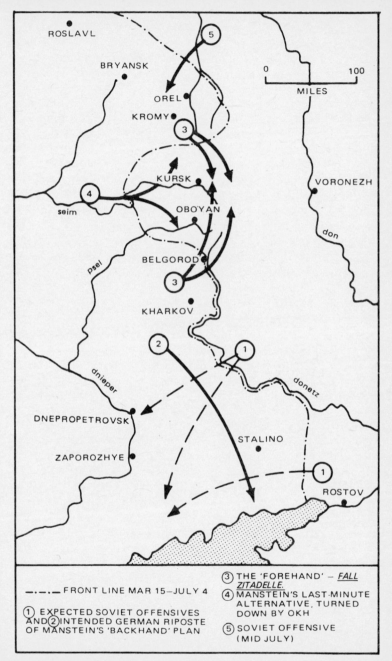

ROSLAVL

BRYANSK

⑤

0   100

MILES

OREL

KROMY

③

KURSK

VORONEZH

④

seim

OBOYAN

don

psel

BELGOROD

③

KHARKOV

②

①

dnieper

donetz

DNEPROPETROVSK

STALINO

ZAPOROZHYE

①

ROSTOV

—·—·— FRONT LINE MAR 15–JULY 4

① EXPECTED SOVIET OFFENSIVES
AND② INTENDED GERMAN RIPOSTE
OF MANSTEIN'S 'BACKHAND' PLAN

③ THE 'FOREHAND' – _FALL
ZITADELLE._
④ MANSTEIN'S LAST-MINUTE
ALTERNATIVE, TURNED
DOWN BY OKH

⑤ SOVIET OFFENSIVE
(MID JULY)

16 SPRING/SUMMER 1943

counter-stroke, a blow on the 'backhand'. In this case he intended to pull the German southern wing all the way back to the Dnieper bend, in the meantime assembling a strong armoured force south of Kharkov, at the shoulder of the presumed Soviet pursuit. Then at the right moment he would unleash this force southwards to the Sea of Azov coastline, thus cutting off the head of the Soviet penetration. Many prisoners would be taken, much equipment lost to the Red Army. Time would be gained, no territory surrendered in the long run. German expenditure in men and equipment would be minimal.

The flaw in the plan, as in its predecessor, was the initial withdrawal involved. In February Hitler, in view of the despairing condition of the German front, had authorised the sacrifice of the eastern Don Basin. But with the ensuing victory behind him he was less receptive to plans for yet another withdrawal, this time all the way to the Dnieper.

Gradually realising that this plan would find no favour Manstein turned his attention, still within the overall notion of the strategic defensive, to the possibilities of a pre-emptive offensive, a stroke on the 'forehand'. The obvious target was the Kursk salient, a large bulge in the German line where Army Group South (as Army Groups B and Don were now grouped) joined hands with Army Group Centre. Concentric attacks against the narrow neck of the bulge might encircle large Soviet forces, impel their tired armour into battle before it had recovered from its winter mauling, and so disrupt any Soviet plans for an offensive of their own. The obviousness of the objective need not matter if the Germans attacked early enough, in mid- or late-April. Formulated in this way such an attack made strategic sense. Manstein cannot be held wholly responsible for what befell the plan in the months that followed.

There is a well-known children's game in which one child draws a head on a piece of paper, folds it over so that only the bottom of the neck is visible, and passes it on for someone to draw a body without knowledge of the head. And so on. The outcome is usually a bizarre and grotesque figure. So the plan for a concentric attack on the Kursk salient – *Zitadelle* (Citadel) – would develop. Manstein's plan, with the date specification and the strategic rationale hidden by the fold of time, passed up the chain of command towards its rendezvous with disfigurement.

II

The day after the Soviet appearance at Sinelnikovo had sent Hitler scurrying skyward and home to Vinnitsa, Guderian had been ushered into his presence, and given the post of Inspector-General of the German Armoured Forces. Fourteen months had passed since his dismissal amidst the mutual recriminations of the disaster before Moscow. If in those months the Wehrmacht had seen little success – only the dramatic but hollow surges forward by Rommel in the desert and the Southern Army Group in Russia, and more recently Manstein's miraculous recovery on the Donetz – still on the newspaper maps little seemed to have changed. Europe was still all one colour, the fronts still far distant from the borders of the Fatherland.

This might have fooled the German people, and even their Führer, but someone of Guderian's military expertise would not be misled by maps in newspapers. Some information would be unavailable to him; he would not know that the Battle of the Atlantic was reaching its unsatisfactory climax or that the Luftwaffe was close to passing the point of no return. But he would know what a price the Army must have been paying in Russia, what the coming débâcle in Tunisia implied for *Festung Europa*, and that Anglo-American resources would eventually realise themselves in a Channel crossing and the dreaded two-front land war. In short, whatever the newspaper maps might say, Guderian knew that Germany was on the ropes. Whether Hitler telling him, simply, 'I need you', touched his heart is open to doubt. That he felt Germany's need for his services is rather more certain.

Germany's need moreover was for his untrammelled talents, not for one more administrator who would spend so much time safeguarding his authority that there would be none left for using it. Before he accepted Hitler's offer he laid down stringent conditions. He would be responsible for all armoured troops, all vehicles (including self-propelled guns), and be answerable only to the Führer himself. Hitler accepted all this, but all the same some malicious spirit shifted the wording of the agreement so as to deprive Guderian of authority over half the mobile artillery. That of course surprised no one. Nor was it reversed.

Guderian's primary brief was to revitalise the panzer force. This implied reorganisation, production of new machines and, to his opponents' dismay, some outspoken notions as to how the force should be used. Or, as in the case of *Zitadelle*, how it should not be used. In February such operational disputes were not yet at the head of Guderian's list of priorities. Before Germany's armoured force could be thrown away it had to be recreated.

All was not well with the knife of the German Army, that had cut its swathes across Europe and Africa. The armoured forces of its enemies had been greatly expanded in the preceding two years; the panzer force, though containing twice as many divisions as in 1941, was in fact little stronger. The divisions had been diluted, their balance altered. The tanks were to the panzer divisions as the panzer divisions were to the Army – the knives. Both were in a minority. The remaining majorities, in both panzer divisions and the Army as a whole, performed the same function – they were the forks and spoons for their respective knives. In France in 1940 most of the panzer divisions had contained two panzer regiments, each in turn comprising two battalions of eighty tanks each. In 1941 one regiment from each division had been made the core of a new division, thereby halving divisional tank strength. The effectiveness of this change was disputed. Some claimed that the weakening of the knife relative to the forks and spoons badly unbalanced the eating process; others counter-claimed that, taken together with the better tanks available, the spreading of experience more than made up for the unbalancing. Nearly everyone agreed that the dilution should go no further.

If the dilution itself was not a crippling problem, the reasons for it were. Germany was not producing enough tanks. The appearance of the Soviet T-34 added the question of quality to that quantity. The Soviet production of between six- and eight-hundred tanks a month in their trans-Ural factories contrasted so strongly with the German figures that Hitler predictably would not believe it. Nevertheless the priorities were clear; an urgent increase in the production of existing models and swift development of new and better models. This, it could be assumed, must have been obvious to everyone concerned.

Here again we enter the strange world of the German war effort; its faithful recreation at the industrial level of those Nazi leitmotifs that appear at all levels of the war's expression, from Auschwitz to Krupps to Stalingrad. The Nazi sense of superiority, sanctioned by racism, rooted in a purely personal arrogance, could not admit to *urgency*. Porsche could have all the time he needed for scribbling on his drawing-board.

Rommel (left) and Bayerlein in the desert.

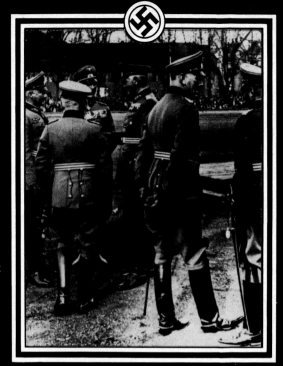

Right: Pre-war full regalia at Potsdam, left to right: Kluge, Bock, Blomberg and Brauchitsch.
Below: At the Wolfs-schanze, left to right: Bormann, Hitler, Mussolini and Keitel.

Genius needed no more than destiny for fulfilment. It *could* not be hurried, it *need* not be hurried. And along with this sense of superiority, somewhat paradoxically, went a profound belief in the baser emotions as the springs of human endeavour. Thus the overlapping baronies of the Nazi hierarchy, each baron struggling to produce the pieces for the jigsaw Hitler was completing on his world-historical board. Competition would bring out the best in them all, so the theory ran. The economists had already discovered the opposite in the Great Depression, and so would Hitler if he had dared to look. This competition bred chaos and inefficiency, and the German Army in the field was paying the price.

Guderian, as the newest baron, was far from immune and, as his conditions for accepting the post demonstrated, determined to win the game rather than refuse to play. What separated him and Speer from the other barons were clarity of thought and actual qualifications for the jobs in hand. These attributes Guderian soon found were as much of a hindrance as a help.

At the time of his appointment it was being proposed by O.K.H. that tank production should, for the time being, be virtually non-existent. The Panzer III, largely useless on the Eastern front, was scheduled for discontinuation; the same fate was being suggested for the Panzer IV. Only Panthers and Tigers would be produced in the immediate future. Unfortunately the Panther was still at the prototype stage and Tiger production was running at about twenty-five a month. In view of the already-noted Soviet figures this was completely ludicrous.

So much for production. The designing of the new tanks had also taken far too long. Two prototype Tigers had been produced, one by Henschel and one by Krupp, and would prove respectively the best and worst tanks of the war. The Krupp version, designed by Porsche and rejected only to re-emerge as the Ferdinand, would perform execrably in *Zitadelle*. Its design, comprising heavy armouring, heavy gun, and inadequate secondary armament, made it virtually impregnable to enemy tank or anti-tank fire, but, once stripped of the covering support of those not so impregnable, it became easy game for any Soviet soldier with the nerve to jump on its back. The Panther, like the Henschel Tiger, would eventually prove a fine tank. But in the spring of 1943 it was far from ready for a baptism in combat.

Given the time required to realise these designs in an overall rise in production, it was important not to weaken further the existing divisions. They had to be kept as far as possible up to strength, their already diluted paper-strength of 160 tanks, not their actual strength of between twenty and sixty. No new formations must be raised. And, given the urgency of raising tank production, the increasing emphasis on producing self-propelled guns – artillery on tank chassis – must be reversed.

Guderian emphasised both these points in reporting to Hitler at Vinnitsa on 9 March. Here he ran headlong into the military baronies. Since the Nazi war machine had been, up to 1942, so palpably inefficient, there was not enough hardware to go around. The artillery, whose horse-drawn guns had been rendered obsolete in Russia, controlled the self-propelled guns despite the overlap with the panzer force as regards chassis production. Fearful of losing ground in the game, they contrived to block Guderian's authority over these guns, thus condemning him to an endless struggle for priority. The S.S. and Luftwaffe, both of whom now had armoured divisions in the field, and were eager to have more, did come under Guderian's authority on paper. But only on paper. Despite the agreement to raise no new divisions whilst the already-existing ones were understrength, Himmler blithely went ahead expanding the S.S. panzer arm. When Guderian objected to Hitler he received no more than a Führer's shrug.

These were not the only channels in which the Inspector-Generals met with obstructions. Attempts to establish a working relationship with Jeschonnek – the Army's greatest successes had, after all, been made possible by close collaboration with the air arm – proved fruitless. He found Jeschonnek in a mood of 'outspoken discouragement', unamenable to 'any human contact'. (3) Attempting to persuade Hitler that Keitel should be ousted in favour of Manstein proved a waste of energy as were Guderian's pleas that the priceless collection of experienced tank crews about to be captured in the fall of Tunis should be evacuated by air. Only the working relationship with Speer prospered, as between them they built up the tank force that *Zitadelle* would squander with such reckless abandon.

III

Guderian's report to Hitler at Vinnitsa had opened with the sentence: 'The task for 1943 is to provide a certain number of panzer divisions with complete combat efficiency capable of making limited objective attacks.' The following year, perhaps, the German Army could launch 'large-scale attacks'. (4)

The distinction, however, was already beginning to evaporate. Zeitzler, ready to reassert O.K.H.'s prerogatives after its winter eclipse, had, with or without Manstein's inspiration, produced a plan for pinching off the Kursk salient through concentric attacks by two panzer armies. This plan had been submitted to Hitler on 11 April, and turned into an operation order by the latter on 15 April. There was no date assigned to the operation, merely a vague stipulation that it would commence as soon as the weather allowed. And this itself was compromised by Hitler's growing doubts as to whether Zeitzler's ten to twelve panzer divisions would suffice for the task. He wanted to use the new tanks, and these, in April, were still trickling off the production line.

Zitadelle's need of them was emphasised by the operation order's blatant lack of inspiration. It was the old recipe yet again. In three years revolutionary phrases had become clichés. Surprise was *essential*, attack on a *narrow* frontage, maximum speed in attack, reduction of the cauldron, deception measures to be taken, etc., etc. The only sign that three years had passed since Poland suffered the novelty of *Blitzkrieg* was in the barely-concealed desperation of Hitler's preamble. 'It must be carried out quickly and shatteringly. It *must* give us the initiative for the spring and summer of this year . . . the victory of Kursk must be a signal to the world.' (5) Must, must, must. The 'limited objective attack' was beginning to sound like a do-or-die throw of the dice. And so it would prove.

On 29 April, as if suddenly aware of a need for haste, Hitler decided on 3 May as a possible starting-date. Almost as quickly he changed his mind. Disturbing intelligence of Soviet preparations for defence of the salient was filtering through. A conference was called in Munich to discuss the implications; a last chance for the doubters, and common sense, to prevail. It opened on the morning of 3 May. Hitler, opening the proceedings, had an impressive audience as he outlined Zeitzler's plan and the Soviet counter-preparations. O.K.W. and O.K.H. were both present in strength, Guderian for the Inspectorate, Speer for the Armaments Ministry, and the future executants of the plan: Kluge who commanded Army Group Centre, Model, his subordinate, who commanded Ninth Army – the northern pincer – and Manstein, who would have overall command of the southern pincer armies. Most of the Wehrmacht's élite was gathered to juggle with its destiny.

Zeitzler's plan, Hitler stated, if successful would destroy large numbers of Soviet divisions, straighten and shorten the German front, and create a breathing space in the Eastern war. The evidence of Soviet activity, mostly produced by Model from intensive air reconnaissance, raised a grave question-mark over the likelihood of success. The Soviets had withdrawn most of their armour from the salient, and had strengthened the axes of probable German advances with powerful anti-tank and artillery forces. Model had concluded from this that either the operation be abandoned or a new tactical approach devised. The last point, of course, left the door open for an orgy of self-delusion. Others were quick to point out that the new tanks provided such a new approach, although in point of fact they did nothing of the kind, merely increasing the potency of the old approach.

Manstein, asked for his opinion, proved unwilling to come out strongly against the offensive. Confining himself to the virtual irrelevance of stating his belief in the success of such an attack a month earlier, he now did no more than ask for two more infantry divisions. Hardly a new tactical approach. He was, Guderian wrote sympathetically, 'as often when face to face with Hitler, not at his best'. A rather strange comment from someone who had tried to get Manstein appointed to head O.K.W.

Manstein's ambivalence was not reciprocated by the usually gloomy Kluge who, as often when face to face with Hitler, radiated enthusiasm. Kluge himself may not have been drunk on the Nazi destiny and the successes of preceding years, but he knew Hitler liked Field-Marshals who were. And, in this case, enthusiasm did not seem too misplaced. The German panzer forces had never yet failed to break through any line of their choice, and this particular panzer force would be the strongest ever assembled. Seventeen panzer divisions! The failure had always come later, in the exploitation phase. The Kursk salient was only a hundred miles wide; each panzer force would only have to cover fifty miles. This operation was nearly all breakthrough. How could it fail?

Guderian, as often when face to face with Kluge, disagreed.

I declared that the attack was pointless; we had only just
completed the reorganisation and re-equipment of our
Eastern Front; if we attacked according to the plan of the
Chief of Staff we were certain to suffer heavy tank casualties,
which we would not be in a position to replace in 1943; on
the contrary, we ought to be devoting our new tank production to the Western Front so as to have mobile reserves
available for use against the Allied landings which could be
expected with certainty to take place in 1944. (6)

He also, with Speer's support, pointed out that the Panthers
were far from ready for such a crucial task.

Hitler, confronted with the disunity of his professional advisers, postponed the taking of any definite decision. As the
conference ended Kluge and Guderian's quarrel, smouldering
since 1941, burst into flames anew. A few days later Kluge
asked Hitler to act as his second in a duel with the Inspector-
General. Hitler declined the honour and forbade the duel. It
was an absurdly apt postscript to the Munich conference.

Guderian, despite the attentions of Kluge, had not given up.
On 10 May he saw Hitler to report on the Panther production
situation. This was satisfactory; the Kursk plan, he repeated,
less than satisfactory.

After the conference I seized Hitler's hand and asked if I
might be allowed to speak frankly to him. He said I might
and I urged him earnestly to give up the plan for an attack
on the Eastern Front; he could already see the difficulties
that confronted us; the great commitment would certainly
not bring equivalent gains; our defensive preparations in the
West were sure to suffer considerably. I ended with the
question: 'Why do you want to attack in the East at all this
year?' Here Keitel joined in, with the words: 'We must
attack in the East for political reasons.' I replied: 'How many
people do you think even know where Kursk is? It's a matter
of profound indifference to the world whether we hold Kursk
or not. I repeat my question: Why do we want to attack in
the East at all this year?' Hitler's reply was: 'You're quite
right. Whenever I think of this attack my stomach turns
over.' I answered: 'In that case your answer to the question
is the correct one. Leave it alone.' Hitler assured me that he

had as yet by no means committed himself and with that the conversation was over. (7)

But neither would he leave it alone, merely postpone it once more. The new date was 12 June, but the disaster in Africa caused a further postponement. Guderian, seeing Rommel in Munich that June, probably heard the latter's idea for continental defence based on strength in anti-tank weaponry and a prodigious sowing of minefields. The enemy armour, Rommel argued, would cut itself to pieces on such a defence if it were well organised in advance.

This theory was about to be tested, although contrary to Rommel's desires it would be the Germans who would provide the armour and the Russians the defence in depth. Unfortunately for the Wehrmacht the theory was a sound one.

IV

As the war in the East had developed the Germans had found that the inexhaustible mass of shiny new T-34s, which the Soviets threw at them with so little regard for caution, demanded a new defensive approach. Single anti-tank guns, or even single clusters, were inadequate for stemming mass attacks. So the *pakfront* system was devised. Mellenthin describes it –

Groups of guns up to a total of ten were put under the command of one man, who was responsible for concentrating their fire on a single target. Groups of anti-tank guns were thus welded into one unit: the groups were organised in depth and strewn all over the defended area. The idea was to draw the attacking armour into a web of enfilade fire. Fire discipline was of the first importance, and to open fire too early was the gravest mistake that could be made. (8)

Mellenthin added wryly that 'the Russians copied these tactics'. They did indeed, in the Kursk salient bringing them to an apotheosis in width, depth, density, and subtlety of camouflage.

The Soviets could afford to be so lavish in this particular sector because they already knew it to be the target of the German offensive. 'Lucy' was putting information on Stavka's desks as fast as Zeitzler put it on Hitler's. As early as the beginning of April 1943 Zhukov had a clear indication of the German intentions, and had received advisory reports from the two Fronts in question: Central and Voronezh. A concentric attack was expected, delivered by around 2500 tanks with the customary air support. Zhukov and his subordinates were in basic agreement as to their correct course of action. They would turn the Kursk salient into a giant trap, a killing ground for the panzer élite. This decision to fight a premeditated defensive battle was taken on 12 April, three days before Hitler signed the operation order for *Zitadelle*. Despite wavering by Stalin in mid-May – 'perhaps our forces will be unable to withstand the German blow' (9) – this decision stood. While the Germans waited for their new tanks the means of their destruction were being fed into the Kursk salient.

Opposite Model in the north Stavka had gathered five infantry armies and a tank army in the forward area; a cavalry corps, two tank corps and several tank destroyer units in immediate reserve behind them. In the south a similar force faced Manstein. Between them these Soviet forces had a better than two to one superiority in artillery and slightly better than parity in tanks. Behind these two lines, in the rear-centre of the salient, was the Steppe Front, as strong as either of the other two forces.

The artillery in particular had an awesome density. On the front of Thirteenth Army in the north, where the brunt of Model's attack would be borne, there was an average of 147 guns of 3-inch calibre and bigger per square mile. All in all the two Fronts could call on close to 20,000 guns and just under a thousand Katyusha multiple rocket launchers. The defences were laid out in such depth that a breakthrough in north or south would virtually prove a break-back into the defences on the other side. The Kursk salient was almost devoid of open space. Six belts of defences, each crammed with *pak-fronts* strewn among minefields, stretched back 110 miles, beyond the line the Germans would reach even should they bite off the entire salient. Mines were laid to a density of over 5000 per mile of front, a six-fold increase on the Stalingrad perimeter. In the months of waiting up to 300,000 civilians toiled to dig over 6000 miles of anti-tank ditches and trench systems. Even a new railway was built to facilitate preparations and the movement of reserves.

Stavka did not restrict itself to its own preparations; it did everything in its power to disrupt those of the enemy. Orders went out to the partisan detachments to cut railway lines whenever and wherever possible. The Red Air Force was sent to bomb the log-jams created by the dislocation of movement. The Germans were forced to undertake five major anti-partisan 'actions' in May and June, as the day of *Zitadelle*'s commencement approached.

That day continued to recede. Hitler, despite his plea of indecision to Guderian, had refixed the operation date for 12 June. But on 13 May the Axis forces laid down their arms in Tunis, and Italian loyalty to the New Europe seemed to be wavering in the southern wind. Hitler decided to send the S.S. Panzer Corps to stiffen resolve. O.K.H.'s plaintive reminder that this Corps was earmarked to lead the southern assault in *Zitadelle* created another period of indecisive wrangling between all those involved. 12 June passed with no new date being set.

By this time Manstein, and even Kluge, were beginning to express strong doubts. Hitler thought that another month's tank production would put the odds back in the Germans' favour. This satisfied the submissive Kluge, but Manstein continued to prevaricate, on the one hand calling for the offensive's cancelling, on the other proposing a new method of execution. Instead of attacking the heavily defended neck of the salient, he argued, the armour should be concentrated against the top of the head, break through in force, and then fan out to left and right against the rear of the defensive belts. Hitler was apparently interested. O.K.H. was not. Zeitzler liked his own plan. And, as usual, indecision bred conservatism.

As the leaders dithered the commanders on the spot prepared themselves for the day. Reconnaissance planes flew constantly across the salient, photographing every square yard. The depth and extent of Soviet preparations were visible, but seemed thinner than was the case on account of Soviet mastery in camouflage. The terrain was not ideal for tanks, but far from unsuitable. The 48th Panzer Corps commanders, stealing forward for a look at the ground they would have to cross, found:

a far-flung plain, broken by numerous valleys, small copses, irregularly laid out villages with thatched roofs, and some rivers and brooks, of these the Pena ran with a swift current between steep banks. The ground rose slightly to the north, thus favouring the defender. Roads consisted of tracks through the sand, and became impassable for all motor transport during rain. Large cornfields covered the landscape, making visibility difficult. (10)

On 2 July the die was cast. Hitler summoned the commanders to Rastenburg and ordered the attack for three days hence. The plan was reiterated; only the density of force distinguished it from those of the preceding years. Doubts could be seen on some of the faces around the room, but none were vocalised. Göring's immortal 'if we lose this war, God help us' had been applied by all to the battle in prospect, with all its idle abdication of responsibility in refusing to acknowledge even those facts staring the Wehrmacht in the face. *Zitadelle*'s game of consequences would be played out to the end, with all that it implied for German hopes of a drawn war, and for the dead men and wrecked tanks soon to bear bloody testimony to the Wehrmacht's fall from power, grace and strategic ingenuity.

In the south preparatory attacks would begin a day earlier, on 4 July. 'Independence Day for America,' remarked Mellenthin with that peculiar fatalism which pervades *Zitadelle*, 'the beginning of the end for Germany'. (11) He might well have added Eliot's 'in my beginning is my end . . . in my end my beginning'. There was nothing accidental about *Zitadelle*. It was the finest example of the perverse logic that 'named' Nazi Germany's war effort. The dancers had all gone under the Nazi hill. The matador had become the bull. And the old Soviet bull, mindful of its limitations, had opted for the toreador's certainty. This would be no dance. It was more like suicide.

V

Before dawn on 5 July the German forces north of the salient were surprised by a heavy Soviet artillery barrage. For a moment it was thought that a full Soviet offensive was beginning, but no troops or armour emerged out of the darkness. Shrugging aside this apparent coincidence the Germans opened their prearranged bombardment, the noise of the chorus swelling as the guns damaged by the Soviet fire came back into action. In the sky above the assigned Luftwaffe bomber force shrieked down upon the visible Soviet positions. At 5.30 a.m. five infantry divisions, 20th Panzer and the grenadier regiments of 18th Panzer began their advance into the Soviet defence system. Model was keeping the bulk of his armour in reserve, ready to exploit a breach.

The soon-apparent extent of the Soviet defences more than confirmed the fears expressed by Hitler on Model's behalf that fateful day in Munich. As the leading ranks of infantry and supporting armour moved forward into the first belt they encountered a volume of fire that might have made a Verdun veteran feel nostalgic for quieter times. The tanks, waiting as the engineers frantically worked to clear paths for them through the minefields, were subjected to a vicious crossfire from hidden anti-tank positions. The infantry stumbled into a trench system of amazing complexity, found themselves channelled into the fields of fire of numerous and well-camouflaged machine-gun nests. And as the Luftwaffe fiercely contested the sky with the Red Air Force there was nothing to stop the distant Soviet artillery laying carpets of destruction across the cornfields.

The heavy tanks, Tiger and Ferdinand alike, with their almost impervious armouring, mostly breached the first belt. The Tigers then found themselves forced to go back again and help the infantry, which now faced a new crop of enemy emplacements that had sprung from hiding once the tanks had passed. The Ferdinands were less fortunate. Unlike the Tigers they had insufficient secondary armament. Stranded without infantry support they were easy prey for Soviet soldiers who climbed aboard and poured flames through their ventilation slats.

The whole of 5 July was spent in wrenching the first belt of defences from the Russians. Each patch of ground, each thatched cottage strongpoint or gully copse, being contested as though it stood in the Kremlin's courtyard. By the morning of 6 July only snipers remained to pick off the odd engineer or grenadier. But the artillery of the Soviet second belt, pre-ranged on the first belt positions, was now creating fresh havoc. Many more days like that and Ninth Army would shrivel away.

Model, however, was not completely dissatisfied. True, the attack on the left had floundered early and left little hope of interfering with the expected arrival of Soviet reserves from the east. True, the cost of the ground gained had been excessive, and by no stretch of the imagination had a decisive breakthrough been achieved. But ground had been taken. In the right-centre of the attack – 20th Panzer's sector – the Soviets had been pushed back five miles, halfway to the low but dominating ridge in the distance. On the left-centre the ridge lay closer to the starting-line and had almost been reached. Fierce fighting had begun in the straggling village of Ponyri.

Through 6 July the struggle continued. 'The grenadiers swept on through the cornfields, capturing trenches, and encountering new ones. The battalions melted away. Companies became mere platoons.' (12) Model fed three panzer divisions into the front line; the experienced 2nd and 9th into the line of 20th Panzer's advance, aimed at the ridge between Teploye and Olkhovatka. On the ground beneath the ridge, a plain of small rolling hills covered in ripening corn, riddled with Soviet defences, the panzers crept slowly forward. By day the varying cracks and roars of tank guns, nebelwerfers, mortars, katyushas, artillery and bombs, set up a never-ending chorus of destruction along the twenty-mile wide zone. Well over a thousand tanks manoeuvred themselves into positions for the kill, and soon the smouldering wrecks of the unfortunate ones littered the ground.

By 8 July Model's forces had reached the ridge between Teploye and Olkhovatka.

The assault on the high ground began. The Russians laid down a curtain of defensive fire. After a few hundred yards the German grenadiers lay pinned to the ground. It was impossible to get through the Soviet fire of a few hundred guns concentrated on such a narrow sector. Only the tanks moved forward into the wall of fire. The Soviet artillerymen let them come within five hundred, then four hundred yards. At that range even the Tigers were set on fire by the heavy Russian anti-tank guns . . . But then three Mark IVs overran the Soviet gun positions. The grenadiers followed. They seized the high ground. They were thrown back by an immediate Russian counterattack. For three days the battle raged . . . (13)

Twice more the Germans grasped the ridgetop. Twice more they were repulsed in hand-to-hand fighting, savaged by the machine-gun emplacements that Roosskovky had scattered like seed on the opposite slopes of the ridge. There would be no breakthrough here in strength. Merely forcing a breach would cost all the strength there was.

Ten miles to the east the village of Ponyri, just beneath the same ridge, had slowly been transformed into a miniature

Stalingrad. The key points were the station, the school, the tractor station and the water tower. Into this square mile of European Russia Model fed two infantry divisions, 9th Panzer, 18th Panzer, and finally, in desperation, his last reserve division, 10th Motorised. Each was swallowed up in Ponyri as a cloudburst by the desert. Gains were measured in yards; the Munich Conference had neglected to calculate the yardage from Kromy to Kursk. In a week's fighting Model had halved his tank strength and suffered infantry casualties reminiscent of the First World War. Ninth Army had won twelve miles of cratered cornfields strewn with wrecked vehicles. And as Model rearranged his forces for one more lunge at the Teploye Ridge he received news of a Soviet offensive fifty miles in his rear.

VI

On the section of the southern front west of Belgorod the German positions were overlooked by a ridge of high ground some four miles distant. The first Soviet defensive belt lay behind this ridge, but an advance across a liberally mined no-man's-land, into the jaws of the Soviet artillery, was not to be taken lightly. But taken it had to be, and on the afternoon of 4 July the infantry and grenadiers moved forwards. The Soviets, surprised by the hour of the assault, pounded by the German artillery and Luftwaffe, did little to intervene until late in the day. Only the minefields caused serious hold-ups; in the absence of an artillery barrage they caused few casualties. The infantry gained the observation posts required by their own gunners that evening; the observers installed themselves soon after. Through the night the tanks clattered forward, into positions for the morning offensive.

So far, so good. Unlike Model in the north, Manstein and his two subordinate commanders – Hoth (Fourth Panzer Army) and Kempff (Army Detachment Kempff) – had not decided on reversion of the old tactics of a breach forced by infantry and exploited by the armour. They intended to make the breach with the armour, formed in wedges or *Panzerkeilen*, spearheaded by Tigers, flanked by Panthers and Mark IVs, and containing the motorised infantry. For this purpose they had close to 1,500 tanks, distributed among three panzer corps. To the west of Belgorod Fourth Panzer Army contained two of these corps: the 48th (comprising 3rd Panzer, *Grossdeutschland*, and

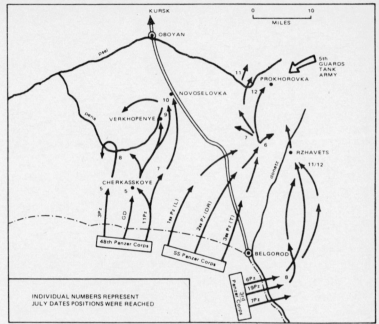

INDIVIDUAL NUMBERS REPRESENT
JULY DATES POSITIONS WERE REACHED

17 ZITADELLE: SOUTHERN FLANK

11th Panzer) and the S.S. Panzer Corps (comprising *Leibstandarte, Das Reich* and *Totenkopf*). To the east lay Army Detachment Kempff contained the other: 3rd Panzer Corps (comprising 6th, 19th, and 7th Panzer). All in all nine panzer divisions on a front less than forty miles wide

Manstein and Hoth envisaged Fourth Panzer Army striking obliquely towards Oboyan, via the neck of land between the upper reaches of the Psel and Donetz. In this way it was hoped to encounter the expected Soviet armoured reserve as it came in from the east, rather than risk that reserve hitting the flank of a more direct strike at Oboyan. The 3rd Panzer Corps was to advance across the Donetz in a north-easterly direction as flank cover for Fourth Panzer Army, and as a possible flank threat to the Soviet reserve. It was as skilful a plan as could have been devised in the circumstances, and came close to local success.

On the morning of 5 July one of the imponderables turned hostile. The weather. The rain fell in sheets and the ground turned into the familiar quagmire. Minor streams in 48th Panzer Corps' sector on the left swelled into major obstacles. Nevertheless, despite this and *Grossdeutschland*'s brand new Panther battalion wandering into an undetected minefield, reasonable progress was made on the first day, as it had been in the north. Third Panzer advanced some four miles on the far left; 11th Panzer and *Grossdeutschland* forced their way into Cherkasskoye.

One reason for this success was the Luftwaffe's temporary ascendancy in the air, made possible by the backfiring of a Red Air Force plan to achieve a dominance of its own. A careful schedule had been drawn up whereby a large Soviet bomber force would arrive over the Luftwaffe airstrips around Kharkov at the moment of maximum vulnerability. The planes would be assembled for take-off, out in the open without fighter cover. Unfortunately for the Soviets the Luftwaffe had installed a new radar device. This picked up the approaching bombers in time to get the German fighters airborne, and it was the Red Air Force which received the nasty surprise.

This action served the S.S. Panzer Corps better even than the 48th, for they had air-support priority on the first day of the offensive. The Luftwaffe had another pair of aces up its sleeve: fragmentation bombs and, a few days later, Stukas fitted with anti-tank cannons. The effect of the former on 5 July was dramatic; the S.S. Panzer Corps driving a deep wedge into the Soviet defences south of the Belgorod–Oboyan highway. Two days later the panzers were across the highway and, after an advance of over fifteen miles, approaching the neck of land between Donetz and Psel.

On the other side of Belgorod things were not going so well for the Germans. A small bridgehead had been won on the far bank of the Donetz, but there the Soviet defences, concealed in thick woods, were proving hard to penetrate. After three days of struggle the weight of Manteuffel's 7th Panzer was shifted suddenly and a breakthrough achieved. Sixth Panzer was quickly switched into the breach, and by the evening of 8 July Brieth's entire Corps was fanning out beyond the first defence belt. Encountering stiff resistance to his intended eastward drive Brieth turned the panzers north. where they would soon be sorely needed. The three days lost, however, could not be regained.

With the offensive four days old, everything still hung very much in the balance. The Soviet defences had been deeper than expected, and had taken a near unacceptable toll of the German armour. The Red Army had also managed to withdraw most of the troops manning the now-sundered first defensive belt. But a breakthrough – the magic breakthrough – was still a possibility for the Germans; its achievement would more than compensate for the losses endured.

On the left 48th Panzer Corps had advanced some ten miles since 5 July through astute juggling of the three panzer divisions. Resistance was stiffer on the left, where 3rd Panzer frequently required aid from its neighbour *Grossdeutschland*. Still, by 9 July *Grossdeutschland* had taken the Pena crossings at Verkopenye, and a day later 11th Panzer seized the heights around Novoselovka. The Corps was poised for the run-down to Oboyan should the S.S. Panzer Corps on its right accomplish the crucial rupture of the Soviet defences on the upper Psel.

The S.S. Panzer Corps was moving steadily towards Prokhorovka. An intended counter-attack on its right flank had been annihilated by the tank-bursting Stukas. A Soviet artillery observer witnessed the action.

The attacking aircraft drops from some 25000 feet upon the unsuspecting armoured column. Not until he is within fifteen feet of the last tank does the pilot pull out of his dive. The crack of cannon, a flash, a crash, and through the billowing smoke of the struck T-34 the German pilot climbs away. A moment later he dives in again. Always from behind. Tank after tank is knocked out by the cannon, the target invariably being its most vulnerable spot, the engine compartment, where each hit results in an instant explosion. (14)

Fifty out of sixty tanks were destroyed. On the 10th *Totenkopf* grasped a hold on the far bank of the Psel; the bridgehead was secured on the following day. On its right *Leibstandarte* and *Das Reich* were advancing along the three-mile-wide strip of land between the Psel and the Kursk–Belgorod railway embankment. On the other side of Prokhorovka the long-expected Soviet reserve – 5th Guards Tank Army, mustering 850 tanks – was moving to meet them.

These two forces clashed in 'the greatest tank battle of all time' on the morning of 12 July. It was a vital encounter for both sides. A week's fighting had not broken the Soviet line, but it had stretched it back in a wide arc. If Hausser's Corps could break through here, could leave the Soviet armoured reserve broken on the fields, the whole Soviet position would break apart like a ruptured boil. The Soviets, for similar reasons, had to halt the march of the hated S.S. The German attacking forces were also stretched, living on their own momentum. Blunt the sword at Prokhorovka and the arm would have to retract.

The ground on which the battle was fought consisted of a plain sloping gently down to the Psel, intersected by steep ravines and dotted with copses and orchards. The Soviet Tank Army commander, Rodmistrov, watched the battle from a nearby hill:

The battlefield seemed too small for the hundreds of armoured machines. Groups of tanks moved over the steppe, taking cover behind the isolated groves and orchards. The detonations of the guns merged into a menacing howl.

The tanks of the 5th Guards Tank Army cut into the Nazi deployment at full speed. This attack was so fast that the enemy did not have time to prepare to meet it, and the leading ranks of the Soviet tanks passed right through the enemy's entire first echelon, destroying his ability to control his leading units and sub-units. The Tigers, deprived in close combat of the advantages which their powerful gun and thick armour conferred, were successfully shot up by T-34s at close range. The immense number of tanks was mixed up all over the battlefield, and there was neither time nor space to disengage and reform the ranks. Shells fired at short range penetrated both the front and side armour of the tanks. While this was going on there were frequent explosions as ammunition blew up, while tank turrets, blown off by the explosions, were thrown dozens of yards away from the twisted machines.

At the same time fierce dog-fights were going on in the air over the battlefield, with both the Nazi and Soviet air forces attempting to help the troops on the ground to win the battle. Bombers, Shturmoviks and fighters literally hung over the Prokhorovka battlefield. One air battle followed another, with dozens of aircraft taking part in each. Thanks to resolute and courageous action by the Soviet fliers, the Soviet Air Force gained the victory in the air.

Soon the whole sky was overhung with heavy smoke from the fires. On the scorched black earth, smashed tanks were blazing like torches. It was hard to determine who was attacking and who was defending. The battle was going differently on the various sectors.

The 2nd Battalion of the 181st Brigade, XVIII Tank Corps,

attacking along the left bank of the Psel, clashed with a group of Tigers, which met the Soviet tanks with fire from the halt. The Tiger's powerful guns created a serious threat to our tank men, who had to engage the enemy in close combat as quickly as possible, to deprive him of his advantages. With the order 'Forward! Behind me!' the battalion commander, Captain Skripkin, headed his tank at the centre of the enemy's defence. With its first round the commander's tank penetrated the armour of one of the Tigers, then turning, set fire with three rounds to another enemy heavy tank. Several Tigers opened fire on Skripkin's tank simultaneously. One enemy shell punctured the side, another wounded the commander. The driver-mechanic and radio operator dragged him out of the tank and hid him in a shell-hole. But one of the Tigers was heading straight for them. The driver-mechanic jumped back into his damaged and burning tank, started the engine and rushed headlong at the enemy. It was as if a ball of fire careered over the battlefield. The Tiger stopped, hesitated, began to turn away. But it was too late. At full speed the burning KV smashed into the German tank. The explosion shook the earth. (15)

In the afternoon Hoth arrived. The battle was not going well. Hausser's Corps had been outnumbered by three to two at the outset; equal losses were costing the Germans relatively more. Where, Hoth asked, was Brieth's Corps and its 300 tanks, which had been directed with this eventuality in mind? The answer came through – twelve miles away. Even the daring seizure of Rzhavets by a column of 6th Panzer's tanks headed by a captured T-34 had failed to recoup those three days lost on the Donetz. Hausser's tanks would receive no help. There would be no Blücher at this Waterloo.

The other news was no more comforting. The Soviets had launched a full-scale offensive against the Orel salient, immediately north of the Kursk bulge. Model had not only been forced to break off his attacks on the Teploye Ridge; he was in grave danger of being encircled from the rear. The heroics continuing on the field of Prokhorovka were fast being drained of any strategic significance. *Zitadelle* had failed.

The next day, 13 July, Kluge and Manstein received summonses to the Wolfsschanze. There they found a very different Führer from the one who had given them the desperate pep-talk of a fortnight before. The bubble had finally burst. The

Allies had landed in Europe, in Sicily; the German panzer force lay savaged 1400 miles away, in the copses and fields of the central Russian plain.

References (Chapter 6)

1. Manstein, *Lost Victories*, 443
2. Ibid, 443
3. Guderian, *Panzer Leader*, 303
4. Ibid, 295
5. quoted in Jukes, *Kursk*, 38
6. Guderian, *Panzer Leader*, 307
7. Ibid, 308–9
8. Mellenthin, *Panzer Battles*, 226
9. quoted in Jukes, *Kursk*, 53
10. Mellenthin, *Panzer Battles*, 214
11. Ibid, 213
12. Carell, *Scorched Earth*, 46
13. Ibid, 47
14. Ibid, 58
15. quoted in Jukes, *Kursk*, 101–2

Chapter 7

WATCH ON THE CHANNEL

In the West is the place that matters. If we once manage to throw the British and Americans back in the sea, it will be a long time before they return ...

(Rommel) (1)

As the German panzer élite melted away beneath the fierce Russian sun Rommel fretted away idle hours in Berlin. He had been appointed as a military adviser to Hitler; his advice did not seem to be required. It would not in all likelihood have been well received. The squandering of the Afrika Korps had not impressed Rommel with Hitler's strategic grasp, and he was not one to flatter his Führer when criticism seemed more apt. He had doubtless not forgotten the scene of the previous November, when Hitler, informed by his favourite Field-Marshal that Africa was lost, could only think to shriek that Rommel was a defeatist and a coward. Since that day fortune had not smiled on the Wehrmacht. Africa had indeed been lost, and the Allies were now in Italy. Stalingrad had left its scar on the German Army; the attack that *must* succeed at Kursk was inexorably failing.

Rommel must have realised the Führer's cardinal responsibility for this succession of disasters. In Africa he had himself received orders which bore no relation to the situation as it was, which no sane man could have been expected to obey willingly. Nor was Hitler's military ability the only factor in contention; the hysterical dogmatism that characterised the Führer's manner of command was beginning to raise doubts as to the man himself, and hence the war as a whole. Coming back from Africa Rommel had talked to fellow officers in Berlin, heard of the atrocities committed by both sides on the Eastern Front, heard rumours of worse behind the high walls of the S.S. establishments. At first he probably, like many others, preferred to believe that Hitler himself was not responsible.

But confronting his Führer with such stories produced no disclaimer, only advice to mind his own business. Neither can he have been encouraged by Hitler's outburst to the effect that 'if the German people are incapable of winning the war, they can rot!' (2)

All this cannot have been easy for the Württemberg handyman to comprehend. Yet in the last year of his life Erwin Rommel followed these issues deeper into his conscience than did most of his fellow officers. It could be said, patronising though it might sound, that in that year he grew up. For the first time in his life he looked beyond the narrow boundaries of family and profession, and found that what he saw could not be ignored. Another destiny called him, one that did not come easily, but which he pursued regardless of the personal consequences. In this pursuit Rommel raised himself into a figure of tragedy, the fate of many who turn alone against an evil tide.

He did not meet a personal 'Damascus'. These thoughts coalesced gradually, with the help of other minds, during the winter and spring of 1943–4. The dominant thought in his mind in the summer of 1943 was clearly military: Germany was headed for defeat. This, though not yet inevitable, could only be avoided by a radical rethink of Germany's strategic priorities.

There can be no question of taking the offensive for the next few years, either in the East or the West, and so we must try to make the most of the advantages that normally accrue to the defence. The main defence against the tank is the anti-tank gun; in the air we must build fighters and still more fighters and give up all idea for the present of doing any bombing ourselves. I no longer see things quite as black as I did in Africa, but total victory is now, of course, hardly a possibility . . .

If we can give the German infantry divisions first fifty, then a hundred, then two hundred 75mm anti-tank guns each and install them in carefully-prepared positions, covered by large minefields, we shall be able to halt the Russians . . .

We must fight on interior lines. In the East withdraw as soon as possible to a suitable, prepared line. But our main effort must be directed towards beating off any attempt in Western Europe to create a second front . . . If we can once make their efforts fail, then things will be brighter for us. (3)

This was the recipe for staving off the inevitable. Had it been
applied with a stern resolve who knows what success might
have been achieved? And had success been forthcoming who
knows how easily Rommel could have stifled his moral doubts?
But it was not. His strategy was not favoured by the Supreme
Command. In the East Hitler's policy of holding every inch of
ground on an over-extended front brought forth a plethora of
mini-Stalingrads as 1943 passed into 1944. Manstein, who shared
Rommel's desire for a strategic-defensive stance, finally
secured his own dismissal by the persistence with which he
urged it. The production emphases which Rommel stressed –
anti-tank guns, fighters, mines – were not accepted either;
instead the world would be thrown back on its heels by a host
of secret weapons: schnorkel submarines, jet aircraft, rocket
bombs. Attack was the best form of defence, Hitler reminded
all and sundry. Soon it would be the only form for which the
German Army was equipped.

Rommel meanwhile was no longer adrift in Berlin. On 15
July, three days after Prokhorovka, he was assigned to Army
Group B, poised on the Brenner to occupy Italy should the
ally turn into an enemy. A brief sojourn in Greece followed,
then return to Italy. Rommel expected command in that
theatre, but his pessimistic advocacy of a defence-line along
the Alps was not appreciated by Hitler, who decided that
Kesselring was the man for the job. Rommel was sent to France,
to report on the Atlantic defences.

The report was not very favourable. Rundstedt, who had
been in command in the West for two years, had told jour-
nalists that 'we Germans do not indulge in the tired Maginot
spirit', (4) and proceeded to ignore the much-vaunted 'Atlantic
Wall' as much as possible. Rommel, seeing how much required
doing, pressed for a command of his own. This he received –
Army Group B, covering the coast from Antwerp to the Loire,
nominally under Rundstedt, but, in the now familiar pattern of
command structure, in reality wielding as much authority over
its own destiny as its commander could wring out of Hitler.
Rommel, as a field-marshal, had direct access. And still a
greater pull with Hitler than any other front-line general,
Model excepted.

While beginning in January 1944 to strengthen the Atlantic
defences Rommel was visited by the Mayor of Stuttgart, Dr
Strölin. The mayor had long been active in the anti-Hitler
resistance, and now carefully sounded out Rommel's loyalty.

Finding a sympathetic reception he proceeded to recount the various plots against Hitler of the preceding years, leading up to the current one – the arrest and forced abdication of the Führer by certain senior army officers on the Eastern Front. He, Rommel, was needed as a unifying force, Strölin said. He was respected by the German people, by the Army, the Party, even by Germany's enemies. 'You are the only one who can prevent civil war in Germany.' Rommel considered the implications, the enormity of it all. Strölin pushed his point, asked the field-marshal if the war was not irretrievably lost. Rommel said that it was, that Hitler was living on illusions. He promised to try and make Hitler see sense one last time. If this proved impossible . . . 'I believe it is my duty to come to the rescue of Germany.' (5)

From this time onward Rommel would play two roles. He realised that the German people still had faith in Hitler, and that only a successful landing by the Western powers would cause that faith to waver. He could not act before invasion was a reality. Yet as a soldier it was his duty to do all in his power to prevent the invasion, not least because an Allied set-back would raise the German bargaining power at the peace-table. It was not an enviable position to be in.

Of the two challenges facing him – the political and the military – the latter came immeasurably easier to Rommel. It was a novel situation for an Army weaned on panzer and stuka, on the land offensive conducted at *Blitzkrieg* pace. On the Channel coast the weapons would remain the same, but it would be a defensive task they would have to perform, devoid of the initiative and hopelessly outnumbered in the air. In such a situation the need was not for a General Staff Officer brilliantly trained in the expected, but for pragmatism, boldness and flexibility, sound instinct hand in hand with common sense. These qualities Rommel had in plenty. He also had experience of fighting the British and Americans, in particular of fighting within the limitations imposed by their air superiority. Throughout the six months between his appointment and the invasion he would carry in his mind a clear idea of how the German response should be organised. Unfortunately for him this clarity was not vouchsafed to others.

Two previous attempts at amphibious landings had left their mark on the Wehrmacht: their own planned invasion of Britain in summer 1940 and the Dieppe Raid in August 1942. The difficulties of amphibious landings, which the Army had experi-

enced for itself in practice-runs for 'Sea Lion', were overestimated; the number of boats required, which had been the Navy's
business, was underestimated, thereby creating the fatal illusion
that the Allies could attempt more than one landing. The first
point was re-emphasised by the Dieppe Raid, hastily dispatched
on the beaches by a solitary panzer division. The raid had only
been a reconnaissance in force, but Goebbels portrayed it as an
abortive invasion and Zeitzler, then Chief of Staff to the C.-in-C.
West, indulging in the exaggeration of enemy forces not un-
common among generals, had encouraged this belief. By 1943
Zeitzler was O.K.H. Chief of Staff, and as O.K.H. was only
responsible for the Eastern Front, interested in playing down
the threat of invasion lest its forces be sent West. Hitler had
adopted this optimistic view, and been, he thought, confirmed
in his belief by Allied failures in Italy.

Rundstedt's judgement has already been noted; it was not
improved by the alcoholic intake he found necessary for a good
night's sleep. So what with Hitler's falsely-based optimism and
Rundstedt's diffidence, progress on the 'Atlantic Wall' had been
extremely slow during 1943. A large work force had been
assembled, but found itself diverted to strengthen submarine
pens in the Bay of Biscay and build emplacements for the
rocket-launching sites in the Pas de Calais. Defence was still
almost a dirty word.

This is not to suggest that the West was low on Hitler's
strategic priority list, and indeed it was climbing month by
month. Defence was low on the list; a decision in the West,
naturally in Germany's favour, was increasingly seen as a
panacea for the mounting problems facing the Third Reich.
Rommel would not lack forces in 1944; the paper strength at
least would be high. A minimum would be left in Russia, Italy,
Scandinavia and the Balkans, even if that minimum accounted
for 220 of the Reich's 280 divisions. Hitler was gambling for
high stakes, as Montgomery's Intelligence Chief noted –

The enemy is courting further and deepening disaster in the
East to retain a good chance in the West; a strange gamble
militarily, made intelligent politically by the prospect of a
compromise peace if the Western decision bore fruit: in short,
more and more Stalingrads in the hope of one Dunkirk. (6)

Even this gamble required higher stakes than Hitler had left in
his pocket. Rundstedt had told him that seventy divisions was

the absolute minimum necessary; by thinning the Eastern Front
beyond the danger level Hitler could scrape together only sixty.
Ten of these would be panzer divisions, and they were generally
in good condition. The infantry left rather more to be desired.
They had a high content of under- and over-age troops, and a
high foreign content. The few experienced divisions came from
the East; they were generally much under-strength and not
over-enthusiastic for more fighting. Rundstedt, in the scathing
tone which characterised his comments in these years, noted
that:

> often I would be informed that a new division was to arrive
> in France direct from Russia or Norway or Central Germany.
> When it finally made its appearance in the West it would
> consist, in all, of a divisional commander, a medical officer
> and five bakers. (7)

These infantry divisions had two thousand miles of coastline to
defend. Over half of them were manning the coastal defences,
the remainder stood close up behind. They were grouped in
four armies. Fifteenth Army, comprising about forty-five per
cent of the total strength, was deployed between the Seine and
the Scheldt; Seventh Army, with another forty per cent, in
Normandy and Brittany. These two armies came under Rommel's Army Group B command. South of the Loire facing the
Atlantic was First Army; on the Mediterranean coast Nineteenth Army. Between them they accounted for the other fifteen
per cent. The placement of the panzer divisions remained a
matter of dispute.

With these forces lay the Reich's fading hopes of a negotiated
peace in the West and time to turn and force a stalemate on the
Red Army. How could they be used to throw the invasion
forces back into the sea? Rommel's answer was two-fold. He
would make it as difficult and as time-consuming as possible for
the enemy to land; he would counter-attack the forces enmeshed on the beaches with panzer divisions deployed to that
purpose. For the first he needed time, for the second a change
of attitude on the part of his collaborators. He would not get
enough of either.

II

A German soldier, in an autobiographical novel, wrote that 'back at home they think of us sitting ever so snug behind the Atlantic Wall. The Atlantic Wall, they quack, it's so solid a louse could not creep through. But if you look at the bloody thing a bit closer you can see that any New York swimming club could land here and walk ashore.' (8) This was the defence line inherited by Rommel in the last months of 1943. Two years of occupation had been largely wasted. He set about organising defences, and not only against New York swimming clubs.

The point was to trap the invaders on the beaches, and to this end Rommel used every possible means. The landing-craft approaching the shore would first be confronted by long-range fire from heavy coastal batteries. These would be protected by concrete walling and roofing, proof against enemy air attack even at the expense of reducing their arc of fire. The next obstacles would be in the water itself: four lines of various gadgets designed to destroy or cripple the landing craft and the troops and equipment they carried. They were mostly spiky, jagged pieces of metal or concrete, frequently loaded with explosive for the moment of impact. While the invaders were attempting to get through these obstacles they would be raked by anti-tank and machine-gun fire from concrete-protected pill-boxes at the back of and behind the beach. If, despite all this, they managed to reach the beach they would find it extensively mined, the exits blocked by concrete, barbed wire, anti-tank ditches and minefields. Behind this line more minefields would stretch back for six miles, in a diluted version of the *pakfront*. Lanes would be left clear for the panzer counter-thrust.

Nor was this all. Rommel also decided to fill all spaces suitable for a glider landing with a grid of stakes hammered into the ground. They would be strung together and armed with shells. Any glider descending among them would be extremely fortunate to survive in one piece.

Overall this seemed to Rommel a formidable system of defence. And so it would have been had he possessed the time to install it. Over half of the five million mines awaiting the Allies on 6 June were laid at Rommel's instigation; he had reckoned that 200 million would be necessary. Of the four lines of foreshore gadgets contemplated only the two highest up the beach were completed by June. For 'Sea Lion' the Germans had planned on a high tide landing to reduce the width of beach they would have to cross, but for 'Overlord' the Allies were counting on a low tide landing, to counter the foreshore obstacles below the water-line and to give their boats a chance of returning immediately across the Channel. Rommel's two lines of gadgets were hence above or only just below the surface when the landing was made, which considerably reduced their effectiveness. Neither were the anti-glider stakes armed with shells; Rommel could not secure them until two days before D-Day, by which time it was too late to install them.

Those defences that were there on 6 June had to be manned. If the beach was the decisive arena, Rommel argued, then the German troops must be on or just behind it. Depth of defence was to be sacrificed to width, concentration of force to concentration of time. The first few hours, at most days, would be decisive.

This naturally raised the question of where to deploy the panzer divisions. Rommel wanted them close up behind the beaches, from where they could counter-attack within those few crucial hours. It was more important to have one panzer division in the assaulted sector on the first day than to have three there by the third day. None of the other responsible commanders agreed with him. They had no faith in the Atlantic Wall, and were only prepared to watch Rommel's frenzied efforts to strengthen it provided such efforts did not prejudice their own plans. These were to concentrate on denying the Allies the major port they would need to build up their forces – it occurred to no one that the Allies would bring their own 'Mulberry' ports with them – and then to counter-attack with the full strength of the panzer divisions husbanded in reserve. To do as Rommel asked, and hold the precious armour close to the coast, was to renounce the principles of flexibility and concentration of response, whose application could alone prove decisive against the enemy's material superiority. It was strategic suicide. Certainly the enemy had the advantage in the air and at sea; all the more reason, surely, for luring him into battle on terms that suited the Germans: mobile warfare behind the coastal area, in which the panzer veterans of the Eastern Front and the superior German armoured vehicles would prove more than a match for the inexperienced and badly-equipped British and American armoured divisions.

Since this view was widely held, and never completely abandoned in practice, Rommel's reply deserves to be quoted at length.

> We can hardly expect a counter-attack by the few reserves we have behind the coast at the moment, with no self-propelled guns and an inadequate quantity of all forms of anti-tank weapons, to succeed in destroying the powerful force the enemy will land . . . (it will be) only by the rapid intervention of our operational reserves that he will be thrown into the sea. This requires that these forces should be held very close behind the coastal defences.
>
> If on the other hand, our principal reserves have to be brought from well back inland, the move will not only require a great deal of time – time which the enemy will probably use to reinforce himself at his point of penetration and either organise his forces for defence or press the attack further inland – but will also be under constant danger from the air. Bearing in mind the numerical and material superiority of the enemy striking forces, their high state of training and tremendous air superiority, victory in a major battle on the continent seems to me a matter of grave doubt. (9)

This was a strategic appreciation. Talking to Bayerlein in May his frustration at not securing his collaborators' agreement was beginning to show.

> Our friends from the East cannot imagine what they're in for here. It's not a matter of fanatical hordes to be driven forward in masses against our line, with no regard for casualties and little recourse to tactical craft . . .
>
> You have no idea how hard it is to convince these people. At one time they looked on mobile warfare as something to keep clear of at all costs, but now that our freedom to manoeuvre in the West is gone, they're all crazy for it. Whereas, in fact, it's obvious that if the enemy once gets his foot in, he'll put every anti-tank gun and tank he can into the bridgehead and let us beat our heads against it, as he did at Medenine. To break through such a front you have to attack slowly and methodically, under cover of massed artillery but we of course, thanks to the Allied air force, will have nothing there in time. The day of the dashing cut-and-thrust tank attack of the early years is past and gone – and that goes for the East too, a fact, which may, perhaps, by this time, have gradually sunk in. (10)

It is easy to note with hindsight that Rommel was substantially correct, and for the reasons he supposed. German armour would never be movable *en masse* under a clear Western sky. The Allies would win the build-up once established ashore; the panzers would be ground down in their enforced defensive role. But all this was not so easy to see in advance, particularly for those officers who had not witnessed an enemy-saturated sky.

Guderian, for example, on a flying visit to the West conversed with Rundstedt and Geyr (the commander, for training and administrative purposes, of Panzer Group West), and found himself in agreement with them. They all realised that enemy air superiority made the movement of armour problematic, but thought the solution lay in movement by night, 'repairs to the French road network . . . the construction of alternative river crossings, underwater bridges or bridges of boats'. (11) They thought Rommel was exaggerating the difficulties, perhaps as a subconscious excuse for his defeat in Africa.

The familiar wrangle now ensued, amidst the familiar chronic breakdown of the Army command structure. All these men – Rommel, Rundstedt, Guderian, Geyr – were only commanders as regards the troops. As regards each other there was, in practice, no hierarchical relationship. They were all simply subordinate to Hitler, who listened to one, then another, and eventually, sometimes, made up his mind. Thus Guderian attempted to convince Rommel that his plan was fallacious.

I was therefore not surprised by Rommel's highly temperamental and strongly expressed refusal when I suggested that our armour be withdrawn from the coastal area. He turned down my suggestion at once, pointing out that as a man from the Eastern Front I lacked his experience of Africa and Italy; that he knew, in fact, far more about the matter in hand than I did and that he was fully convinced that his system was right. In view of this attitude of his, an argument with Rommel concerning the distribution of our motorised reserves proved to be quite fruitless. (12)

Of course it was fruitless! These two, the surviving executants of France's defeat in 1940, had no power over the deployment of the armoured troops. Nor did Rundstedt, who complained bitterly after the war that his authority as C.-in-C. West stretched as far as the changing of guards in front of his gate.

So Guderian tried to get Rommel subordinated to Rundstedt, which in theory he already was. Rommel tried to get Geyr's panzer divisions subordinate to himself. All the Army authorities tried to get operational control of the Luftwaffe and Navy coastal units in their areas. Not only did they not get that, but even the coastal artillery and anti-aircraft formations were outside their jurisdiction. It was not hard to foresee how much time this cumbersome structure would consume on D-Day, when hours really counted. Then it would be a question of getting Hitler out of bed, now, *vis-à-vis* the location of armour, it was a matter of someone convincing him one way or the other. But no one could. Respecting Rommel's judgement, but loath to disregard the substantial experience raised against him, Hitler compromised fatally. He failed to give Rommel what was needed for a fight on the coast, he failed to concentrate the strong reserve that defeat on the coast would render indispensable. The panzer divisions were neither behind the beaches nor hidden in the forests around Paris. Instead they were scattered in between, to be summoned one by one across open ground into a battle decided before their arrival.

III

This was not Hitler's only compromise in the months preceding June. On 2 May his oracle had spoken within, telling him that Normandy would be the focus of the invasion. The generals did not agree. For them it had long been an article of faith that the Allied *Schwerpunkt* would be directed against the Pas de Calais. Their disagreeable experience with 'Sea Lion' led them to expect that their enemy would also regard the shortest route as the safest. It offered the greater rewards as well: the cutting off of all the German troops in France, a short run to the Rhine and Ruhr, the speedy suppression of the V-weapon launching sites.

The Allies did everything conceivable to confirm this erroneous appreciation. Much construction work was undertaken in south-east England: storage depots, new railway sidings, port facilities. The divisions assigned to the later waves of the Normandy invasion were all housed in Kent. All this was subtly displayed to the German reconnaissance planes. In the southwest, by contrast, where the real preparations were underway,

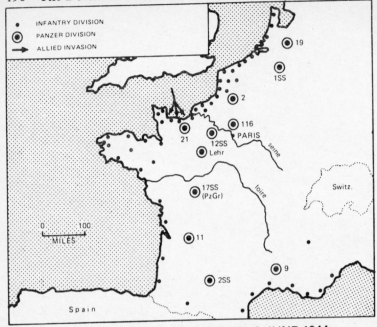

18 FRANCE: GERMAN DISPOSITIONS, 6 JUNE 1944

a much stronger attempt at concealment was made. Wireless traffic from Montgomery's H.Q. near Portsmouth was relayed by land to Kent and then broadcast by radio from there. Abroad British and American agents had a field day convincing German intelligence that they had stumbled skilfully upon the destination of the Allied armada: the Pas de Calais. In their strategic bombing programme the deception was maintained. The French railway system was reduced to chaos, hindering enormously the German movement of troops and material, as much north of the Seine as south of it.

Yet, despite it all, the Führer's intuition had worked the trick once more. Rommel too became infected with the possibility of an attack in Normandy. In May he asked for the 12th S.S. Panzergrenadier Division to be moved to St Lô, where it would have faced the American landing. But Hitler refused. The intuition remained, but the will to follow the sleepwalker's destiny had evaporated. Through May and the first week of June he turned down request after request by Rommel to move troops into the threatened area. An A.A. Corps between Orne and Vire, a Nebelwerfer Brigade south of Carentan, Panzer *Lehr* near Avranches, the mining of the Bay of Seine; all were requested, all refused. Like a lover asking to be loved, yet disbelieving each passionate protestation, Hitler spurned the last gifts of his own intuition.

And so the Germans in France waited, watching the Allied air forces thickening above them, sensing the preparations accelerating out of sight across the Channel. Behind them their own flow of supplies – food, petrol, ammunition, materials for construction work – gradually ebbed as the air offensive against the French railway system took its toll. Through a clear May they waited, as the Seine bridges were demolished in their rear.

As June began it seemed as if they had been granted a respite. The chief Luftwaffe meteorologist reported on 4 June that no invasion was likely to be possible in the next fortnight. Rommel submitted a report to von Rundstedt, confirming the preparations visible around Dover and their probable realisation in a strike against the Pas de Calais. He added that the harbours further west on England's southern coast had not been reconnoitred. On the morning of 5 June he took the leave of absence apparently granted by the weather and set out for home. It was Lucie's birthday. The next day he intended to visit Hitler at Berchtesgaden and make one final attempt to secure the forces he wished for Normandy.

That day the reconnaissance planes were grounded by the weather, the navy patrols confined to port. It was all the more surprising for German Intelligence, therefore, when the long expected message to the French Resistance – invasion within forty-eight hours – was intercepted that evening. The radar installations between Cherbourg and Le Havre were then discovered to be jammed. Those further north on the Pas de Calais were not; they reported heavier-than-usual shipping in the Channel. American reconnaissance aircraft were intercepted signalling weather information.

At Rundstedt's H.Q. the threat of invasion was still not taken seriously; at Rommel's it produced an alert signal to the troops covering the Pas de Calais! Those in Normandy received no warning other than unusually intense air activity. Rommel himself was not there. Neither was Dollmann, whose Seventh Army covered the stretch of coast for which the Allied armada was heading. He was returning from a 'war game' in Rennes. The only armoured force in the area was 21st Panzer. It was alerted at 1 a.m., and told to wait for orders.

IV

Throughout the months of wrangling the central premise of Rommel's plan had remained unaltered: the Allied landing could only be repulsed by a swift armoured counter-attack. The strength and depth of the coastal defences were subordinate to this, designed to bind the prisoner while the punch was prepared for delivery. When it came to the day 21st Panzer was the only armoured force available. Rundstedt tried to get Panzer *Lehr* and 12th S.S. Panzer released from O.K.W. Reserve at 4 a.m.; he was told by Jodl that as the Führer was not yet convinced that this was the main assault, he would have to wait. Hitler then went to bed, and it was early afternoon before the argument could be resumed. Since these divisions were not as close to the coast as Rommel had wanted, this timing effectively cancelled them out as regards the crucial day. Everything rested on 21st Panzer. That division's efforts on 6 June tell the story of the German response.

It was not one of the best Panzer divisions in France. The equipment was plentiful – 146 tanks, fifty-one self-propelled guns – but not of the highest standard as many of the tanks were French. The troops were mostly young and inexperienced. The original 21st Panzer had been lost in the African débâcle; only a few of its troops, convalescing in Europe at the time of surrender, provided any continuity.

Inexperienced troops was one problem bedevilling the German Army in France. The command structure was another, and here 21st Panzer had more than a fair share. General Feuchtinger, commanding the division, simply did not have any clear instructions as to whose operational command he came under. His immediate superior was Richter, commanding 716th Infantry Division, and above him Marcks, commanding 84th Infantry Corps. But at the time of invasion 21st Panzer was in the process of incorporation into 47th Panzer Corps, and there also existed, for various purposes, a command connection with Geyr's Panzer Group West. In such a situation it was to be expected that Feuchtinger would wait, before committing his armour, for definite instruction from Army Group B, i.e. Rommel, who was five hundred miles away. So the tanks, though alerted early enough, stood in line by the side of a road south of Caen through the precious hours of darkness.

Feuchtinger did have certain standing orders. If the enemy landed around the mouth of the Orne his two infantry battalions

Left: Balck.

Below: 1937 manoeuvres,
left to right: Hitler,
Ciano (behind shoulder),
Mussolini and Goering
conferring, Udet,
Dietrich and List.

Left: Model.
Below: Kluge (left) in France, Summer 1944.

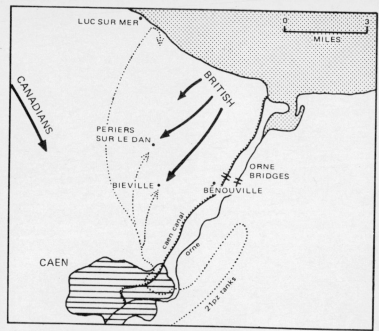

19 21st PANZER'S COUNTER-ATTACK: 6 JUNE 1944

north of Caen were to pass under Richter's command and his anti-aircraft units to Caen Flak Command. When the paratroopers dropped from the skies to secure the Orne bridges at Benouville, these two infantry battalions were immediately sent in to engage them on both sides of the river. Feuchtinger went further, on his own initiative sending another battle-group, including some tanks, east of the river. Meanwhile the mass of armour still stood motionless on the far side of Caen.

Rommel's Chief of Staff, General Speidel, was now beginning to realise that this was 'the Day', and at 6.45 a.m. phoned the Field-Marshal at home. He received permission to use 21st Panzer as he saw fit, and thence passed this permission down the line to Marcks. Around 8 a.m. the tanks on either Marcks's or Feuchtinger's order, moved around the south-eastern outskirts of Caen to attack northwards down the east bank of the Orne. This was presumably Marcks's order, since he was intending to use 12th S.S. Panzer on the west bank. Certainly something was needed west of the river, since Richter's movement of 21st Panzer's infantry and assault-guns against the paratroopers had left a gaping hole between Caen and the beaches now filling up with enemy forces.

Marcks had not been informed of O.K.W.'s earlier decision to 'wait and see' before freeing 12th S.S. Panzer from reserve. Informed of this only at 9.30 he was then obliged to reverse the order given to 21st Panzer and bring it across to the west, thus involving it in another route-march, this time in full daylight. And by this time, of course, the division was busily engaged around the Orne bridges. Only the tanks could be sent west. They spent the next five hours working their way through the rubble-strewn streets of Caen.

The one available armoured division had now been broken up and dispersed across a ten-mile front. Its balance had been destroyed, its punching power correspondingly thinned. At midnight it had been ideally deployed to counter-attack decisively down either bank of the Orne: half a day's indecision had produced no meaningful counter-attack, merely the steady erosion of what potential there was.

By 3 p.m. the tanks had finally shaken themselves free of Caen and were moving north towards the eight-mile distant beaches in three parallel columns. On the right twenty-five tanks were advancing on Bieville, in the centre thirty-five tanks on Perriers sur le Dan, and on the left six tanks, sundry armoured cars and infantry from one of the panzergrenadier regiments were aimed towards Luc sur Mer. Between these columns and the coast, roughly three miles north of Caen, was a line of high ground. Had the German armour possessed any air support they would have been forewarned of the British forces driving south towards them. This would have been infinitely preferable to the surprise they received. The twenty-five tanks on the right reached the foot of the slope just as British anti-tank guns, artillery and tanks reached the crest.

Their position was well-chosen tactically and their fire both heavy and accurate. The first Mark IV was ablaze before a single German tank had the chance to fire a shot. The remainder moved forward, firing at where the enemy were thought to be: but the English weapons were well-concealed and within a few minutes we had lost six tanks. (13)

The German centre did no better, running into a squadron of Staffordshires west of Periers Rise. They lost ten tanks in a matter of minutes.

It is not hard to imagine the effect of such losses on in-experienced tank crews, particularly after spending fourteen hours trundling this way and that to no apparent purpose. But all was not lost. The German left wing had not run into the enemy and was motoring steadily down to the sea. By 8 p.m. it had reached the coast, and discovered that there and for two miles further west the defences remained intact. Appraised by radio of this exciting news Feuchtinger made rapid plans to plunge his tank strength into the gap. If the British and Canadians could be held apart the British forces in the eastern-most beachhead would be isolated and open to a concentrated counter-thrust. As suddenly as it had appeared the opportunity vanished. The units awaiting the order to march were suddenly confronted with a sky full of enemy gliders. This, the planned appearance of 6th Airborne Division, looked to the watching Germans like a fiendishly rapid reply to 21st Panzer's thrust. It certainly had that effect, neatly cutting off the group on the coast from the forces assembling to reinforce them. In the confusion the attack spluttered and stalled. 21st Panzer had failed to provide the miracle that Rommel's strategy, once compromised by Hitler's indecision, had doomed it to attempt.

If Hitler and Jodl had released 12th S.S. Panzer when Rundstedt requested, with some darkness still remaining, the division would have arrived by midday at the latest, and the chances of a successful counter-attack doubled. As it was they let it go at 3 p.m. Under constant pressure from the Allied Air Forces the division inched its way from Lisieux westward towards Caen at an average speed of 4 mph. Kurt Meyer's leading battle-group limped into position south of the city at midnight, hoping to refuel at a now non-existent fuel dump.

Hitler, who had ordered that 'the bridgehead must be cleaned up not later than tonight', was to be disappointed. The British and Canadians had secured holds twenty miles wide and from three to six miles deep; the Americans held two rather shallower beachheads on the Continent of Europe. The Germans who held the spaces in between had waited in vain for the armoured forces. None arrived. Their ammunition and confidence began to evaporate. A feeling of hopelessness spread. The Anglo-American forces were ashore and unlikely to be dislodged. In a few weeks the Soviet offensive was expected. There was not enough force left to combat either. Militarily Germany had lost the war. Only politics could save her now.

References (Chapter 7)

1. *The Rommel Papers*, 453
2. quoted in Douglas-Home, *Rommel*, 118
3 *The Rommel Papers*, 451–3
4. quoted in Strawson, *Hitler*, 186
5. quoted in Young, *Rommel*, 240–1
6. quoted in Wilmot, *Struggle for Europe*, 196
7. quoted in Belfield and Essame, *Normandy*, 37
8. Ibid, 28
9. *The Rommel Papers*, 454–5
10. Ibid, 468
11. Guderian, *Panzer Leader*, 328
12. Ibid, 330
13. quoted in McKee, *Caen*, 67

PART 3

Whose Germany?

the great poisoned drum
quakes earth, heaven
turn back, look –
dead bodies miles around

（Myotan）

Chapter 8

'MAKE PEACE, YOU FOOLS'

'Why would a man run back, instead of running forward to give himself up? Discipline in the German Army must be formidable.'

(Canadian tank sergeant on D–Day)

If a radio battery runs out, it runs out. You can leave it in bright sunlight, heat it in the oven. Both will provide a minor recharge, drag a few more hours of life from the cell. But you will also see about acquiring a new battery. There is no reversing the process.

If on the other hand your football team are two-nil down with five minutes to go, a mad flicker of hope may still dance amidst the gloom of inevitable defeat. Occasions when the impossible has occurred spring readily to the mind. Maybe this time? Where the efforts of human beings are a factor, then hope dies hard.

The Wehrmacht was beaten – anyone could see that. But . . . if every German soldier fought like ten . . . if every industrial worker produced like ten . . . if the Goddess of War laid a charm on the Reich or a curse on her enemies . . . if, if, if . . . there was always hope, until the last bitter moments. The twisted genius of the Führer, ever-more twisted, ever-less possessed of genius, refused to countenance defeat. Like a team manager in those last five minutes, all reason swept beneath a deluge of emotion, he screamed at his players from the touch-line bunker. If they really wanted to win, they would win. If they lost it was because they did not want to win enough. They lacked the will, the guts, the faith. Like the manager remembering other days, that victory snatched from defeat in the dying seconds, Adolf Hitler paced up and down beneath his portrait of Frederick the Great, who had also been threatened from all sides, yet had won through. Will-power, strength in adversity, a superhuman effort. The German destiny required and expected it. The coalition would then collapse. The secret weapons would spread dismay. All that was needed was time; time could only be won by the will. It was never too late.

The generals who had waited through that now long-ago night of 10 May 1940 had been guided by their sense of professionalism and their notion of 'Germany'. Each must have seemed so unambiguous then. Germany was their country, their professionalism devoted to its service. The nation demanded the most unwavering allegiance; any idea that patriotism could be qualified by wider truths they dismissed as nothing more than Bolshevism. Accordingly they felt a horror of civil war only matched by their unquestioning acceptance of international war. In 1940, on the nation's behalf, they were more than ready to wage the latter against the 'criminals of Versailles'. Like knights in shining armour they would right the wrongs of 1919. This had been their leader's avowed policy; with it he had united the nation as never before. Peace had failed to complete the process, now war would continue the pursuit of the same policies by other means. Once Germany had retaken her rightful place, war would end and peace return. For the moment their skills, to which they had devoted their lives, were needed by the nation. They were soldiers, trained to achieve the objectives assigned by their political superiors at the least cost to their military comrades. In the summer of 1940 they did just that. France was broken, German losses minimal. They had kept faith with Führer and troops.

By June 1944 it was no longer so simple. The war in the East had introduced a new dimension. It was not so much a war fought between nations as between ideas. The one could end in compromise, in reversion to the political realm. The other could not; it was already *in* the political realm. And if there was no hope of compromise then the only war-aim, by 1944, was survival. And as men engaged in a struggle for survival seek to define themselves, so too do nations. The abstraction that was 'Germany' became the land, the people, the way of life that was Germany. Yet this new master, still ill-defined but infinitely more real, was incompatible with the old one. The generals had to serve one or the other. The Führer, who personified 'Germany' and to whom they were bound by oath, demanded that the war continue, to total victory or total defeat. The generals knew that victory was out of the question, that continuance of the war doomed at least eastern Germany to the same horrors that the Reich had spread across the Soviet

Union. The only hope lay in an end to the war. The only hope of that lay in the Führer's removal. But such a course involved breaking the oath, entering the political realm they abhorred, raising the spectre of civil war against Party and S.S. And as they searched in vain for a less drastic solution the war continued, increasing the burden of the obligation they felt to their troops, dying in droves on the promises of one man's mania. The generals' professional skill was no longer required; they were merely expected to translate without question the orders raining in, detail by detail, from above. Orders that their professional expertise knew to be no more than mass death sentences on the troops they still nominally commanded.

. . . all the courage didn't help. It was one terrible bloodletting . . . My nerves are pretty good, but sometimes I was near collapse. It was casualty reports, casualty reports, casualty reports, wherever you went. I have never fought with such losses . . . And the worst of it is that it was all without sense or purpose. There is no longer anything we can do. Every shot we fire is now harming ourselves, for it will be returned a hundred-fold. The sooner it finishes the better for all of us.

We are finished, and most of the gentlemen above know it perfectly well, even if they won't admit it. Even they aren't so stupid that they can't recognise facts that anybody could work out on the fingers of one hand. (1)

Rommel, like any commander in the field, knew that German defeat would not be a product of insufficient effort, courage or will. The Army continued to fight with formidable skill and discipline. There was simply not enough strength to go around. It *was* too late. The question now was – to whom would Germany yield?

II

In Normandy the Germans continued their attempts to break into the bridgehead, the Allies theirs to break out. On 7 June the two available panzer divisions – 21st and 12th S.S. – again tried to drive a wedge between the British and Canadians north of Caen. The S.S. staged a neat ambush of the main Canadian armour but was then driven to ground by accurate

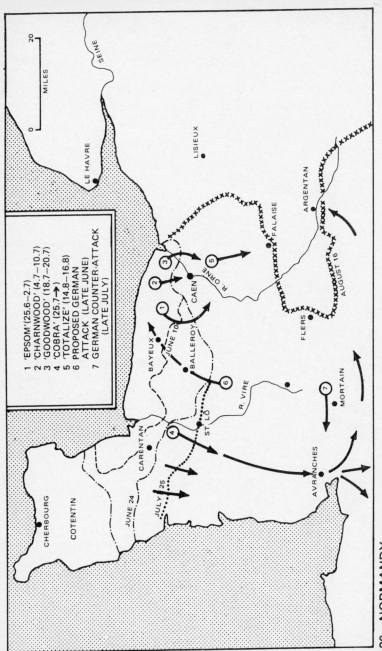

20 NORMANDY

1 'EPSOM' (25.6–2.7)
2 'CHARNWOOD' (4.7–10.7)
3 'GOODWOOD' (18.7–20.7)
4 'COBRA' (25.7→)
5 'TOTALIZE' (14.8–16.8)
6 PROPOSED GERMAN ATTACK (LATE JUNE)
7 GERMAN COUNTER-ATTACK (LATE JULY)

fire from the off-shore naval guns; 21st Panzer's advance quickly stalled around Epron. Rather than breaking through the Germans had to shift forces westward to stem a breach in their own lines opened by another Canadian tank force. Already a stalemate situation was developing, one that could only assist the Allies, whose build-up was proceeding at the faster rate.

The next morning Geyr, now commanding Panzer Group West operationally, cut dead the ever-ebullient Kurt Meyer with the words: 'My dear Herr Meyer, the war can only be won now by political means.'(2) We are not told what these means were to be. In any event, the panzer thrust as military panacea proved a hard theory to dislodge. One more attempt would be made to throw the enemy back into the sea, this time with three divisions. Panzer *Lehr*, the cream of the panzer force, was on the way.

It had ninety miles to cover from its billets near Le Mans. The commander, Bayerlein, received his orders to move from the Seventh Army commander, Dollmann, at daybreak on 7 June. Having served with Rommel in the desert, and sharing his old leader's apprehension of Allied air superiority, Bayerlein begged Dollman to let him move up under cover of the next night's darkness. That would be too late, he was told. Bayerlein did the best he could, dispersing his division over five different axes of advance, and hoped.

The first air attack came about half-past five that morning, near Falaise, by noon it was terrible; my men were calling the road from Vire to Bény-Bocage a fighter-bomber racecourse . . .

Every vehicle was covered with tree branches and moved along hedges and the edges of woods. Road junctions were bombed, and a bridge knocked out at Condé. This did not stop my tanks, but it hampered other vehicles. By the end of the day I had lost 40 tank trucks carrying fuel, and 90 others. Five of my tanks were knocked out, and 84 half-tracks, prime-movers and self-propelled guns. These were serious losses for a division not yet in action. (3)

Panzer *Lehr* was not the only division to suffer. 17th S.S. Panzergrenadier Division encountered a similar fate.

Our motorised columns were coiling along the roads towards the invasion beaches. Then something happened that left us in a daze. Spurts of fire flicked along the column and splashes of dust staccatoed the road. Everyone was piling out of vehicles and scuttling for the neighbouring fields. Several vehicles were already in flames . . . The march column was now completely disrupted and every man was on his own, to pull out of this blazing column as best he could. And it was none too soon, because an hour later the whole thing started all over again, only much worse this time. When this attack was over, the length of the road was strewn with splintered anti-tank guns (the pride of our division), flaming motors and charred implements of war. (4)

These divisions struggled up to the front line, there to be further injured. The three division attack on 9–10 June ran headlong into an Allied attack proceeding in the opposite direction. Once the smoke had cleared the line remained in roughly the same place, yet one more panzer division was inextricably welded into it, immobilised in a defensive role.

On 10 June Rommel wrote a summary for the benefit of those directing the battle from far-distant headquarters. The enemy, he said, would hold the bridgehead between Orne and Vire, and attempt to widen it through the capture of the Cotentin Peninsular and the port of Cherbourg. They would then fill it with troops and equipment to the point where it over-flowed into France. Their air superiority had crippled the German attempts to mount a counter-attack; in the approach marches, the formation for attack, the attack itself. The only hope was to bring in sufficient infantry to hold the line, thus releasing the panzer forces for another more concentrated effort. As the enemy build-up was proceeding faster than the German this was a thin hope. If an attack was to be mounted, he added, it should be against the weaker Americans.

This was a reasonably accurate summation. The only point it missed was Montgomery's central strategic recipe – he would draw the German armoured strength on to his western wing, expend it in attrition battles, and thus prepare the way for an American break-out in the east. Rommel's instinctual preference for attacking the Americans was well-grounded. Not that it mattered.

My functions in Normandy were so restricted by Hitler that any sergeant-major could have carried them out. He inter-fered in everything and turned down every proposal we

made . . . We wanted to attack the weak bridgehead first.
But no; Hitler thought otherwise. The half-hearted dispersed
attack which resulted was simply nipped in the bud. If we
pulled a division out, Hitler ordered us to send it straight
back . . . When Cherbourg finally surrendered they sent us a
court-martial adviser. That was the sort of help we got . . .
(5)

On 13 June he wrote to his wife, telling her it was time for
'politics to come into play'. The Russian offensive was expected
any day; 'it will all be decided quickly'. (6)

The men in the front line knew it too. One of 21st Panzer's
soldiers wrote home on 16 June:

The men know that the battle is lost already. There's not a
chance any more. Not even the first V-weapons which thun-
der across the night skies towards England give them any
hope. The enemy gets stronger every day. One can feel it.
The 4th Company has received not a single replacement
since D–Day: not a man, not a machine, to replace our losses.
With other units it is the same. The troops are bled to death
. . . our task is simply to hold the enemy; no longer can we
attempt to drive him back. (7)

Rommel and von Rundstedt, wishing to impress the seriousness
of the situation on their Führer, demanded a conference. The
Führer arrived at Soissons on 17 June, meeting his field-marshals
at the headquarters built four years earlier for supervision of
the invasion of Britain. Not only military matters were discussed, Rommel protesting, with a lack of tact that did him
credit, the recent massacre at Oradour. 2nd S.S. Panzer Division
(*Das Reich*), en route for Normandy, had been deprived
of one of their officers by a Resistance bullet. In retaliation
they massacred the inhabitants of a village, only to find out
that it was the wrong one. Rommel demanded that the division
be punished; Hitler told him, once again, to mind his own
business.

Not that he was allowed to mind even that. The two field-
marshals asked for freedom of movement, for a chance to
withdraw and engage the Allied armour beyond the range
of the Royal Navy's guns. Hitler said the same to them as he
had to Manstein's similar scheme fifteen months before. Not a
yard was to be yielded. The V-weapons would win the war.

To Rommel's scarcely-veiled demand for peace negotiations he replied, quite correctly, that no one would make peace with him. Rundstedt and Rommel returned empty-handed to their H.Q.s, Rommel no doubt wondering if the Allies would make peace with *him*. Back at Soissons an errant V-1 had landed above Hitler's bunker and sent him scurrying back to Germany.

III

Around the perimeter of the bridgehead the German line yielded, bent, but did not break. The onus was now on the Allies to break the deadlock; the German forces could devote all their ingenuity and experience to breaking down the Allied offensives. The terrain aided them, especially to the west of Caen, where the *bocage* – small fields enclosed by thick hedges and earthworks, threaded by sunken lanes – offered ideal ground for defence. The lessons of the East had not been learnt in vain; the defence in depth, the *pakfront*, was as potent here as it had been in the Kursk salient.

The first line of defences, stretching back for about half a mile, was called the 'battle outposts'. Here a maze of inter-connecting trenches was dug, enabling rapid transfer of troops forward, backward or sideways. An attacking force entering this belt had much to contend with. Mines were liberally scattered, particularly on paths and roads. All the obvious axes of advance were pre-pinpointed for the artillery and mortar positions far in the rear. Machine-gun nests proliferated, creating potential lattices of crossfire against advancing infantry. The odd tank and self-propelled gun lay hidden in wait for the enemy armour. And snipers, often biding their time as the first wave went through, would pick off the less careful individuals of the second wave.

Camouflage was brought to a fine art in Normandy. The precious tanks, mostly deployed in the second 'advance position', were rendered as invisible as possible, both from ground level and the air. The hedges provided foliage; it was applied to the metal monsters with infinite care. All tell-tale tracks were painstakingly removed; grass bent back, corn re-arranged, dust smoothed out. The crews sat inside them for days on end, peering through the observation slits, waiting for the unsuspecting prey.

The 'advance position' was more heavily mined than the

'battle outposts', protected also by barbed wire, manned by the main force of tanks and self-propelled guns. This belt was about a mile deep. Three miles further back the final 'main position' housed the reserve troops, the heavy armour and artillery. All in all it was a formidable system, as the Allies found to their cost in the four-day attempt to throw a force around the west of Caen on 13–16 June. Like the Germans at Kursk they suffered heavy casualties for minimal ground. Unlike the Russians at Kursk, the Germans did not have either time nor numerical superiority on their side. Panzer *Lehr* might have accounted for over 200 enemy tanks in the Villers Bocage battles; it also lost close to a hundred of its own. The German losses, though less, were more significant. Montgomery's aim of bleeding the German panzer forces through heavy attritional warfare was paying off, as it had to do. After 8 June there was little risk involved, only blood. And, as Montgomery well knew, the Germans had less to spill.

So did the hapless Rommel and von Rundstedt. They knew it mattered little that the Germans had, generally, superior technique and equipment on their side. No matter how well, how bravely, the troops fought, they were slowly and inexorably being exhausted. No matter how superior a tank the Tiger was, it could not fight an enemy-held sky. True, the panzer divisions were flowing into Normandy. Both S.S. Panzer Corps, 1st, comprising 1st and 2nd S.S. Panzer Divisions, and 2nd, comprising 9th and 10th, had arrived by 28 June. So had the veteran 2nd Panzer. In anticipation of this force's arrival, plans had already been laid for an offensive directed through Balleroy and Bayeux to the sea, thus cutting the British and Canadians off from the Americans. The anticipation was sweeter than the actuality, for on 26 June Montgomery launched another attack west of Caen: 'Epsom'. This too failed in its territorial objective: the taking of Caen, but succeeded strategically; by the third day the entire panzer force gathered for the German offensive was fighting desperately to stem the enemy's. Clearly the line could not be held indefinitely, let alone pushed back. The field-marshals demanded another meeting with Hitler.

The Führer was not risking another trip to France. He received them at Berchtesgaden, amidst mounting reports of a catastrophe in Russia. The Red Army had gone over to the offensive on 22 June; Army Group Centre was disintegrating under the blow. The same fate was likely to befall the army in France, Rommel and Rundstedt informed their Führer, unless they were allowed a free hand. The German forces must be withdrawn across the Seine, now, before Seventh Army was encircled and annihilated.

Hitler seems to have been rather unhinged by the week's events. He pushed aside all his field-marshals' arguments with a welter of superlatives and instant solutions. The German Army need not fear, he told them excitedly. Soon the very latest types of aircraft, jet fighters and rocket bombers, would fill the sky above the bridgehead. Anti-aircraft highways would be constructed across France, guarded by guns on the ground and fighters in the sky. Destruction of the Royal Navy's artillery power, he emphasised, was of primary importance. Special bombs were being designed and produced for use against the battleships. With all this help on its way the Army need only hang on to its present positions. Rommel and von Rundstedt drove back to France, dejected and disgusted. They arrived to find the S.S. Panzer Corps utterly exhausted after failing to cut across the neck of the 'Epsom' advance. This, Rundstedt informed Keitel over the telephone, was the beginning of the end. 'What shall we do?' lamented the O.K.W. chief. Rundstedt was withering. 'Make peace, you fools. What else can you do?'

His subordinates were just as unhappy. Dollmann had died of a heart attack brought on by his anxiety about the situation. His successor in command of Seventh Army, S.S. General Paul Hausser, took an equally gloomy view. He and Geyr were both convinced that the German line must be pulled back out of range of the naval guns. They submitted reports to this effect and Rommel, who had already suggested as much, passed on their recommendations to Rundstedt. It seems that the two field-marshals decided to try the *fait accompli* where direct confrontation had failed. Rundstedt ordered all the preparations to be made for such a withdrawal, and then requested sanction for these orders from the Supreme Command. The response was immediate. The present line was to be held. The following day Rundstedt was given another decoration and informed that he had asked to be relieved. On 3 July von Kluge arrived to take over. The two leading generals involved in the conspiracy against Hitler were together in France. The moment for action was approaching.

IV

Field-Marshal Gunther von Kluge exemplified the tentative strand in the conspiracy that had been slowly tightening around the person of Adolf Hitler since 1938. He was a general of the old school, correct with a touch of vanity, possessed of that Prussian code of personal honour that proved so ill-equipped to face the political confrontations inherent in a war conducted by and for the National Socialist ideal. As a soldier he was competent but disinclined to take risks, as his running feud with Guderian amply demonstrated. As a conspirator he was even less so inclined. Yet for all this lack of resolution he was, excepting Rommel, the only field-marshal prepared to put himself at risk. During 1942 and 1943 his HQ at Army Group Centre had been a hotbed of military politicking. There von Kluge had tolerated Tresckow and Schlabrendorff's insistent plotting, even to the extent of turning a blind eye to the assassination attempt that misfired in March 1943. Some spark of social obligation flickered in his soul, ever-competing with the spark of self-preservation. Like the proverbial man between two stools von Kluge could find nowhere to sit down; like the moth to the flame he was drawn and repelled, eventually doomed to burning.

Both he and Rommel were aware that the conspiracy would soon take action against Hitler, but exactly how much more than that they knew is unknown. Rommel had not only reported the desperate Normandy situation to the Führer; he had also sent word to Beck, ex-Chief of the General Staff and titular head of the conspiracy. If action was to be taken it should be taken soon, Rommel advised, while there was still a military position with some bargaining power. Both he and von Kluge knew what was expected of them. With Hitler arrested or killed they were to approach the Allies in Normandy for an armistice.

Von Kluge, one suspects, was as happy with this arrangement as he could expect to be with any. Rommel probably had less faith in the civilian side of the conspiracy, a greater personal resolve, and a growing feeling that action in Berlin might achieve less than action in France. He told his son, shortly before his death, that

The revolt should not have been started in Berlin, but in the West. What could we have hoped to achieve by it? Only, in the end, that the expected forcible American and British occupation of Germany would have become an unopposed 'march-in', that the air attacks would have ceased, and that the Americans and British would have kept the Russians out of Germany. (8)

At the beginning of July 1944 he was still uncertain. If the conspirators in Berlin acted soon, well and good. If they did not, he was preparing to act on his own. First he had to convince his co-conspirator in the West that the war was lost.

Von Kluge had been staying at the Führer's HQ prior to assuming his new command, and had there proved as incapable of mental independence as ever. Just as Tresckow had convinced him at Army Group Centre that Hitler had to go, so Hitler at Berchtesgaden had little trouble inveigling him into the mad dance of ultimate victory. It took a few days for von Kluge to shake off the Führer's post-hypnotic, within which time he took Rommel sternly to task, informing him in less-than-gentlemanly tones that he would now have to learn to obey orders. Rommel was hardly pleased. It was bad enough to have the Führer interfering from Berchtesgaden, without the same blindness appearing on his own doorstep. The next day a memorandum arrived on Kluge's desk detailing, once more, the reasons for the German plight in France and Rommel's lack of responsibility for it. The troops had not been deployed where he wanted them; they had been moved, against his advice, directly under the Allies' bomb-sights in daylight; all his recommendations for attacking the weaker American bridgehead had been ignored. The memorandum was lengthy, cogent, and irrefutable. Von Kluge was not so hypnotised that he could not see that it tallied rather better than the Führer's version with what was actually happening.

Having helped the wavering von Kluge back on course Rommel turned to other obvious problems. It was all very well to approach the Allies for an armistice, with or without prior action against Hitler, but what would follow? Who knew how far loyalty to the Führer had been eroded by the apprehensions and despairs of a lost war? Rommel could be reasonably certain that the Army would follow him and von Kluge if they took resolute action, but the Army was not alone in France. The Luftwaffe's allegiances were unknown; the S.S., whose panzer divisions in Normandy outnumbered those of the Army, might prove hostile. There was also the civilian Gestapo. Through

June and July Rommel managed to keep the reliable 116th Panzer in reserve against the period of uncertainty. But otherwise the plans were little more than gambles. 21st Panzer was assigned the disarming of 12th S.S., an ominous prospect.

V

On the battlefield the familiar cycle continued. The Germans brought fresh infantry into the line facing the British, thus hoping to free their armour for use against the expected American break-out. The British then attacked to hold the armour where it was. German armour or no German armour, the Americans continued to struggle in the *bocage*. The Allied build-up forged ahead of the German. It was only a matter of time, even if it was taking more time than had been expected. The Germans knew this as well as their enemy; the latter's low level of tactical and sub-strategic imagination gave them only temporary respite.

This lack of imagination reached a new high with the 7 July 'Charnwood' offensive. Having failed to envelop Caen, Montgomery decided to storm it frontally. Naturally there was to be an intensive air bombardment beforehand. Bomber Command, more used to aiming at cities than soldiers, insisted that the zone of attack be not less than six miles from the Allied front lines, lest they bomb their own men. This caution might have been more admirable had it taken cognisance of the fact that the German front lines were also less than six miles from the Allied line. To compound the error further the air attack was timed six hours in advance of the ground attack. The German defences were both warned and virtually untouched. The inhabitants of Caen were less fortunate, some thousands of them dying in the air attack. It is hard to disagree with McKee's assessment that this was the 'greatest single atrocity of the Normandy campaign'. (9) As for the ground attack, it struggled forward with heavy losses to take most of the city. The crucial part – the high ground south of the river – remained in German hands.

Looking back on offensives like 'Charnwood' it is tempting to wonder how long the bridgehead itself would have sustained had the Germans managed to shake themselves free of the notion that an attack north of the Seine was still imminent. In this they were once more their own worst enemies, for in the previous year O.K.W., as usual fighting O.K.H. for priorities, had deliberately inflated the intelligence estimate of the Allied divisions assembling in Britain. Having used this falsification to bolster their demands for larger German forces in the West they could not then counter Hitler's arguments that the Allies still had sufficient forces in Britain for another landing, without admitting that they had been fooling him all along. So Fifteenth Army was still sitting in the Atlantic defences north of the Seine with 150,000 men, almost half the number engaged around the bridgehead. Normandy was one of the last great triumphs of Hitler's appalling system of command.

By the middle of July it was finally dawning on the Germans that another invasion in strength was now unlikely, and some of the troops who had waited in vain along the Pas de Calais coast were shifted west to Normandy. Caution was still the watchword – Fifteenth Army did not march *en masse* across the Seine – but four fresh and experienced infantry divisions arrived in the third week of July to provide Rommel with another chance of extracting his armour from the front line. This the Allies, with their dominance of the air, could not help noticing. So another attack in the east was called for as the interminable wait for the great American break-out in the west continued.

Having tried a right hook around Caen and a major frontal assault, Montgomery now opted for the full set with a plan to swing a left hook round the city. Three armoured divisions would cross the Orne and advance southwards towards the Caen-Falaise road. Their path would be cleared by Bomber Command. The idea was to reactivate German fears of a break-out in the direction of Paris. In this, if in nothing else, 'Goodwood' succeeded.

Yet again the enemy dispositions were mislocated. The defences were thought to stretch back for three or four miles; in fact they were ten miles in depth. The bombing pulverised the forward infantry positions, but the zone of attack fell short of the German armour and artillery concentrations. The three Allied armoured divisions advanced out of their narrow bridge-head east of the Orne on 18 July with insufficient infantry support. To the German gunners they looked like metal ducks on a shooting gallery conveyer belt. By evening 200 tanks were smouldering on the plain. Rommel, who had supervised the defensive preparations, would have been as satisfied as any German general could be in July 1944, had he been there. He was not. Instead he was fighting for his life in a military hospital, unaware that his soldiering days were all behind him.

Three days before 'Goodwood' began he had directed Speidel in the drafting of a final report to Hitler. It was, he told his Chief of Staff, Hitler's last chance. If it did not induce the Führer to either open peace negotiations or make way for someone who could then he, Rommel, would feel himself free to do so.

The report's tone was of unmitigated pessimism. For all the defensive successes, to which the repulse of 'Goodwood' would soon be added, 'the situation on the Normandy front is growing worse every day and is approaching a grave crisis'. The Allied supremacy in tanks, artillery, air power, infantry, the report continued, was inexorably eroding the German strength. Of the 97,000 German casualties so far incurred, only 10,000 had been replaced. Seventeen new tanks had arrived to make up 225 losses. 'The newly arrived infantry divisions are raw, and, with their small establishment of artillery, anti-tank guns and close-combat anti-tank weapons, are in no state to make a lengthy stand against major enemy attacks.' The destruction of French roads and railways had made the movement of supplies a nightmare; only the barest necessities were getting through. No new forces could be made available without stripping the Mediterranean and Pas de Calais regions of minimal cover. The Allied forces in contrast were increasing each day; the pressure on the bridgehead perimeter correspondingly growing. The dam was about to burst.

In these circumstances we must expect that in the foreseeable future the enemy will succeed in breaking through our thin front . . . we dispose of no mobile reserve for defence against such a breakthrough . . . The troops are everywhere fighting heroically, but the unequal struggle is approaching its end. (10)

In his own handwriting Rommel appended: 'It is urgently necessary for the proper conclusion to be drawn from this situation. As C-in-C of the Army Group I feel myself in duty bound to speak plainly on this point.'

The report was dispatched to von Kluge for forwarding to Hitler. Four years after writing to his wife of the Führer's wonderful visit to 7th Panzer HQ he was challenging Adolf Hitler for the right to determine Germany's future. The contest was not to be held. On 17 July, one day before 'Goodwood', three before Stauffenberg placed the bomb, the RAF caught up with him. Returning in the evening to Army Group HQ his car was attacked by a fighter-bomber. Rommel suffered severe injuries, including a multiple fracture of the skull. The conspiracy had lost its sustaining power in the West; Germany had lost her chance of an early peace.

VI

At 12.35 p.m. on 20 July Stauffenberg placed his bomb-loaded briefcase underneath the map-table in the Rastenburg briefing-room, muttered that he had a phone call to make and left. The ten-minute fuse was accurate. At 12.42 the conference was interrupted by a resounding explosion. Stauffenberg, un-aware that someone with cramped legs had moved the briefcase behind the thick table support, to the side furthest from Hitler, gleefully began the journey back to Berlin, where his co-conspirators would already be moving to assume the authority of the dead Führer.

Back in the capital his associates were waiting rather than moving. Another of their number, stationed at Rastenburg, had been supposed to phone through with news of the assassination attempt. He had not. Hardly had the last echoes of the explosion faded away before the Rastenburg S.S. had cut all communications with the outside world. This the group waiting in Berlin did not know.

They were a strange little community. Retired soldiers, right-wing nationalist politicians whose liberal streak would not dissolve, young Army officers with an idealistic bent. The titular head was General Beck, whose planned Army coup in 1938 had been aborted by the Anglo-French betrayal at Munich. Then he had been Chief of the General Staff, now he was a soldier commanding great respect but no troops. Field-Marshal Witzleben, who had been retired sometime after the Western Campaign, had similar credentials. He was to take over command of the Army. The leading civilian was Karl Goerdeler, ex-Mayor of Leipzig, who had resigned that office when the city's Mendelssohn statue was taken down on racial grounds.

These three were not to implement the coup; they were to wield the power it won. The actual executors were those gathered in the War Ministry waiting for news of Stauffenberg's attempt. Olbricht, Quartermaster-General of the Reserve Army, was the one who would give the orders for 'Valkyrie' to commence. This was the code-name for seizure of key-points in the event of Allied air-landings or a revolt of the foreign workforce; an ironic cover for the coup against Hitler. 'Valkyrie' had already been set in motion once, five days earlier, when Stauffenberg had stayed his hand on account of the absence of Himmler and Göring. It had, with difficulty, been explained away as an exercise. They had to be sure this time.

In Olbricht's office the minutes ticked slowly by. Rumours arrived of an explosion at Rastenburg, but no news of Hitler's death or survival. At 3.30 the conspirators got through to the Wolfsschanze on the telephone, only to learn what they already knew, that an attempt had been made on Hitler's life. Still no news of success or failure. Olbricht had to make a decision. Stauffenberg would not return before 4.45 at the earliest; 'Valkyrie' had to be ordered before then if it was to be ordered at all. For all Olbricht knew, the Führer was dead and the S.S. seizing control. Hoeppner, the panzer commander dismissed in disgrace in December 1941, was too nervous to offer him any help. At 3.45 Olbricht made up his mind. If Hitler was dead they must rush to fill his place; if not they must risk everything anyway. There was no going back. The telephone calls went out, carrying the codewords.

In Paris one of Kluge's staff, Colonel Finckh, picked up the receiver to hear the word *'abgelaufen'* (launched). He ordered his car and drove to the General Staff HQ of the Western Command. There he told Kluge's Chief of Staff, Blummentritt, that Hitler was dead and a provisional government forming in Berlin under Beck, Witzleben and Goerdeler. Blummentritt tried to phone Kluge. He was out, inspecting the front-line. He would not be back until evening.

The military governor of Paris was General Stulpnagel, a long-time conspirator. His job was to arrest the S.S. and Gestapo in the city. It was also, Beck told him over the phone around six o'clock, to stiffen von Kluge's resolve. Stulpnagel gave his orders for the Paris round-up and set off to visit Kluge at La Roche-Guyon.

The sixty-two-year-old Field-Marshal had meanwhile returned from the front and was busy relaxing from the exertions of the day when Beck came through on the telephone at around seven o'clock. At the same moment Kluge was handed a transcript of Goebbels's radio broadcast. The Führer was not dead, said the transcript. The Führer might be dead, said Beck. It might be a bluff. Stauffenberg had seen the explosion, but . . . Von Kluge was not about to commit himself on a series of 'mights'. He reminded Beck that he had only agreed to act if the Führer was dead. 'I'll ring you back,' he said.

Shortly after this Blummentritt arrived from Paris. He had with him an order signed by Field-Marshal von Witzleben. This impressed von Kluge. Perhaps Hitler was dead. 'This is an historic moment, you know,' he said to his Chief of Staff. 'I would like to order a cessation of the V-1s immediately. If the Führer *is* dead we ought to get in touch with the other side right away.' He sat back to consider. The telephone rang again. It was Warlimont, O.K.W.'s Deputy Chief of Operations, speaking from Rastenburg. The Führer was *not* dead. Kluge sat back once more, his mind made up.

Stulpnagel had promised Beck that he would act whether or not Hitler was dead. At dusk he drove through Kluge's front gates with two fellow conspirators, Colonel Hofacker and Speidel's brother-in-law Dr Horst. Kluge and Blummentritt welcomed them in and a conference ensued. Hofacker strenuously tried to convince the Field-Marshal that he should act regardless. Germany needed such action. His pleas fell on deaf ears. Rommel might – probably would – have listened. Kluge merely said: 'Gentlemen, it's misfired.'

It had misfired more than he knew, for after a pleasant candlelit dinner Stulpnagel informed him that the arrests of S.S. and Gestapo were already underway in Paris. Kluge was momentarily furious, then calmed himself and told Stulpnagel he must do his best to undo the damage. The two parted sadly, aware of failure and the cost still to be borne . . . 'If only that swine was dead,' Kluge mourned, as he accompanied Stulpnagel to his car. 'You must consider yourself suspended from duty,' he added. 'You had better just disappear.'

Stulpnagel arrived back in Paris soon after midnight to find his staff drowning their apprehension in champagne. Hitler was to broadcast sometime during the night. Stulpnagel took a glass and waited with the rest, listening to the martial music blaring out of the radio. At 1 a.m. it faded away, and the voice of the German Führer pronounced sentence.

It is unthinkable that at the front hundreds of thousands, no millions, should be giving their all while a gang of ambitious and miserable creatures here at home tries perpetually to sabotage them. This time we are going to settle accounts with them in the way to which we National Socialists are accustomed . . . (11)

It had already begun. Beck, after two attempts, had been assisted in the taking of his own life. Stauffenberg had been executed in the War Ministry courtyard, shouting a last defiance at his murderers, hidden behind the blinding lorry headlights.

In Paris Stulpnagel ordered the release of the detained S.S. and Gestapo. The S.S. commander, General Oberg, was a former Army man and not inclined to make difficulties. He took champagne with Stulpnagel and shook him by the hand. But it was too late. At 9 a.m. the telephone rang once more. It was Keitel ordering him to report in Berlin. Stulpnagel considered, ate lunch, and set out across France. In the vicinity of the Meuse he asked his driver to stop, left the car and walked away. Within minutes a shot was heard. The driver, rushing after the general, found him unconscious, floating in the nearby river. He was not dead, merely minus an eye. Hurried to Verdun military hospital for an operation he eventually recovered consciousness, deliriously muttering the word: 'Rommel'.

Stulpnagel was not the only one with Rommel on his mind. At La Roche-Guyon von Kluge was wondering how best to cover his tracks. First he sent off a full report of Stulpnagel's activities the previous day. But, he wondered, did this smack of a guilty conscience? Rommel's 'ultimatum' to Hitler was still lying on his desk. Von Kluge decided to forward it, perhaps with such cunning motives, perhaps with a last spark of defiance. Most likely the soldier was again taking possession of his soul, pulling him out of those dangerous winds of politics and social morality, back into the safe haven of his profession. Coup or no coup, the military situation in Normany had not blown away.

I forward herewith a report from Field-Marshal Rommel, which he gave to me before his accident and which he had already discussed with me. I have now been here for about fourteen days and, after long discussions with the responsible commanders on the various fronts, especially the S.S. leaders, I have come to the conclusion that the Field-Marshal was, unfortunately, right . . .

I came here with the fixed intention of making effective your order to make a stand *at any price*. But when one sees that this price must be paid by the slow and sure destruction of our troops – I am thinking of the *Hitler Jugend* Division, which has earned the highest praise . . . then the anxiety about the immediate future on this front is only too well justified . . .

In spite of all our endeavours, the moment is fast approaching when this overtaxed front is bound to break up . . . I consider it my duty as the responsible commander to bring these developments to your notice in good time, my Führer. (12)

It was not a difficult prediction to make.

On 25 July the American assault was launched. The four-mile stretch of front running west from St Lô, held by Panzer *Lehr*, was attacked by over two thousand American bombers to a depth of two miles. Each bomber had only to plough a strip some ten feet wide. Bayerlein's division was virtually annihilated.

Units holding the front were almost completely wiped out, despite, in many cases, the best possible equipment of tanks, anti-tank guns and self-propelled guns. Back and forth the bomb carpets were laid, artillery positions were wiped out, tanks overturned and buried, infantry positions flattened and all roads and tracks destroyed. By midday the entire area resembled a moon landscape, with the bomb craters touching rim to rim, and there was no longer any hope of getting out any of our weapons. All signals communications had been cut and no command was possible. The shock effect on the troops was indescribable. Several of the men went mad and rushed dementedly around in the open until they were cut down by splinters. Simultaneously with the storm from the air, innumerable guns of the U.S. artillery poured drumfire into our field positions. (13)

That evening Bayerlein was brought an order. He was to hold the line. Not a single soldier was to leave his post. Bayerlein looked up at the sprightly staff officer who had conveyed these instructions. 'Out in front everyone is holding out,' he said slowly. 'Everyone. My grenadiers and my engineers and my tank crews – they're all holding their ground. Not a single man is leaving his post. Not one! They're lying in their foxholes mute and silent, for they are dead.' (14)

The order stood. It made no difference. This time there was to be no mistake. First the infantry, then the armour, plodded through the widening hole in the German line. One hundred and sixteenth and 2nd Panzer, sent west to plug the gap, were attacked so repeatedly from the air, both en route and in their assigned assembly area, that the counter-attack never got started. Within days the Americans were breaking free of the *bocage*, and letting Patton off the leash.

This was only one crisis. On the other side of Europe the Red Army was streaming towards the Vistula. Across the river the Poles were poised to seize their capital.

In Berlin the grisly farce of the conspiracy trials was soon to begin. In a French hospital bed Rommel talked with Admiral Ruge of the technical problems involved in drawing energy from the ocean tides. The handyman was still alive, if only for a short time more.

The war still had nine months to run. The failure to secure peace in the West implied occupation from the East. The German people rallied to their Führer, who alone possessed power over their lives, and thus offered the only conceivable hope of salvation. A 'joke' went the rounds of the ruined cities: 'Enjoy the war; peace will be dreadful.'

References (Chapter 8)

1. *The Rommel Papers*, 496
2. quoted in McKee, *Caen*, 89
3. quoted in Belfield and Essame, *Normandy*, 73
4. Ibid, 74
5. *The Rommel Papers*, 495
6. Ibid, 491
7. quoted in McKee, *Caen*, 143
8. *The Rommel Papers*, 486
9. McKee, *Caen*, 221
10. *The Rommel Papers*, 487
11. quoted in Manvell, *The Conspirators*, 132
12. quoted in Young, *Rommel*, 231–2
13. quoted in Belfield and Essame, *Normandy*, 201
14. quoted in Carell, *Invasion*, 267–8

Chapter 9

REICH AUTUMN

The fifth spring came and still the war
No glimpse of peace supplied.
The soldier drew the consequence
A hero's death he died.

(Bertolt Brecht)

On 18 July Guderian had received a visit from his old Luftwaffe liaison officer, General von Barsewisch. The two had gone for a long ramble in the woods, and there, far from prying ears, Barsewisch told his friend of the impending assassination attempt and the possibility of von Kluge negotiating a separate armistice in the West. The conspirators, he said, wanted Guderian's active participation.

The Inspector-General was hardly shocked by the thought-process, but perhaps shaken by the imminence of action. He reluctantly refused Barsewisch's request. He could not break his oath; he must pursue his duty as a German officer. This latter he then proceeded to interpret rather widely. He did not have Barsewisch arrested or convey a report of the conversation to higher levels. Instead he undertook on the following day a lightning inspection tour of all those forces in or around Berlin and Rastenburg, forces whose loyalty might prove decisive in the event of a coup. He also granted a request from General Thomale, his conspiratorially-minded Chief of Staff, that panzer units due for dispatch eastward should be held in Berlin another day for use in an 'Operation Valkyrie' exercise. Guderian knew what this implied. He was not going to partake of the plot, but if it succeeded he was determined that the Army and not the S.S. or Party should pick up the reins dropped by a fallen Führer. This, to him, was keeping faith with his oath and pursuing the duty of a German officer.

The next day – which Thomale's request had suggested was *the* day – Guderian spent at home. Following the example of an old commander who used to take long walks when trouble loomed Guderian spent the afternoon incommunicado, out inspecting his estate. Thus insulated from the drama unfolding in Rastenburg, Berlin and Paris he tensely awaited news. Around four o'clock a dispatch rider caught up with him. He could expect a telephone call from Supreme Headquarters. Back at his house he heard that the radio had announced a failed assassination attempt on the beloved Führer. No decision was now necessary. The evening was spent in waiting for the expected call. Around midnight, as Stulpnagel's staff were drinking their forlorn champagne in far-off Paris, it came through. Thomale gave Guderian the astonishing news that he was the new Chief of the General Staff. Through a chain of reasoning known only to himself the narrow escape had persuaded Hitler to sack Zeitzler. Guderian was to report to Hitler on the following day.

It is not hard to imagine the contradictory thoughts and feelings crowding Guderian's mind as he made the journey to Rastenburg. He was assuming the most prestigious post in the German Army, at a time when the Army was in full retreat across the breadth of Europe, involved in a permanent crisis of confidence with its Commander-in-Chief, which had climaxed the previous day with his attempted assassination. It was hardly an auspicious moment to realise a life's ambition.

He was greeted with express instructions from Hitler not to resign. This was hardly a premonition of harmony. Reaching his new office things did not improve.

I then attempted to telephone the army groups in order to find out the situation at the front. There were three telephones in the Chief of Staff's office, and no way of telling what purpose each one served. I picked up the nearest one. A female voice answered. When I said my name she screamed and hung up on me. (1)

Nerves were worn thin at Rastenburg, thin as the German fronts. These should have been Guderian's first priority. Hitler had other ideas. Though claiming that only a small clique had been responsible for the plot against him he used it to punish the whole Army. Guderian, who wanted unity above all else and realised that Hitler was its only possible source, was an obedient if unenthusiastic servant. He found himself preparing nauseating declarations of the Army's fidelity, accepting, at last, the Nazi salute for the Army, and attending the 'Courts of

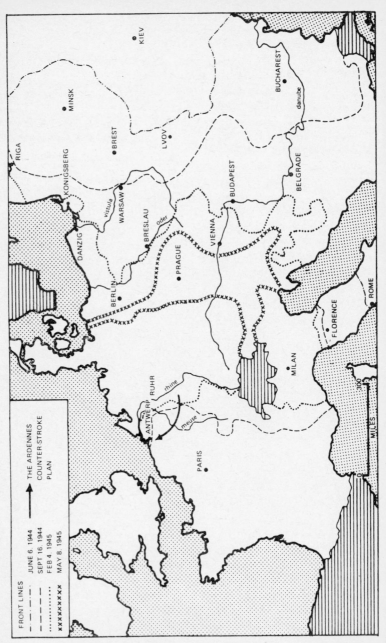

21　THE SHRINKING REICH

Honour' which delivered Army personnel to the 'people's revenge' meted out by the Nazi courts.

It might seem difficult for Guderian to have justified acceptance of this role to himself. But really there was little choice. Unlike Rommel he had more than merely mental horizons to transcend. Guderian was a Prussian, and it was his homeland that lay in the path of the Soviet advance. For him at least the duty of his professionalism was unequivocal; the skill he possessed must be used to beat back the Bolshevik hordes. All else was subordinate to this, a feeling, as we shall see, shared by von Kluge and Rommel. It is ironic that the situation that most closely parallels that of the German generals in July 1944 was that of the leading Bolsheviks in the 1920s. Everything had gone wrong, and each conscience chose a different path. As Trotsky challenged Stalin, so Rommel prepared to challenge Hitler; as Zinoviev and Kamenev dithered between deference and defiance so did von Kluge; as Bukharin stayed with Stalin, stayed within the source of power, so Guderian stayed with Hitler, almost to the end, because only with Hitler could anything be achieved, could anything be saved from the wreck.

The situation when he took over was, as he put it with a certain understatement, 'appalling'. Since the beginning of the Soviet offensive of 22 June there had occurred the aptly-named 'destruction of Army Group Centre'. Twenty-five divisions had been consumed in the fire of the Soviet advance. The Dnieper, where Guderian had argued with Kluge three years before, had been left far behind. In the south–central sector the Russians had reached the upper Vistula, in the centre they were approaching Brest, in the north–central sector knocking at the gates of East Prussia. By the end of July they were on the Vistula, in the east bank suburbs of Warsaw. There the momentum ran out. The Red Army had covered nearly five hundred miles in six weeks, and had far outdistanced the capacity of its supply services.

In the north and south it was a different story. The width of the German front had expanded as the Army retreated west of the narrow neck of land between Memel and Odessa. Army Groups North and South Ukraine were becoming increasingly disconnected from the central front. In the former Army Group's case this had been made explicit by the Red Army, who had reached the sea west of Riga on the day Guderian took office, thereby cutting it off. In the far south an even greater catastrophe had occurred. At the end of August the Red Army lunged into Rumania, overrunning most of the country within a fortnight. In the process Rumania changed sides. Bulgaria would soon follow suit. On 3 September Finland sued for peace. Only Hungary remained of the German allies, anxiously scanning the lower Danube for the coming Soviet onslaught.

Guderian's efforts to shore up this collapsing position were hampered by shortage of troops and decisions taken by his superiors. Having reconnected Army Group North with a swift drive of Manteuffel's panzers he was unable to secure its necessary withdrawal. Needless to say the Soviets proceeded to cut it off again, and, also needless to say, Hitler refused to sanction its withdrawal again, this time by sea. Its fifty divisions, he said, would tie down a large Soviet force, safeguard Swedish iron ore deliveries, and protect the U-boat training grounds in the Baltic. Guderian, who had other ideas for those fifty divisions, was unimpressed. He wanted a strategic reserve.

Nevertheless the breathing-space granted in the central sector was welcome enough, as it provided time for the construction of fortified defence positions. Hitler, who had always opposed these as unnecessary encouragement of his generals' tendency to retreat, had at last grasped their importance. Unfortunately, not only did he insist that they be built in the wrong place, too close up behind the front line, but he had too few troops left to man them. Guderian's suggested volunteer force was co-opted by Bormann for the Party; their consequent quality of leadership fulfilled his most pessimistic predictions. Those full combat divisions still being raised and equipped in Germany were all being sent West. In the East now, as had been the case in Normandy, it was a matter of waiting. For the water to rise, for the dam to burst.

II

One of Guderian's first requests on being appointed O.K.H. Chief of Staff – a post, it might be remembered, exclusively concerned with the Eastern front – was for von Kluge's dismissal in the West. Old scores were still being counted. 'He did not have a lucky touch in commanding large armoured formations,' Guderian maliciously informed his Führer. (2) Von Kluge did not have a lucky touch in treason either. Hitler knew all about it. 'He had foreknowledge of the assassination attempt,' he interrupted Guderian, only to be persuaded by

Keitel and Jodl that von Kluge was, for the moment, militarily indispensable. Hitler, also for the moment, concurred.

This was on 21 July, the day von Kluge had dispatched his and Rommel's appreciation of the military situation in the West. In the weeks that followed there was no improvement. Another attempt to cut through the bottleneck of the American break-out failed around Mortain, and Seventh Army, forbidden the wholesale retreat which alone made sense, found itself caught between the American sweep around its left flank and the British–Canadian drive down on its right. One hundred thousand men were trapped in the Falaise pocket, and only through the most strenuous efforts were 30,000 broken free. Sixty thousand prisoners were left behind, and 10,000 dead.

Even before the magnitude of this disaster had become apparent von Kluge's military indispensability had run out. Hitler had concluded that his plans failed because von Kluge wanted them to fail. The Field-Marshal then committed the indiscretion of being caught in an Allied bombing raid, and was thus out of touch with Supreme Headquarters for most of a day, 15 August. Hitler feared von Kluge was arranging an armistice behind his back. Three days later Model arrived to take over, Kluge's dismissal in his hands. The Field-Marshal sat down to write his Führer a last letter.

When you receive these lines I shall be no more . . . I am dispatching myself where thousands of my comrades have already gone . . .

I do not know whether Field-Marshal Model . . . will yet master the situation. From my heart I hope so but, if this should not be the case, and if your new, greatly desired weapons, especially those for the Luftwaffe, should not succeed, then, my Führer, make up your mind to end the war. The German people have borne such untold suffering that it is time to put an end to this frightfulness. There must be ways to obtain this object and above all to prevent the Reich from falling under the Bolshevist heel. (3)

With this last submissive plea en route for Germany, von Kluge set out to follow it in his car. Stopping in the vicinity of Metz he ate a picnic beneath the shade of trees close to the road. There, with the air of a moth flying calmly into the flame, he took poison.

A week earlier Rommel had been moved from the hospital at Vesinet to his Heerlingen home in southern Germany. There he gradually recovered his strength, and by mid-August was well enough to take walks, jot down notes on his campaigns, and express continued disgust with the way the war was being conducted. Nothing annoyed him so much as the moving of troops from East to West. It was the Russians who were the real enemy, who had to be kept at bay at all costs. 'These fools,' he cried out to his son, 'they think of nothing but their own skins. What good is it to them to prolong their miserable lives by a few more months? The Eastern front will simply crack and the next Russian push will bring them into German territory. We all know what that means.' (4)

His opinion of the Supreme Command was apparently mutual. His superiors seemed little interested in his recovery, which surprised Frau Rommel but not her husband. He received news of von Kluge's suicide; then, at the beginning of September Speidel, his ex-Chief of Staff, was dismissed and summoned to Berlin. Rommel wrote a letter of protest on his behalf to Hitler but received no more reply than sundry suspicious characters lurking in the neighbourhood of his home. On 7 October Rommel himself was ordered to Berlin, to 'discuss his future employment'. He declined on grounds of health. Another five days of silence elapsed. Then, on 13 October, he was informed by telephone that Generals Burgsdorf and Maisel would be arriving to see him at noon the next day. The following morning he went for a long walk with his son, who remembered the following conversation.

> 'At twelve o'clock today,' my father said, 'two generals are coming to see me to discuss my future employment. So today will decide what is planned for me; whether a People's Court or a new command in the East.' 'Would you accept such a command?' I asked. He took me by the arm, and replied: 'My dear boy, our enemy in the East is so terrible that every other consideration has to give way before it. If he succeeds in overrunning Europe, even only temporarily, it will be the end of everything which has made life appear worth living. Of course I would go.' (5)

The generals arrived punctually. They had no Eastern Command to offer Rommel, only a choice between a People's Court and suicide. The former included a trip to Berlin – a trip

Rommel was convinced he would never complete alive – and dire consequences for his family. The latter comprised a quick death by poison ('the pill takes only three seconds to act, Herr Feldmarschall'), a state funeral with full honours, and security for his family. Rommel chose the latter. Within an hour he was lying dead in the back of the generals' car, parked off the road to Ulm. The pill took closer to five minutes.

Four days later his cortège rode through Ulm. Rundstedt, chosen to read the funeral oration, announced that Rommel's heart had belonged to the Führer. His voice apparently lacked conviction. If he did not know the circumstances of death,* Rundstedt knew very well Rommel's true feelings for his Führer.

III

Von Kluge's successor on the Western front, if it could still be called that, was Field-Marshal Walther Model. The imposing but ineffectual Rundstedt was also coaxed out of retirement once more for figurehead purposes. Model was only fifty-four, the youngest Field-Marshal in the Reich's short history, by all accounts not very imposing but certainly extremely effective. In many ways he was more like Rommel than any of his other peers, but seemingly without the strong streak of basic 'decency' which characterised the 'Desert Fox'. That is perhaps a harsh judgement. Model was wanted for war-crimes in Russia; so were many others. Rommel never fought in Russia, was never subjected to the slow brutalisation that the war there seemed to inflict on gentleman and peasant alike. Perhaps Model was the Rommel who did fight in Russia, with dash, vigour, a strong tactical sense. In the summer of 1941 he had led Guderian's panzer spearhead, then for a year and a half commanded Ninth Army in its central defensive role, finally leading it, against his better judgement, into the cauldron of *Zitadelle*. In August 1944, when he received his transfer west, he had just performed miracles in restoring the shattered German front along the Vistula. Now he was expected to do likewise on the Seine.

One of the reasons for his run of success – rare among German generals in 1944 – was his favourable relationship with

---

* Rundstedt said after the war that he would have refused the assignment had he known. His behaviour after the funeral – refusing to attend the cremation or visit the bereaved home – lends support to the belief that he guessed considerably more than he knew.

Hitler. Model was a rough-and-ready sort of person, not at all the caustic nose-sniffling Prussian archetype for whom Hitler felt such a vitriolic mixture of envy and contempt. Model did not despise Hitler or the Nazis as upstarts; he gave them their due as the leadership of the Reich. He accepted Hitler as his superior in the chain of command, without compromising that submission through believing him a social inferior. He thus felt little of the reluctance experienced by many of his fellow generals in doing what he had been trained as a soldier to do – achieve militarily the goals laid down by the political leadership. For Model the distinction between the two areas of action was still clear. He was the first general to repledge his fidelity after 20 July; he was the one who most often took rankly insubordinate action. Because of the first he was allowed to get away with the second. In this one relationship was concentrated most of the mutual trust still existent in the German Army of late summer 1944.

In France there was sore need for someone who could do what had to be done. On the day Model arrived the jaws were closing around the Falaise pocket and Patton's armour was streaking eastwards towards the Seine. For the next eleven days Model had to move heaven and earth, both to extricate his troops from the Falaise pocket and to get them back across the Seine before the Americans, moving down the river's west bank, joined hands with a British–Canadian drive on Rouen and trapped them in another, larger, pocket. That any of Seventh Army and Fifth Panzer Army (as the remaining armoured strength was now styled) got across the river was a matter of rejoicing for the Germans. Harried all the way by the Allied air forces, towards a wide and bridgeless river, they could of necessity save little equipment. Of the 2,300 tanks committed in Normany only 100–120 got back across the Seine. The ten-week battle had cost the Army nearly half a million casualties, and there was precious little strength remaining between the Allies and the Reich itself. The panzer divisions, Model reported, had between five and ten tanks each. The sixteen infantry divisions brought across the Seine contained enough troops for four. Seventh and Fifth Panzer Armies would not be holding the line of the Seine: they were, he told Hitler, retreating to the Somme. He advised the speedy strengthening of the fortifications on the German border. The front could be held, he added, if reinforced by thirty to thirty-five infantry and twelve panzer divisions.

These, not surprisingly, were unavailable. The German Army in France fought its way homeward, the Allied infantry in pursuit, the Allied armour already in its rear. By 31 August Patton had reached the Meuse at Verdun, the following day the Moselle. In the north British armour rolled into Brussels on 3 September, Antwerp on the 4th. Between these two spearheads and the Rhine was virtually nothing. Facing Patton's six strong divisions were five weak German, with few tanks or anti-tank guns; facing the British was the hastily assembled First Parachute Army, a grandiose title for a scratch force of some 18,000 policemen, sailors, boys and walking wounded. On the whole 'front' the Germans had less than a hundred tanks and 570 aircraft. In each department the Allies had a more than twenty to one advantage. And in the sector between Aachen and Metz, where Guderian's panzers had poured forth four years before, there were eight infantry battalions.

Yet the Allied advance stalled. Supply lines were lengthening; those of the Germans contracting. Petrol in particular was running short, and was certainly insufficient to fuel the broad front strategy insisted upon by Eisenhower. One daring thrust through north, south or centre might have proved decisive, but the Allies argued, hesitated, threw the chance away. By mid-September the Germans had recovered sufficient strength to slow the advance almost to a standstill. Montgomery, pushing forward too fast and too late, found disaster at Arnhem. Patton, seeking to emulate Attila the Hun's capture of Metz, spent a month bloodying his nose on the fortress walls. In the West, as in the East, the front stabilised. It was still merely a matter of time, but time was something the Wehrmacht dearly needed.

IV

As in the autumn of 1944 the Allies wound up their armies for the final spring, Hitler feverishly scraped the barrels of German manpower, and Speer, with a last desperate effort, cajoled the armaments industry to production figures undreamed of in the years of victory. The men and equipment for the last armies were being gathered. How and where would they be used?

To Guderian it was obvious. Defensively, and in the East. A fresh Red Army onslaught could not long be delayed. The thaw would harden into the frost of December; the German forces as they were would not be strong enough to resist the forces unleashed. The last German reserves must go East, to protect Mother Prussia from violation by the 'Red hordes'. If this meant defeat in the West, then so it would be. Better peace with the Anglo-Americans in Germany, conditions or no conditions, than peace under Soviet occupation.

To Hitler this was not the issue. If the Reich lost then the Reich perished. Caring nothing for Germany he cared not to alleviate defeat. Rather he would still seek victory, whatever the consequences. All or nothing. The Wehrmacht must attack. Not in the East; there was no objectives within reach, no cracks in the stolid Soviet will. Stalin like himself was a man of steel. But in the West, yes, one swift pulverising blow and the Alliance would burst apart. The last reserves must be used there, preferably against the Americans, their army of 'bank clerks and Jewish hoodlums'. They would learn to leave Europe alone if showed the gleam of the German sword. And then, once more, the might of the Reich could be shifted east against the barbarians.

The idea of a Western offensive was first broached on 19 August, amidst the carnage of Falaise. Jodl noted in his diary that the Führer was resolved to attack in November, when the weather had grounded the Allied air forces. A month later, on 16 September, Hitler confided the latest fruit of his intuition to Guderian, Keitel and Jodl. Another *Blitzkrieg*, again out of the Ardennes, this time aimed north and west across the Meuse to Antwerp. The British would again be cut off, this time annihilated. Though the 'Stalingrads' in the East would soon have German names Hitler still chased the decisive 'Dunkirk'. Two panzer armies would perform the task, a third army would cover the southern flank of their surge across Belgium. Such a force could not but succeed. Even should fortune favour the enemy, his offensive plans would be disrupted, his morale weakened. Time would be gained. Time for the new weapons. Time for the unlikely coalition to collapse. Then, perhaps, Germany would sue for an honourable peace.

Jodl drafted the plan to Hitler's specifications, and on 24 October Krebs and Westphal, Chiefs of Staff to Model and Rundstedt respectively, were summoned to the Wolfsschanze for the first briefing. The primary role was allotted to Sepp Dietrich's newly refitted Sixth S.S. Panzer Army. This, the current apple of Hitler's Army, would strike west from the front running Monschau–Losheim. The infantry would then assume a blocking position between Monschau and Verviers while the panzers swept around both sides of Liège, crossed the Meuse and headed for Antwerp. Four S.S. panzer divisions were involved: 1st, 2nd, 9th and 12th. Further south between Manderfeld and Vianden, Fifth Panzer Army included three Army panzer divisions – 2nd, *Lehr* and 116th – and several supporting infantry formations. Its commander would be General Hasso von Manteuffel, recently promoted from command of a division. He had led a panzer regiment in 7th Panzer's summer drive through the Ukraine in 1941, and that winter taken it into the north-western suburbs of Moscow. For the last three years he had led this regiment, and then the division, in the 'firefighter' role, dashing hither and thither to blunt Soviet spearheads that had broken through the infantry-held front lines. Now again he had an offensive task. Fifth Panzer Army would strike west, through Bastogne and St Vith to the Meuse between Namur and Dinant, then wheel north towards Brussels. On its southern flank Seventh Army would unroll infantry divisions as cover.

This was the basic plan. Hitler had added a few flourishes. A force of English-speaking Germans had been gathered, provided with captured American jeeps and tanks, and ordered to drive deep into enemy territory once the initial penetration had been achieved. There they were to spread the maximum confusion. Airborne troops would also be used; they would be dropped near Malmedy to secure the Amblève bridges for Dietrich's drive on Antwerp. The Luftwaffe would naturally be present in force, although even Hitler now accepted Göring's assurances with more than a pinch of salt. Petrol would be supplied in adequate quantities. The Chiefs of Staff, Hitler gloated, must be surprised at the forces he had collected, despite their gloomy prognoses. The war was not yet lost, as they could see.

The Chiefs of Staff were undoubtedly surprised. So were their commanders Rundstedt and Model. The optimism of it took Rundstedt's breath away. 'Antwerp!' he exclaimed. 'If we reach the Meuse we should go down on our knees and thank God.' (6) A meeting was called for 27 October; present were Model, Rundstedt, Krebs, Westphal, Manteuffel, Dietrich and Brandenberger. The plan's shortcomings were subjected to a withering scrutiny. No one could deny that the strategic aim would have been sound if – an all-consuming if – the forces had been available to achieve the objectives laid down. Hitler had chosen his breakthrough sector wisely; Antwerp was indeed of crucial importance to the enemy. But even assuming a successful breakthrough, the objectives were way beyond German capabilities. Hitler had compared this offensive to *Sichelschnitt*; the differences between 1940 and 1944 were more apparent to his subordinates. The ratio of forces was far less favourable. After the initial breakthrough the Allies would soon be able to match the German concentration of strength; the latter's attack would from that moment be sustained only by its own momentum. This was unlikely to sustain. There was insufficient fuel. There was likely to be precious little Luftwaffe. True, the weather would keep the skies clear of Allied aircraft, but the same weather would slow the panzers. In the *summer* of 1940 it had taken Guderian three days to reach the Meuse; how long would it take in mid-winter? And how long would the weather ground the enemy air forces? Even given that enemy morale in the threatened sectors might crack, in itself unlikely, the enemy would still possess ample reserves to throw in. The Germans would have next to none. Manteuffel summed it up cogently.

> They expressed doubts whether the numbers, equipment, arms, mobility, and supplies were sufficient to sustain an attack over a front of something like 125 miles under wintry conditions, and then to hold the western flank sufficiently long to encompass the destruction of the 25–30 divisions it was hoped to encircle. (7)

When it is remembered that Hitler had only twenty-eight divisions to invest in the offensive the scale of profit expected was somewhat excessive.

Before the 27 October meeting both Model and Rundstedt had devised less ambitious alternatives. At the meeting they were synthesised. An attempt should be made to oust the Americans from their positions around Aachen, to retake Liège and re-establish the German line on the lower Meuse. This, they thought, was a plan better tailored to the forces available. It had no sooner been drafted for submission than Hitler's plan arrived, endorsed in his own handwriting: 'not to be altered'. This last instruction was reinforced by a visit from Jodl on 3 November. He overrode the combined objections of Rundstedt, Model and Manteuffel with the usual 'political' reasons for ignoring military common sense.

The commanders did not give up, trying once more on 2 December to alter the Führer's unalterable resolve. Hitler listened and dismissed all their misgivings. Only in the tactical handling of the breakthrough itself did he allow himself to accept some of Manteuffel's ideas; the bringing forward of the assault-time to maximise the hours of daylight for the initial penetration, a shortening of the artillery barrage to sharpen surprise, artificial moonlight to guide the tanks forward on the first night. The main features of the plan stood. Only a blow on the intended scale would produce the desired effect. As he told Speer, quite rightly, 'if it does not succeed, I no longer see any possibility of ending the war well . . . ' (8)

But it would succeed. On 12 December he delivered his customary pep-talk to the assembled commanders on the eve of battle. The political implications were explained at length.

> Never in history was there a coalition like that of our enemies, composed of such heterogeneous elements with such divergent aims . . . Ultra-capitalist states on the one hand; ultra-Marxist states on the other . . . Even now these states are at loggerheads, and he who, like a spider sitting in the middle of the web, can watch developments, observes how these antagonisms grow stronger and stronger from hour to hour. If now we can deliver a few more heavy blows, then at any moment this artificially-bolstered common front may suddenly collapse . . . (9)

He was right about the coalition, as post-war events would demonstrate. But the spider simile was too apposite. For, as he neglected to add, rarely has human history seen a state as malignant as Nazi Germany. Rare evil draws together rare coalitions. 'Wars,' as Hitler gratuitously informed his audience, 'are finally decided by one side or the other recognising that they cannot be won.' (9) It is also true that some wars are won by one side or the other recognising that they cannot afford to lose it, and having the power to turn resistance into ultimate triumph. This was one of those.

V

Through November and the first two weeks of December the preparations for *Herbstnebel* ('Autumn Mist'), as the offensive was code-named, went on behind the deceptively quiet front. The men, the weapons, fuel and supplies for twenty-eight divisions had somehow to be gathered unnoticed in the area

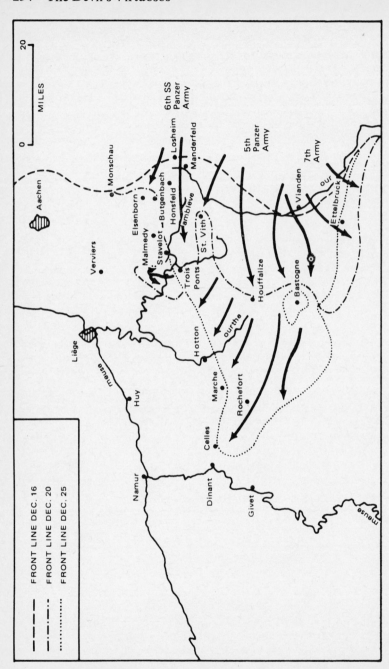

22 'HERBSTNEBEL'

behind the Eifel front line. From all over Europe they came, the trains click-clacking across the points of the still-barely-intact German rail system, to the Rhineland. There they were moved up to their deployment areas by night, the tanks hidden in the forests, the guns shrouded in leafy camouflage. A quarter of a million men, 2000 guns, 700 tanks . . . all were shifted into a 75-mile front, under an enemy-held sky, unnoticed and on time. The German General Staff might have been stripped of its strategic and tactical prerogatives; it still maintained a skill in logistics that bordered on the miraculous.

The Allies would have thought so. Odd intelligence of an imminent German offensive came in piece by piece to their various HQs. It was ignored. Germany had lost the war; it was merely a question of tying up the loose ends. There could certainly be no German offensive in prospect. With the canny Rundstedt in charge there *would* be no offensive. No one could imagine that Germany would squander any remaining reserves with the Reich in such peril. The four divisions that manned the stretch of front in the Eifel settled down in the warmth of what shelter they could find and waited for Christmas.

On the morning of 16 December they received a surprise. V-1s streaked overhead, two thousand guns opened fire promptly at 5.30 a.m., and the first waves of German infantry loomed out of the dawn mist. It was the supreme moment of *Blitzkrieg*, the first shattering psychological blow. The thin screen of American divisions manning the central sector were not prepared. Some had arrived only a a few days before, others were resting after a mauling in the Hürtzen Forest battles the previous month. The elements of U.S. 106th Infantry Division on the Schee Eifel ridge were quickly enveloped by German infantry; the U.S. 28th Infantry Division on the river Ourthe were swiftly overwhelmed by five German divisions. By nightfall the front opposite Manteuffel's Fifth Panzer Army was in fragments. The searchlights were turned on and pointed upwards. Their beams reflected back off the clouds, and by this ghostly light the panzers started to roll forward.

Surprise had been achieved, but in the northern sector – the *Schwerpunkt* of Hitler's plan – it had not all been on the enemy's side. Sixth Panzer Army, advancing against the Elsenborn Ridge, ran headlong into an American concentration deployed for an attack of their own. Almost immediately a bitterly contested stalemate took the place of swift advance. Only in 1st S.S. Panzer's sector – the Losheim Gap – was resistance negligible. Here the leading panzer regiment, Battle-Group Peiper, burst through to a depth of six miles by nightfall.

In the far south Brandenberger's Seventh Army made practically no progress. It only consisted of four infantry divisions with no tank support; it was fighting against a numerically inferior force, but one which possessed the very tank and artillery support the Germans lacked.

This mixture of good and bad omens characterised the first four decisive days of *Herbstnebel*, the good gradually giving way to the bad. In the north a wholesale breakthrough continued to elude Dietrich, as his infantry and 12th S.S. Panzer struggled for possessions of the Elsenborn Ridge with the American VII Corps. Peiper meanwhile was confidently driving west, destroying the U.S. garrison at Honsfeld, commandeering two lorry convoys encountered on the road, and machine-gunning American prisoners. By dusk on the 17th he was outside Stavelot. There he made the mistake of pausing to take breath. Only six miles away, across the river Amblève, was a three million gallon fuel dump. By morning U.S. troops were in possession of the bridge and Peiper wheeled west to Trois Ponts, only to find the bridge had been blown. Fuel was now running short, there was no way across the river, and support from the rear had not arrived. The fly, in Steinbeck's immortal phrase, was beginning to discover it had conquered a flypaper. Where was the support? Still banging its head against the American positions between Butgenbach and Monschau on Hitler's orders. Surprise and speed had been lost, but the Führer was reluctant to admit the failure of the S.S. armour. Model on the 18th begged him to shift the *Schwerpunkt* south, but he would have none of it. The plan was 'not to be altered', even in its execution.

Rundstedt thought it was too late in any case.

We should abandon the offensive and prepare to defend the area we have gained. Dietrich's forces are held up between Monschau and Malmédy. St Vith has not been taken. We have only just reached Bastogne, which ought to have been taken on D plus 1. We have not made the most of our initial surprise. The offensive has never gathered speed, due to the icy roads and the pockets of resistance which forced us to lay on full-dress attacks. (10)

Model thought this too pessimistic. In Fifth Panzer Army's sector things were not, superficially at least, going badly.

Admittedly the difficulties were considerable. Most of the good roads ran at right angles to the German axes of advance; the columns of vehicles were having to traverse roads difficult even for the Eifel/Ardennes. In such circumstances it was not easy to concentrate force against local centres of opposition. The columns, winding through the narrow valleys, had no flexibility of movement. A check to their spearhead found them unable to offer support, merely doomed to wait while the obstruction was cleared by those at the front of the line. And the Americans were proving gallant and efficient Horatios, fighting with élan against superior forces, doing all in their power – blocking roads, blowing bridges, destroying fuel dumps – to slow the panzer advance. Yet advance, as Model insisted, it still was. Slowly but irresistibly the panzer tide was flowing west. 116th Panzer aimed on Houffalize, 2nd and *Lehr* on Bastogne. The former arrived on 19 December; the latter arrived too late.

Manteuffel had urged the importance of securing Bastogne at his last meeting with Hitler. Both he and Model had realised that the nature of the terrain and the seasonal conditions made it vital to seize the two key road junctions. Already by the 17th the other one – St Vith – was proving an 'abscess on our lines of communication'. The small American garrison had put up spirited resistance on the first day of the assault; on the second they were reinforced by the arrival of U.S. 7th Armoured Division. The two German infantry divisions assigned the town's capture found the task beyond them. It would require the commitment of two S.S. panzer divisions before St Vith fell on the 21st. By then the abscess at Bastogne had begun to fester.

Had Panzer *Lehr* and 2nd Panzer reached Bastogne ahead of the American reinforcements the outcome of *Herbstnebel* might have been more imponderable. As it was Panzer *Lehr* struggled down muddy side-roads to a vantage-point above the town only to discover that U.S. 101st Airborne Division had won the race. The town was no longer ripe for capture. Manteuffel had a real dilemma on his hands. Should he follow classic *Blitzkrieg* doctrine: bypass the town and leave it for the infantry; isolate resistance and leave it to cry in the wilderness? Or should he attempt its capture regardless of what brake that might place on the dash for the Meuse? The speed of the German advance did not so much depend on the driving-time available as on the efficiency with which the panzers could be maintained in fuel and other supplies. An American garrison astride the main supply artery would cripple the advance as surely as a pause to remove it.

This dilemma was rooted in the mistaken strategy of the whole operation. There was not enough force to go around. Had Seventh Army achieved even half its operational objectives Bastogne would have been sealed off from the south. Then Manteuffel could have risked leaving it alone. But Seventh Army was struggling some miles in Fifth Panzer Army's rear. If the panzers took Bastogne they would also presumably have to hold it against the expected American intervention from the south. They would have to act as their own flank guard, thus critically weakening the forces available for their real purpose. Manteuffel compromised, as he had to do. The town was invested, the advance continued. Neither promised much success. On 20 December 1944, with an unconscious irony and at least two days too late, Hitler switched the *Schwerpunkt* to Fifth Panzer Army's sector.

In the days that followed only the Führer could delude himself into believing that the apparent advances had any strategic significance. On the 23rd the leading elements of 2nd Panzer looked down upon the Meuse near Dinant; on the same day the skies cleared and the Allied planes took to the air. Dietrich was still beating his head against the Elsenborn Ridge, although the S.S. Panzer reserve (9th and 2nd S.S.) had taken St Vith and surged westwards. The German advance, on the 20th consisting of two narrow corridors, had been broadened into a wide bulge. But the shoulders, at Elsenborn–Monschau and Bastogne–Ettelbruck held firm, and for the wide fan of panzer divisions at the front, fuel was running out. Behind them the Allied air forces were blocking the roads and destroying supply columns in the winding defiles. For all the ground gained the German situation was untenable. As Model said to Speer on the 23rd, *Herbstnebel* had definitely failed.

Hitler ordered it to continue. The Führer's obsession with maps never deserted him. Neither did his inability to correlate them with reality. On the 24th he saw the flags standing on a line (north-east to south-west) Trois Ponts–Hotton–Marche–Celle, some twenty miles south-east of the Meuse. Like a dying animal, hypnotised by the powerful claws before its eyes, unable to accept that there was no longer strength enough in the limbs to wield them, Hitler gazed at his flags. Nine panzer divisions! How could the offensive be called off with such power still available! When so close to success! He did not see

that Second Panzer, out of fuel, faced two British armoured
brigades. Or that Montgomery had gathered a reserve force
behind the Meuse greater than the entire German attacking
force. Or that Allied air power was proving as decisive as it
had been in Normandy. The German spearheads were under
constant attack from the air; they were receiving no supplies.
The Luftwaffe had been outnumbered and outfought. Insufficient training, insufficient checking of machines, insufficient
numbers – all took their toll. Bastogne refused to fall, despite a
three-division attack on Christmas Day. The leading elements
of Patton's relief force arrived on the 26th to lift the siege. On
the 27th the 2nd U.S. Armoured Division and the British
Guards Armoured Division attacked 2nd Panzer in its advanced
position west of Rochefort. By nightfall, unable to manoeuvre
through lack of fuel, the point of Manteuffel's spear had been
blunted and torn apart. Somewhere far to the west Peiper's
troops, having abandoned their vehicles, were trudging morosely
through the snow towards Germany.

VI

On 28 December an unrepentant Führer told Rundstedt that
'in a military sense it is decisive that in the West we are moving
from a sterile defence to the offensive. The offensive alone will
enable us to give once more a successful turn to this war in the
West.' Rundstedt could not bring himself to agree that the
entire strategic situation had been transformed, or that a 'tre-
mendous easing' of Germany's plight had taken place. But
Hitler was on the crest of his dubious wave. 'We shall yet
master fate.' (11)

Fate, in the form of the Red Army, was going to take some
mastering. On the 24th, Guderian had journeyed West to beg
for the transfer of forces to the Eastern front. He and the head
of 'Foreign Armies East', General Gehlen, had been accumulating intelligence of the coming offensive.

We calculated that the attack would begin on 12 January.
The Russians' superiority to us was 11:1 in infantry, 7:1 in
tanks, 20:1 in guns. An evaluation of the enemy's total
strength gave him a superiority of approximately 15:1 on
the ground and 20:1 in the air, and this estimate did not err
on the side of exaggeration. (12)

Hitler decided it was a bluff. These figures, he shouted, 'are the greatest imposture since Genghis Khan. Who's responsible for producing this rubbish?' His tanks were, however precariously, on the Meuse once more. They could not be moved east at such an historic moment. Surely you realise, he and Jodl told Guderian, that this priceless initiative in the West cannot be thrown away for fear of imaginary Soviet armies.

Guderian returned to Zossen empty-handed. In the Ardennes Allied pressure on the German bulge increased as Montgomery's and Patton's forces drove in wedges from north and south. On New Year's Eve Guderian tried again. This time he visited Rundstedt first, found out what divisions were immediately available, and arranged the trains to move them east. So armed he bearded Hitler and Jodl again. Angrily asked from whom he had received his information, Guderian triumphantly pulled Rundstedt's name out of the hat. He got four divisions but no more. They went moreover to Hungary, not to Poland.

By 8 January 1945 the Allied pressure made a German withdrawal imperative. This, together with the failure of a subsidiary German attack in Alsace, at last convinced the reluctant Hitler and Jodl that the initiative had passed them by. Not that they yet placed any credence in Guderian's estimates of Red Army strength. A new batch presented by Guderian on the 9th produced a demand that Gehlen be put in a lunatic asylum. If it wasn't a bluff it would be a disaster. So it had to be a bluff. Guderian again failed to secure either reinforcements or permission to organise the defence as he and his subordinates in the East saw fit. The most Hitler would do was to thank him for creating such a strong reserve. 'The Eastern Front is like a House of Cards,' an unmollified Guderian retorted, 'if the front is broken through at one point the rest will collapse.' (13)

On 12 January the Soviet offensive began, quickly biting huge holes in the thin German line. 120,000 men, 600 tanks and 1600 aircraft that might have slowed or even halted it were scattered across the Ardennes or in Allied prison compounds. Gehlen's figures had not been an imposture. Neither for that matter was Genghis Khan.

References (Chapter 9)

1. Guderian, *Panzer Leader*, 342–3
2. Ibid, 341
3. quoted in Wilmot, *Struggle for Europe*, 444

4. *The Rommel Papers*, 497
5. Ibid, 502
6. quoted in Strawson, *Ardennes*, 15
7. quoted in Jacobsen and Rohwer, *Decisive Battles*, 396
8. quoted in Strawson, *Ardennes*, 6
9. quoted in Wilmot, *Struggle for Europe*, 578
10. quoted in Strawson, *Ardennes*, 88
11. quoted in Wilmot, *Struggle for Europe*, 605
12. Guderian, *Panzer Leader*, 382
13. Ibid, 387

Chapter 10

ALLEGIANCE OF THE BLIND

I have always been absolutely fair in my dealings with the Jews. I gave them one final warning. I told them that, if they precipitated another war, they would not be spared . . .
(Adolf Hitler, 26 April 1945) (1)

War has seldom brought anything for the people engaged in it. But the people aren't usually asked.
(Erwin Rommel, September 1944) (2)

Heaven and earth are not humane. (Lao Tzu)

On the morning of 16 April 1945 the Soviet forces broke through the last barrier, the Oder-Neisse line that had held them up for two months. Berlin was less than fifty miles ahead. On the other side of the shrinking Reich, Field-Marshal Model, trapped with a quarter of a million under-armed troops in the Ruhr pocket, received the news. 'This is the end,' he said to his Senior Intelligence Officer, 'it's the smash-up.' The next morning he gave his troops a choice: they could surrender, continue to fight, or try to find their way home. He, Model, would not surrender. A Field-Marshal could not do that. 'Have we done everything to justify our actions in the light of history?' he asked a staff officer. 'What is there left to a commander in defeat?' (3)

What indeed? In the bunker beneath the Reich Chancellery in Berlin the Führer was dictating his testimony to Bormann. The Jews had started the war, the generals had lost it. His only errors had been on the side of moderation. The German people had proved unworthy of him.

Of the generals most encountered in these pages, few remained in active service. Guderian had finally been sacked at the end of March; he had contradicted the Führer once too often. He returned to Zossen, to his wife. 'It was a relief for both of us.' (4) Manstein had already been in retirement for a year. These two Prussians – what was left to them in defeat? They would both survive to write their memoirs, Manstein to stand trial. They had both experienced the glory of defeating France, both pitted their skill against the Red Army with success when that was at all possible. Guderian had misjudged the situation in Normandy, Manstein the possibilities of *Zitadelle*. These were minor blemishes on brilliant records. They had fulfilled their vocation, exercised their virtuosity, and, for the second time, witnessed the total military defeat of their nation. This time the price had been high.

> For us Prussians it was our immediate homeland that was at stake, that homeland which had been won at such a cost and which had remained attached to the ideals of Christian, Western culture through so many centuries of effort, land where lay the bones of our ancestors, land that we loved. (5)

Such feelings are not held in such regard today. Attachment to a 'homeland', to ancestors, to Western culture – these have paled, been pushed aside by the different loyalties of the global village. But for Guderian and Manstein they were real and they were central to their lives. It is a tragic irony that the only 'developed' country where such feelings are still held in high regard is Israel. Now it is the Prussian who is doomed to external exile, the Jew who defends his homeland with the tank doctrines first realised by Guderian in the 1930s.

At least Guderian and Manstein were alive. Neither, it would appear from their memoirs, learnt very much from the war. The slaughter of the Jews, of which both denied knowledge prior to the war's end, merits no attention, no inner searching. Their books are about their soldiering, little else. Hitler is seen as incompetent, eventually hysterically incompetent, but for them time has reduced his stature. As a soldier, they say, he was hopeless; as the leader of the German people . . . they have nothing to say. They prefer to remember the virtuosity, to forget the dark cause for which it was wielded. Their homeland is gone. Yet never do they say that were Prussia still Prussian, they would not have known the exhilaration of the panzer ride, the comradeship-in-arms, the laurels they won and wore with such pride. The politics were thrust upon them; they did their duty. The rest was not their business, merely their fate.

At least they were alive. Rommel never knew the fate of the Third Reich. Neither did von Kluge. Perhaps Model, wandering through the ruins of the Ruhr, thought of them, and of von Paulus, the Field-Marshal who surrendered and broadcast over Moscow for his jailers. 'A Field-Marshal does not become a prisoner,' Model reiterated to the few loyal staff officers who still accompanied him in evading the American search; 'such a thing is not possible.'

His military record was also virtually without blemish. More than any other general he had slowed the consequences of Stalingrad and Kursk. He was popular among his troops, with his Führer, with everyone but the enemy and the traditionalist Prussian élite. And unlike the latter he understood the nature of this war. He could not surrender, wash his hands of the whole business, retire to write his memoirs. The Russians wanted his head, but it was more than that. Model's sense of honour was not the product of a thousand years' tradition, entwined in ritual, petrified by the coincidence of class and profession. For Model the social and personal could not be held apart with such ease. The Reich had lost the war; he, Model, was a part of that Reich, a part of that defeat. It was not a game, a military exercise with live ammunition. There would be no final whistle, no shaking hands and comparing of notes. Thirty million people had died. Model had followed Hitler and his hooked cross to the ends of Europe; he could not escape the retribution. On the morning of 21 April he told his Intelligence Officer: 'My hour has come. Follow me.' The two of them walked into the forest that lies by Duisburg. Somewhere deep among the trees Model drew his pistol and shot himself in the head. The Intelligence Officer buried him in an unmarked grave.

In the Chancellery bunker the mad dance continued for another week. Hitler, free at last of the malicious General Staff, ordered his non-existent armies across the chequerboard of ruins that was Germany. His political acumen remained as sharp as ever. He knew the Grand Coalition ranged against him would break up long before most of its members did. For perhaps only the second time in his life he overestimated his enemy, granting it a foresight the equal of his own. But Roosevelt's shortsightedness and the march of that destiny he had so often invoked prevented the last-minute rescue. The atavistic barbarism that was Nazi Germany would be ground under before a new battle for the world began. This Hitler could not understand. Surely the Allies would want German help against the communist hordes? Göring thought so too, expecting a telegram from the Western powers 'in a few days'. Bormann struggled to inherit the empty crown. Goebbels, with rather more insight, devoted his time to preparing a finale to end all finales, a 'world-historical end' in Berlin.

Viewing this group's final frenzy of mutual incriminations
and wild hopes it is hard to believe that for twelve years they
had guided Europe's strongest nation. They seem more like a
bunch of gangsters trapped in a Chicago hotel than the heirs of
Bismarck. Of the entire group only Speer demands a certain
respect, Speer who at this moment was doing his best to
sabotage Hitler's orders to 'scorch' Germany beyond hope of
recovery. Yet for all this it is important to remember that these
men were not clowns, not incompetents or fools. Hitler and
Goebbels were both intelligent men in their own way, both great
orators at a time when radio was the crucial political medium.
Göring was a national hero from the First World War;
Himmler a depressingly efficient bureaucrat. Between them
they had raised Germany from the moral debris of Versailles
and the Depression, formed an army capable of carving an
empire from the Pyrenees to the Volga, from Egypt to Narvik.
When the drums had beaten out their victory roll in Berlin
after France's fall, there had been few who questioned the
political efficacy of Nazi leadership.

Less than five years had passed. The world that had laid at
their feet was now closing in around their heads. Yet the
memory of success had not faded easily. The generals' faith
had been weakened before Moscow, destroyed at Stalingrad,
but by then Hitler had other means of eliciting support. The
generals could no more loosen their grip on the Soviet tiger's
tail than Hitler could. They shared, with a great many of the
German people, the fear of communism that had brought
Hitler to power in the first place. No, what the generals wanted,
once the Russian war was an actuality, was the time and the
forces and the freedom of decision to bring it to a successful conclusion. This, they knew as early as 1942, could only be achieved
within the context of a peace in the West. And this, they took
too long to realise, was a fool's dream. Hitler was the first
stumbling-block, but even had he been dispensed with, there
remained the Allies' demand for unconditional surrender, wilfully hardened by leakage of the Morgenthau Plan for dis-
mantling German industry and reverting the Reich to a vast
peasants' plot. If the Allies could not distinguish between the
Nazis and the Germans then how could the generals? Reared
and encouraged to look the other way, few even tried.

History rarely judges men as men. It recounts what they did
and draws its conclusions; it says little of who they were. The
German generals have been no exception. Yet they above all

should be seen for who they were, for in judging their deeds Western civilisation had applauded their talents yet condemned them for allowing those talents to be used in the service of such a cause. The twain have never met.

Such judgements are easy to make. The German generals were the finest thinking and fighting soldiers of modern history. The cause they served possessed a calculated barbarity without recent parallel. Neither statement is in doubt. The largest empire since Napoleon and the greatest slaughter since Genghis Khan bear adequate and terrible testimony to these truths. Can the two be brought together? Did the generals themselves bring them together? *Did they know?*

There is no simple answer. In this era of 'double-think' it is quite plausible to believe that they both knew and did not know. Albert Speer, meeting an old friend in 1944, was advised strongly not to visit a certain 'establishment'. In his memoirs Speer notes that he did not ask what made that 'establishment' so dangerous to visit; he did not want to know. Rumours were more than enough and . . . what could he have done?

It is unlikely that the generals knew even this much. Yet they must have guessed something. Not at first, and not the whole truth by any means, but something. Anti-semitism, after all, was as common in Germany before the war as colour prejudice is in Anglo-America today, and with as little reason. Hitler's pronouncements on the theme were certainly exaggerated, but he was exaggerated about most things. It would have been hard to believe in 1940 that he was bent on deliberate racial genocide.

As the war continued, and Hitler's exaggeratedness became more bizarre and savage, the doubts must have grown. But by this time the German nation, as the generals saw it, was fighting for its life. They could not afford these doubts if they were to perform their primary function. Had they known the full extent of the crime going on behind their back it is hard to believe that they would have continued to serve Hitler as most of them did. But from where they stood it was all rumours, and they chose, consciously or otherwise, to let them remain that way.

There have been many crimes against humanity in this century, committed by a wide spectrum of the world's nations. What distinguished the crime against the Jews was its systematic nature, the fact that it was carried on for years, and its particularly absurd ideological rationale. The generals were not responsible for, or a party to, this mad deliberation. Their crime, such as it was, was that of the pharisees who passed by on the other side of the road with eyes clenched shut. Perhaps in some ways they can be compared with the scientists who created the atom bomb. These scientists knew, as surely as anyone could, that the fruit of their endeavours would be the slaughter of innocent and guilty alike. They followed science where it led them; if they thought of moral justification it lay in the need to defeat an all-encompassing evil. That Truman would use their bomb merely to forestall Soviet participation in the occupation of Japan doubtless did not occur to them, any-more than it occurred to Rommel and Guderian that their dashing panzer drives would cost six million Jews their lives in the gas chambers of the Nazi inferno. The scientists' allegiance to Truman was secondary, as was the German generals' to Hitler. The real blindness lay in their total allegiance to deplorably partial gods, pure science and the art of war.

Still we know little of who they were. Their memoirs tell us little more. Both Guderian and Manstein wrote as soldiers; cold and pedantic, allowing themselves only the slightest touches of an arid wit. Rommel wrote like the soldier he was; he wrote his own adventure story. But this was not all they were. Reading Manstein's book, reading about him, the overwhelming impression is one of coldness, yet those who knew him stress the warmth that lay beneath that cold exterior. Rommel once replied to his son's contempt for the Italians' martial abilities with a comment to the effect that civilisation's progress owed more to non-martial abilities. Guderian said of Hitler: 'Everything on this earth that casts a glow of warmth over our life as mortals, friendship with fine men, the pure love for a wife, affection for one's own children, all this was and remained for ever unknown to him.' (6)

These were not monstrous men, merely men whose supreme competence in one field of endeavour rendered them grossly and tragically inadequate in others. To answer the question – what is left to a commander in defeat? – is not, in their case, difficult. The supreme consolation. None of them had to live in the world as it would have been had they won.

References (Chapter 10)

1. quoted in Bullock, *Hitler*, 772
2. *The Rommel Papers*, 499

3. quoted in Whiting, C. *Battle of the Ruhr Pocket* (Pan/ Ballantine, 1970), 139–40
4. Guderian, *Panzer Leader*, 429
5. Ibid, 388
6. Ibid, 441

Select Bibliography

Primary Sources

(Books/Articles written at first-hand or containing first-hand material)

Bayerlein, F. 'With The Panzers in Russia', Marine Corps Gazette, 38 no 12.

Bekker, C. *The Luftwaffe War Diaries* (Corgi, 1969).

Blummentritt, G. *Von Rundstedt* (Odhams, 1952).

Freidin, S. and Richardson, W. eds., *The Fatal Decisions* (Michael Joseph, 1956).

Galland, A. *The First and the Last* (Fontana, 1970).

Goerlitz, W. *Paulus and Stalingrad* (Methuen, 1963).

Guderian, H. *Panzer Leader* (Futura, 1974).

Halder, F. *Hitler as War Lord* (Putnam, 1950).

Jacobsen, H. A. and Rohwer, J. eds., *Decisive Battles of World War II: The German View* (André Deutsch, 1965).

Keitel, W. *The Memoirs of Field-Marshal Keitel* (William Kimber, 1965).

Kesselring, A. *The Memoirs of Field-Marshal Kesselring* (William Kimber, 1953).

Liddell Hart, B. *The Other Side of the Hill* (Cassell, 1951).

Manstein, E. *Lost Victories* (Methuen, 1958).

Manteuffel, H. 'German Morale 1939–45', *An Cosantoir*, IX no 11.

Mellenthin, F. W. *Panzer Battles* (Cassell, 1955).

Rommel, E. *The Rommel Papers* (Collins, 1953).

Rudel, H. *Stuka Pilot* (Euphorion, Dublin, 1952).

Ruge, F. 'In Defence of Rommel', *An Cosantoir*, X no 1.

Schweppenburg, L. G. 'A Modern Anabasis', *An Cosantoir*, X nos 3–4; 'Invasion Without Laurels', *An Cosantoir*, X nos 1–2.

Speer, A. *Inside the Third Reich* (Weidenfeld & Nicolson, 1970).

Speidel, H. *We Defended Normandy* (Herbert Jenkins, 1951).

Turney, A. *Disaster at Moscow: Von Bock's Campaigns 1941–2* (Cassell, 1971).

Warlimont, W. *Inside Hitler's Headquarters* (Weidenfeld & Nicolson, 1964).

Westphal, S. *The German Army in the West* (Cassell, 1951).

Secondary Sources

Belfield, E. and Essame, H. *The Battle for Normandy* (Pan, 1967).

Bullock, A. *Hitler: A Study in Tyranny* (Penguin, 1962).

Carell, P. *Hitler's War on Russia* (Harrap, 1964); *Scorched Earth* (Harrap, 1966); *The Foxes of the Desert* (Four Square, 1961); *Invasion – They're Coming!* (Corgi, 1963).

Clark, A. *Barbarossa* (Hutchinson, 1965).

Dallin, A. *German Rule in Russia* (Macmillan, 1957).

Douglas-Home, C. *Rommel* (Futura, 1975).

Edwards, R. *German Airborne Troops* (Macdonald & Jane's, 1974).

Elstob, P. *Bastogne* (Macdonald, 1968).

Erikson, J. *The Road to Stalingrad* (Weidenfeld & Nicolson, 1975).

Essame, H. *The Battle for Germany* (Batsford, 1969).

Fleming, P. *Operation Sea Lion* (Pan, 1975).

Fuller, J. F. C. *The Second World War* (Eyre & Spottiswoode, 1948); *The Decisive Battles of the Western World* (Volume 2) (Paladin, 1970).

Goerlitz, W. *The German General Staff* (Hollis & Carter, 1953).

Hoehne, H. *The Order of the Death's Head* (Secker & Warburg, 1969).

Horne, A. *To Lose a Battle* (Macmillan, 1969).

Jukes, G. *The Defence of Moscow* (Macdonald, 1969); *Stalingrad: The Turning Point* (Macdonald, 1968); *Kursk: The Clash of Armour* (Ballantine, New York, 1968).

Keegan, J. *Barbarossa* (Macdonald, 1970); *Guderian* (Ballantine, New York, 1973); *Rundstedt* (Ballantine, New York, 1974).

Kitchen, M. *The German Officer Corps 1890-1914* (Clarendon, Oxford, 1968).

Liddell Hart, B. *History of the Second World War* (Pan, 1973).

Lucas, J. and Cooper, M. *Hitler's Elite: S.S. Leibstandarte* (Macdonald & Jane's, 1975).

McKee, A. *Caen: Anvil of Victory* (Pan, 1966).

Macksey, K. *Panzer Division* (Macdonald, 1968); *Guderian* (Macdonald & Jane's, 1975); *Tank Warfare* (Panther, 1976).

Malaparte, C. *The Volga Rises in Europe* (Panther, 1965).

Neckar, W. *The German Army of Today: 1943* (EP, 1973).

Paget, R. *Manstein* (Collins, 1951).

Reitlinger, G. *The S.S.: Alibi of a Nation* (Heinemann, 1956).

Seaton, A. *The Russo-German War* (Barker, 1971); *The Battle for Moscow* (Hart-Davis, 1971).

Shirer, W. *The Rise and Fall of the Third Reich* (Secker & Warburg, 1960).

Sibley, R. and Fry, M. *Rommel* (Ballantine, New York, 1974).

Strawson, J. *Hitler as Military Commander* (Sphere, 1973); *The Battle of the Ardennes* (Batsford, 1972).

Werth, A. *Russia at War* (Barrie & Rockliff, 1964).

Wheeler-Bennett, J. *The Nemesis of Power* (Macmillan, 1953).

Williams, J. *France: Summer 1940* (Macdonald, 1969).

Wilmot, C. *The Struggle for Europe* (Collins, 1971).

Young, D. *Rommel* (Fontana, 1955).

Index